# The Alexis de Tocqueville
# Lectures on American Politics

# Nature and History in American Political Development

A DEBATE

*James W. Ceaser*

WITH RESPONSES BY
*Jack N. Rakove*
*Nancy L. Rosenblum*
*Rogers M. Smith*

HARVARD UNIVERSITY PRESS
Cambridge, Massachusetts
London, England

Library of Congress Cataloging-in-Publication Data
Ceaser, James W.
Nature and history in American political development :
a debate / James W. Ceaser ; with responses by
Jack N. Rakove, Nancy L. Rosenblum, Rogers M. Smith.
p. cm.—(The Alexis de Tocqueville lectures on
American politics)
ISBN 978-0-674-02158-7 (cloth: alk. paper)
ISBN 978-0-674-02723-7 (pbk.)
1. Political science—United States—History.
2. United States—Politics and government.
3. Foundationalism (Theory of knowledge)
4. Ideology.   I. Rakove, Jack N., 1947–
II. Rosenblum, Nancy L., 1947–
III. Smith, Rogers M., 1953–
IV. Title.   V. Series
JA84.U5C432 2006
320.97301—dc22      2005043547

# CONTENTS

*Foreword by Theda R. Skocpol*                                    vii

1. FOUNDATIONAL CONCEPTS AND AMERICAN
   POLITICAL DEVELOPMENT                                          1
   James W. Ceaser

2. CAN WE KNOW A FOUNDATIONAL IDEA
   WHEN WE SEE ONE?                                               91
   Jack N. Rakove

3. REPLACING FOUNDATIONS WITH STAGING:
   "SECOND-STORY" CONCEPTS AND AMERICAN
   POLITICAL DEVELOPMENT                                          113
   Nancy L. Rosenblum

4. WHAT IF GOD WAS ONE OF US? THE
   CHALLENGES OF STUDYING FOUNDATIONAL
   POLITICAL CONCEPTS                                             141
   Rogers M. Smith

5. FOUNDATIONAL CONCEPTS RECONSIDERED                            169
   James W. Ceaser

*Notes*                                                          199
*About the Authors*                                              222
*Index*                                                          223

# FOREWORD

THE ALEXIS DE TOCQUEVILLE LECTURES ON AMERICAN Politics were inaugurated in 2004 under the sponsorship of the Center for American Political Studies at Harvard University—an interdisciplinary home for the study of modern American politics by political scientists, political theorists, sociologists, economists, and historians. Generous support from Harvard alumnus Terry Considine made it possible to launch this series. Invoking the name of Alexis de Tocqueville—the French aristocrat who visited the fledgling United States in the 1830s and wrote the enduringly influential *Democracy in America*—is appropriate for a lecture, critical seminar, and book series meant to embody bold, broadly relevant thinking about the history and current state of politics in the United States. In the years to come, Tocqueville lecturers and commentators will put forward a variety of arguments. In the spirit of Tocqueville, they and their interlocutors will expand our understanding of society, politics, and public policymaking in America.

This book features the first Tocqueville lecture, delivered by political scientist James Ceaser in October 2004, along with the feisty dialogue following the lecture among Ceaser, historian Jack Rakove, and political theorists Nancy Rosenblum and Rogers Smith. The lecture and exchange help to open up new terrain in the study of the role of ideas in American political development. Much previous work in this area has focused on explicit political ideologies, but James Ceaser argues for exploring the repeated invocation of what he calls "foundational ideas"—ideas that provide the ground or ultimate appeal for other political ideas. Foundational ideas involve first premises—about nature, history, or religion—that are not argued, but rather provide the basis for argument in contests among theories of governance or party programs. Ceaser illustrates ways in which understandings of foundational arguments can improve our understanding of trends and conflicts in American political history.

The critical commentators—Jack Rakove, Nancy Rosenblum, and Rogers Smith—challenge Ceaser's arguments in a variety of ways. They point to alternative ways of conceptualizing foundational ideas in American political development. They call upon Ceaser to say more about religion, given that his original lecture focuses mostly on nature and history. And they ask him to further clarify *how* foundational ideas work politically. Ceaser responds in a spirited way, and he says more about how we might analyze the impact of religious ideas. This helps to connect Ceaser's approach more directly to the analysis of contemporary political conservatism in the United States.

The value of this lecture, the commentaries, and the rejoinder lies in the exchange of ideas. Scholars, students, and members of the educated public will enjoy seeing the play of hard-hitting arguments among intellectual heavyweights. Some will be inspired by Ceaser's call for more work on foundational ideas, and others will sharpen their disagreements with his approach. Everyone will enjoy and learn—and that is the point.

THEDA R. SKOCPOL, *Director*
*Center for American Political Studies, Harvard University*

# Nature and History in American Political Development

# 1

# FOUNDATIONAL CONCEPTS AND AMERICAN POLITICAL DEVELOPMENT

*James W. Ceaser*

I WOULD LIKE TO EXPRESS MY GRATITUDE TO THE benefactor of this new lectureship series, Mr. Terry Considine, and to commend his wisdom in naming it in honor of Alexis de Tocqueville, a thinker who contributed so much to our understanding of America and to the development of the discipline of political science. It is also highly fitting that Harvard should renew its connection to the legacy of Tocqueville, for there is no other university in America with which Tocqueville had closer ties. In 1831 Tocqueville visited Boston, where he held a lengthy interview with Harvard's president, Josiah Quincy—a conversation that helped to shape his thinking about the influence of America's historical origins on the development of American democracy. Even more important, Tocqueville met the great American historian Jared Sparks, and the two became friends and entered into a lifelong correspondence. In 1832, at Tocqueville's request, Sparks prepared a memo on local government in New England that directly informs a large section of Volume 1 of *Democracy in America*.[1] Sparks later became president of Harvard, and it was during his tenure that Tocqueville was awarded an honorary degree in 1852. The links between Tocqueville and Harvard University continue into our own time, with the recent publication of the acclaimed English translation of *Democracy in America* by Harvard's Delba Winthrop and Harvey Mansfield. I hope this lectureship will contribute in the future to an important dialogue between Tocqueville and American political science.

I also wish to thank Professor Theda Skocpol, director of Harvard's new Center for American Political Studies, under whose auspices this lecture is held. When I was discussing the topic of this lecture with Professor Skocpol earlier this year, she informed me of the Center's focus on the topic of American political development, a sub-discipline of political science to which I owe a special debt of gratitude. When I began graduate studies more than a quarter-century ago, what was then benignly called the "behavioral persuasion," but which more accurately should have been designated the "behavioral dogma," was at its apogee of influence, proscribing all theoretical and historical analyses except those dreary, data-laden lists dubbed "longitudinal" studies. I was guilty of a great impertinence by using both the T and D words in the title of my dissertation, "Presidential Selection: Theory and Development"—a transgression that earned me academic exile at that then genteel backwater of traditionalism, the University of Virginia. Not many years thereafter, however, the field of American political development emerged on the scene, and its founders began to grant refugee status to some, like myself, who employed old-fashioned approaches. It has been satisfying ever since to observe the progress of this sub-discipline, which is now so prominent that it has become solidly ensconced within Acronymia as "APD." Scholars in this field have proven their ability to compete successfully for resources against those from rival schools, such as rational choice, whose followers, expert at calculating their interest, are now joining APD in droves and attempting to appropriate it from within.

## Foundational Concepts and Their Uses

The subject of this lecture—foundational concepts and American political development—is not currently a part of "normal science," in which researchers pursue well-defined incremental questions in an established field. Even the terminology sounds slightly unfamiliar and calls for clarification.

Foundational concepts are one type of idea in a general field of ideas that plays a role in moving American political life. As there is no reason to think that ideas are any more homogeneous than other kinds of political phenomena—say, interest groups or government agencies—it follows that they need to be classified into intelligible categories before a systematic study of them can begin. Ideas appear in different forms and possess different levels of generality. Ideas that are influential in altering policies in discrete areas, such as economic or welfare policy, differ from, and are often said to depend on, more general kinds of ideas that deal with the role of government in society (sometimes called "ideologies") or with the distribution of power among institutions and levels of government ("theories of governance"). A pyramid of idea types can be elaborated with foundational concepts at the base. A foundational concept is an idea offered in political discourse as a first cause or ultimate justification for a general political position or orientation. It is usually presented as requiring no further argument, since it is thought to contain within itself its first premise. It supplies the answer to the question "Why," beyond which any further response is thought unnecessary. Included in the category of foundational concepts are ideas drawn from views of nature, History, and religion. This lecture will focus on the concepts of nature and History in American politics.

Foundational concepts are identified here in the first instance as elements of political discourse, not as pure ideas of philosophy or theology. The term "foundational" has been selected—another word might have been chosen—because it seems to offer the most descriptive label. As it happens, too, this term has often been used inside politics itself. At the formation of the nation, during an important debate in the Continental Congress of 1774, John Adams records that the great issue was to decide the "*foundation* of right" that would be used to justify the American policy of opposition to the British. He continued: "We very deliberately consid-

ered and debated . . . whether we should recur to the law of nature" (an obvious instance of a foundation in nature) or continue
to rely on the "common law," the "charters," and the "rights of
British subjects" (an instance of a foundation based on History).[2]
The question of political right, a topic of great theoretical interest
in philosophical tracts, arose here within the horizon of political
life. The participants discussed it in a fashion intelligible to ordinary political actors, deliberating not only about the merit or
truth but also about the likely effectiveness of different foundations in generating support for impending action and in ensuring
political stability over the long term.

Nature and History are difficult terms to define, but a common
meaning is needed to begin a discussion. Roughly speaking, a
foundation in nature provides justification by reference to something in the structure of reality as it can be accessed by reason.
Nature is chiefly a philosophical (or scientific) concept, even when
it is said to be confirmed by religious faith. Different views of science may accordingly give rise to their own distinct conceptions
of nature. Darwinists with their conception of natural law based
on competition, or sociobiologists with their theory of the selfish
gene and law of selection, offer an account of nature that is very
different from that found in the "law of nature" as expressed by
John Adams and many of the Founders.[3] Strictly speaking, all of
these views are accounts of nature, and they are often referred to
publicly in such terms. It is nevertheless the case that one understanding (actually, a set of understandings) has in practice enjoyed
a privileged status in political discourse because of its long usage
in Western political thought and, in the case of America, because
of its official endorsement in the Declaration of Independence and
some state constitutions. This is the view of nature as referring to
something unchanging or permanent, which can provide a standard of right. This understanding has been so prevalent that even
its opponents have often found themselves obliged to refer to it as
*the* concept of nature and, when disputing it, to challenge the
principle of nature itself.

A foundation in History is more complicated, which accounts for the awkward convention of using the term with a capital *H*. A foundation in History offers ultimate explanation or justification by situating things in the flow of time. Something is said to be a primary cause, or to be right, either because it conforms to a tradition deemed sacred and unassailable, or because it conforms to the direction in which the temporal process is said to be going, usually "progress." The first option, which looks to the past or tradition, is often called "Customary History" or the "Historical School," while the second, which looks more to the future, is usually called "Philosophy of History." In speaking of History, then, I am not referring to accounts generated under the auspices of the intellectual discipline of history, but to temporal accounts that are designed to establish a fundamental purpose or standard of right. I mean to distinguish History (with a capital *H*) from "ordinary" or "rationalist" history (with a small *h*)—what Edward Gibbon once colorfully characterized as "the register of the crimes, follies, and misfortunes of mankind."[4] The two share the same name, but in a deeper theoretical sense have little in common. Most practicing historians today do not aspire to provide accounts of this kind, nor do they think that history properly understood is capable of supplying such foundations. In reading a work by Eric McKitrick or David McCullough, for example, one expects to learn a great deal of history and perhaps much that might help in making certain kinds of judgments, but one is not seeking to discover ultimate meaning and guidance for human life. In contrast, when reading Hegel or Marx, one finds a temporal account that claims to explain the human condition and how to orient our actions and policies.[5] Those who have helped to fashion foundational ideas of History have not been limited to those generally classified as historians, but have included philosophers, poets, and sociologists.

General definitions about highly theoretical matters rarely do a very good job by themselves of conveying meaning. Just as every picture is worth a thousand words, so an example may replace a hundred attempts at abstract explanation. Consider the following two statements by Abraham Lincoln and Woodrow Wilson:

> Whenever the question of [slavery] shall be settled, it must be settled on some philosophical basis. No policy that does not rest upon some philosophical public opinion can be permanently maintained. . . . All honor to Jefferson—to the man who . . . had the coolness, forecast, and capacity to introduce into a merely revolutionary document, an abstract truth, applicable to all men and all times.[6]

> Progress! Did you ever reflect that that word is almost a new one? No word comes more often or more naturally to the lips of modern man, as if the things it stands for were almost synonymous with life itself. . . . We think of the future, not the past, as the more glorious time in comparison with which the present is nothing. Progress, development—those are modern words. The modern idea is to leave the past and press onward to something new.[7]

The first statement, combining bits of a speech and a letter from the 1860 presidential campaign, can be placed into the category of nature; the second, an excerpt of a speech from the 1912 campaign, into the category of History. In light of the difference between the two concepts, it is not surprising that they should sometimes have been viewed as rivals. Jefferson once alluded to this tension in characterizing the thinking of the American Revolutionaries: "We had no occasion to search into musty records, to hunt up royal parchments, or to investigate the laws and institutions of a semi-barbarous ancestry. We appealed to those of nature, and found them engraved in our hearts."[8] Nature, not History, supplies the standard of right. Woodrow Wilson, for his part, once told an audience—at a Jefferson Day celebration no less—that "if you want to understand the real Declaration Of Independence, do not repeat the preface."[9] Right comes from History, not nature. In the practice of politics, of course, foundational statements are not always so "pure" or exclusive. Statesmen are often understandably indifferent to or confused by abstract ideas, and matters are often blurred or obfuscated as political actors discover reasons for seeking syntheses, genuine or contrived. Precision, in political life, is not the virtue that it claimed to be in philosophy.

Of the different kinds of ideas at work in American politics, foundational concepts pose the greatest challenge to the political scientist. While many political scientists acknowledge in principle the importance of foundational ideas, they shy away from treating them, considering these concepts to be either too remote from ordinary practical affairs or too difficult to operationalize. There is an unfortunate tendency to think that what is not measurable or repeatable does not exist. It is easier to create an index of changing party strength in congressional voting than to devise a measure of shifting public support for the law of nature. Political scientists have also been discouraged from venturing into this area by philosophers and political theorists, thinkers rarely known for their modesty. Because of the overlap between foundational concepts and theoretical ideas, these lofty thinkers have recently taken to asserting an exclusive right to treating all questions relating to foundations, letting it be known in no uncertain terms that they intend to handle the big stuff, while ordinary political scientists should confine themselves to matters such as post offices and maternity benefits. It is the study of politics that suffers, since philosophers rarely show much interest in examining how foundational concepts function in political life, preferring instead to use the appearance of these ideas as an opportunity to engage in theoretical disputes and promote their own favored positions.

It is important, therefore, to restate why political scientists should study foundational concepts. The reason has nothing to do with indulging an impulse to get a sneak peek at Spinoza or Hegel under the guise of analyzing American politics; it derives instead from the simple fact that foundational concepts are encountered as tangible political phenomena that are in play in the practical political world. As much as the economic conditions or political situation, foundational concepts form part of the context in which statesmen must act. They constitute a potential variable— if not an independent one, then at any rate an intervening one— and isn't it the political scientist's duty to protect every degree of variance? This duty admittedly leads here into strange territory. American politics, for better or worse, is not a self-contained universe. Phenomena in the political realm "down here"—a realm of practical matters such as constitutions, wars, and elections—are linked to phenomena in the philosophical and metaphysical realm "out there." These links also bring under the scope of political analysis an unusual set of actors: those who play a role in spreading and producing these ideas. It is impossible to treat foundational concepts without considering the public intellectuals who import them into political discussion and the theorists and philosophers, perhaps far removed from ordinary politics, who are their originators. Woodrow Wilson once remarked that government, to be properly understood, must be comprehended "under the theory of organic life," not (as the Founders sought to do) "under the theory of the universe": "*It* [government] *is accountable to Darwin, not to Newton.*"[10] Political scientists are certainly not obliged to follow Wilson to the point of preoccupying themselves with the "pure" science of studying how amoeba evolve or the rate at which an apple falls; but they would do well to trace the chain of intellectual filiation as far back as those who try to forge direct connections between theoretical ideas and foundational concepts.

## The Study of Ideas in American Politics

Nothing, surely, could be more fatal to a public lecture than a lengthy discussion of approaches, which is a subject better left to the opening chapter of a doctoral dissertation. I only want to make a few comments in order to compare the method adopted here to the approaches of others who have treated foundational concepts, even if they have not used the term itself.

More than a century ago, America's first sociologist, Lester Ward, introduced into American social science the distinction between those who hold that the political world is moved in the first instance by ideas—let's call such people idealists—and those who hold that it is moved by economic or physical factors—let's call them materialists. Ward expressed his preference for idealism, and no one has ever done a better job assembling a catalogue of splendid aphorisms uttered on its behalf, from Virgil's "Mens agitat molem" ("Mind makes matter") to Auguste Comte's "Ideas govern the world, or throw it into chaos."[11] A Hundred Years War then ensued between partisans of the two camps, fueled for much of the time by Marxists of different stripes, who exercised enormous influence within the political world and inside social science.

Now that Marxism is dead as a governing ideology in the West, and its authority waning within academia, idealists can take heart that they have achieved something approaching a draw. Hardly any social scientists today deny that "ideas have consequences," and most probably find the sharp distinction between idealism and materialism to be overdrawn.[12] To paraphrase Thomas Jefferson, "We are all idealists, we are all materialists." Political scientists nevertheless devote more of their attention to the materialist side and ignore those who dwell on the "softer" subject of ideas. Perhaps this attitude has some basis, too, insofar as materialists are light years ahead of idealists in developing a systematic approach to the study of their subject.

What is the status of idealism in the field of American political development? One can, I believe, identify two basic ways of studying "big" ideas. The dominant one is the "traditions approach." The first question posed is "Who are we?" or "What is our tradition?" where a "tradition" refers to a package of ideas that defines the entire polity and sets the boundaries within which political debate takes place. Traditions are prefabricated essences, such as liberalism, republicanism, or Anglo-Protestantism, that analysts have imported from the outside in order to organize and make sense of the disparate ideas of American political life. This approach is often traced to the work of Louis Hartz, who defined the American tradition as a "liberal" one, in a generic sense. Others have since attempted to modify Hartz's thesis, identifying, for example, gaps between liberal aspirations and the realities of American life; or they have disputed the thesis, insisting on the existence of competing traditions, none fully dominant, that have been colliding with each other like huge bumper cars over the course of American history.[13]

Despite such differences, what these accounts share is the notion of a tradition itself. This is the strength of the approach, since the breadth of this concept is what allows for a general characterization of the whole polity. But it is also its weakness, since few have bothered to define what a tradition is.[14] It is a rule of logic that you get out of an inquiry only what you put into it. If scholars begin by looking for traditions in the study of American political development, then this is what they will find. But if parts of a tradition change, at what point does it cease to be the same thing? To take the most notable case, theorists and students of traditions label as "liberalism" both the Founders' system, which rests firmly on a foundation of natural rights, and certain modern conceptions that claim to float airily on no foundation. But are the two the same? If so, then why do so many of the theorists of nonfoundationalist liberalism expend so much of their time and energy decrying the Founders' idle preoccupation with "timeless truths" and differentiating themselves from any system that rests on a foundation? Should John Rawls be put in the same bed as John Adams, and Richard Rorty with Richard Henry Lee? Without specifying the parts of the whole—without saying what it is that constitutes a tradition—such questions are impossible to answer.

No one doubts the need for making global characterizations as a starting point. But if the object now in the study of American political development is to search for finer distinctions, might it not be time to declare a moratorium on a method that starts with preconceived traditions and that attempts to "score" ideas based on which tradition they fall into? Instead, I have suggested an open-ended, empirical-analytical inquiry that goes back to the phenomena themselves. It begins by drawing a circle around the objects being investigated (ideas). It then assigns analytic labels to different kinds or levels of ideas, virtually as they appear in political discourse, with only the gentlest intervention of the researcher. Finally, it looks at how the data vary, allowing links among the different levels of ideas to emerge as a result of the inquiry itself, rather than to be designated beforehand as an intrinsic property of a tradition.

A second general approach to the study of ideas employs the open-ended method just suggested, in which the analyst "jumps in" and investigates major ideas as they have appeared, without trying in advance to organize them according to a predefined package. This approach for a time was designated in political science as the study of "ideology"; but as that word became so weighted down with negative connotations, some scholars in the 1960s proposed the substitute term "public philosophy." They sensed, rightly, that they would be suspect if they presented themselves as students of ideology or as ideologues, whereas to claim that they studied the public philosophy, or better still were public philosophers, might win them acclaim and earn them invitations for serious interviews on National Public Radio. The study of ideas within American politics has since been dominated by this seductive term.

The study of the public philosophy was intended to launch inquiries into political ideas and their transformations at some fairly high level. "Public philosophy," as defined by Theodore Lowi, referred to a set of ideas that "dominates all other sources of belief in the formulation of public policy"; for Samuel Beer it was "an outlook on public affairs which is accepted within a nation by a wide coalition and which serves to give definition to problems and directions to government policies dealing with them."[15] These scholars had in mind studies of the political programs of the dominant parties, such as the laissez-faire ideas of the late nineteenth-century Republican Party and the welfare-state ideas of New Deal Democrats. The primary factor that seemed to define a public philosophy was a view about the size and role of government in society. The research agenda envisaged in this project was to describe each of these public philosophies. The plural is important, as there had been several public philosophies in the past, and there were certain to be more of them in the future. The concept of the public philosophy was intended to be analytic, not normative.

Yet scarcely was the ink dry on these first studies when political theorists, attracted by the word "philosophy," began to get involved in the enterprise. They immediately shifted the focus, dismissing the notion that a public philosophy could consist of anything as pedestrian as a mere set of policy programs; instead, they insisted, it had to be something much grander or deeper—something resembling a tradition or the mental structure or "unreflective background" that shapes all thinking and political discourse.[16] It also became clear that even the original analytic concept harbored large and unexamined assumptions. One was the notion that political ideas move in comprehensive units or blocs, in which a new winning bloc emerges to replace a losing one. As with the study of its sister concept, partisan realignments, this idea relied uncritically on a theoretical model—the paradigm of paradigms—taken from Thomas Kuhn's theory of how ideas are generated in the world of the physical and natural sciences. No one paused to ask whether the development of ideas in the political realm obeyed the same logic. With the acceptance of the paradigm model came yet another assumption, again equally unexamined: that having a public philosophy constitutes the natural or equilibrium position in political life. "A public philosophy," wrote Lowi, "is something that every stable polity possesses."[17]

Where a public philosophy does not exist in full vigor, there is a crisis that calls out for a saving dispensation. If you do not have a public philosophy, you'd best go out and get one right away.

Enter Michael Sandel. His book *Democracy's Discontent: America in Search of a Public Philosophy* (1996) masterfully appropriated discussion of this term, shifting the ultimate focus of the inquiry to the quest for a saving public philosophy that, once identified and installed, should not be replaced. To call this approach normative, given the author's discomfort with this term, would be inappropriate. Instead, the standard of right in politics is proven on the slaughter bench of history. Sandel accordingly sketches a "story" or "narrative" arguing that America began with a public philosophy of republicanism or communitarianism, which lasted from the Founding until 1933; it was then replaced by liberalism, which remains in effect today. But liberalism has become so manifestly dysfunctional—the crisis is palpable—that it is hardly more than an empirical observation to say that it needs to be jettisoned and that the nation should return to its original view. How fortuitous it is, too, that the central debate of academic theory, between Sandel's communitarianism and John Rawls's liberalism, happened all along to be playing itself out in a real-word struggle, thus bestowing on American history the privilege of settling a quarrel between two Harvard professors.

The original impetus to the study of the public philosophy had much to commend it. But the entire enterprise has splintered and gone in different directions. The term "public philosophy" now only sows confusion, having become a concept that, in Thomas Hobbes's description, "entangles us as a bird in lime twigs—the more he struggles the more belimed." It would be a blessing to eliminate this term altogether and start over, referring instead simply to "the major ideas that influence movement in American political life." Free of previous assumptions and pretensions, we could begin the process of classifying and mapping these ideas. In previous work I made a start on such a project, commencing with the more familiar kinds of ideas discussed, although never systematically spelled out, in public philosophy studies.[18] These consist of ideas that treat the ends of government and society (views on such things as equality and liberty); the bond or glue that holds the nation together; the role of government in society; the delimitations of power and the arrangement of institutions (separation of powers, the courts, federalism); and the role of America in the world. During this investigation it became clear to me that another kind of idea, higher on the scale of abstraction, was present in American political life, influencing the course of development, sometimes by directly explaining or justifying a major plan of action, at other times by grounding the more familiar kinds of political ideas just mentioned. These are the foundational concepts to which I now turn.

## Nature and History from the Puritans to the Founding

What Jefferson claimed was first in importance in 1776, "nature," became an important foundational idea only very late in colonial thought. Before then, foundations had been sought in History—Sacred History and Customary History. These foundations, along with the more recently discovered Philosophy of History, were alternatives to the concept of nature that were available to the Founders at the time of the Revolution. Like good lawyers writing a brief, the Founders rejected no argument that could help their cause. But in the end the Historical foundations were of less importance than the concept of nature.

Sacred History derived from Puritan thought. The great American Puritan authors operated under the guidance of a religious idea that was expressed in Historical terms. A few of the titles tell the story: *The History of New England* (John Winthrop), *A Brief History of the Warr with the Indians in New-England* (Increase Mather), *The Ecclesiastical History of New-England* (Cotton Mather), and the list goes on and on. Puritanism is a religion of the Book, and the Bible—the Old Testament in particular—favors the Historical sense. God acts in time, and His plan is revealed in the temporal realm. "Jerusalem," meaning Biblical religion, is the source of the primacy of history, "Athens" of nature. Of all the Protestant sects, Puritanism was the most responsible for reviving a connection between the execution of the Divine plan and the deeds of an earthly people. In their flight from Europe to America, the Puritans likened themselves to the Israelites undertaking an "errand in the wilderness" in the service of a covenant with God.[19] Although this mission was part of Sacred History, concerned with achieving sanctity and not worldly power, the great drama was unfolding amid one people in one unlikely place: "that little country New England."[20] As time went on, more thinkers called attention to the links between this mission and the fate of America in a more worldly sense—between the Divine plan (Providence) and the establishment of a great republic of liberty. This last view still had some currency at the time of the Revolution and was expressed in some of the sermons of the day, which were a major vehicle for the advocacy of political ideas. To take an example from a sermon preached in Newburyport, Massachusetts, in 1777: "God pleads his own, and his people's cause by his providence. . . . Our cause is not only righteous, but most important: it is God's own cause: it is the grand cause of the whole human race."[21]

This mode of thinking was not, however, dominant among the major Founders. Although the Declaration and *The Federalist* take note of Providence and of indications of Divine favor, the references are almost always to matters that can be confirmed by rational understanding as well. History was no longer mapped out on the basis of how events fit into a Providential plan. The Founders' concern was with the political, not religious, consequences of their actions. The aims of government were expressed in terms that address these "profane" or political ends, among them the protection of rights, security, and achieving the common good.

By the middle of the eighteenth century the virtual monopoly that Sacred History exercised over American historical consciousness had ended, and many of the educated were taking their bearings from another mode of thinking, less religious in its concerns—namely, Customary History. The underlying premise of Customary History is that legitimacy or right derives from the old or ancestral. This premise was rarely stated directly or theoretically; theoretical articulation was never the point. Rather, the premise was made manifest inside the historical accounts themselves. As J. G. A. Pocock has noted, the idea of right in this type of account was held to come from "a time immemorial" that is "traceable to no original [rational] act of foundation" and that "was heatedly asserted as literal historical truth."[22]

Customary History had two variants that were of interest in America. One was a moderate form of Whig history that supported the British constitution, including a limited monarchy. This account, which was contained in the jurisprudential histories of Edward Coke and William Blackstone in which so many of the Revolutionary leaders were schooled, emphasized the traditional rights of Englishmen as grounded in the ancient charters. It served as the basis in America for much of the initial opposition to the acts of the British government. The argument, repeated time and again in American writings, including the Declaration, was that British authorities had violated the colonists' rights as Englishmen. Initially, in the 1760s, Parliament was blamed; later, by the mid 1770s, the king was at fault. But as separation from Britain loomed, the very fact that this view emphasized America's ties to the British constitution, and to the monarchy, made it more difficult to sustain as the sole or primary foundation.

Some Revolutionaries turned to another form of Customary History, known as "real Whig" history. Real Whig history was anti-monarchic and could therefore more easily be called upon to underwrite the Revolutionary cause.[23] It appealed beyond the British constitution to an earlier and more original constitution, known as the "old" or "Gothic" constitution said to have governed England under Saxon rule before the Norman invasion. Here, incidentally, is the usual method of debate found in traditional or nonphilosophical societies: an appeal is made to the sanctity of an older or purer tradition against the sanctity of a later one. For the real Whigs, the Saxons had brought the constitution with them from the "forests of Germany," where it originated.[24] The source for this view was Tacitus' *Germania,* which described the simple, freedom-loving characteristics of the decentralized Germanic tribes. Thomas Jefferson gave expression to this idea in his widely read *Summary View of the Rights of British America* (1774), in which he lauded Anglo-Americans' "Saxon ancestors," who had left "their native wilds and woods in the north of Europe" to come to Britain and to establish the "system of laws which has so long been the glory and protection of that country."[25] Two years later he wrote to a friend: "Has not every restitution of the ancient Saxon laws had happy effects? Is it not better now that we return at once into that happy system of our ancestors, the wisest and most perfect yet devised by the wit of man, as it stood before the eighth century?"[26]

Liberty and constitutionalism in this account owed their origin to robust Nordic habits and practices, not to philosophical thought, which was associated with the Normans and royal absolutism. A popular Revolutionary War text by "Demophilius" (1776) summarized this position: "Whatever is of Saxon establishment is truly constitutional; but whatever is Norman is heterogeneous to it, and partakes of a tyrannical spirit."[27] In the Gothic thesis, constitutionalism derived from mores or "culture" rather than from theoretical principles. Americans were the last and truest heirs of the Gothic tradition, and even in America the "forests of Germany" were a symbol of liberty. Because of its opposition to the monarchy, the Gothic thesis managed to survive the Revolutionary period and continue as a major theme of American political thought until the World Wars, when the German forests lost much of their luster, as well as their foliage.[28]

As with Sacred History, Customary History in the end was not central to the Founders' argument. The opening paragraph of *The Federalist* makes clear that the determination of political right should be grounded on "reflection and choice" rather than on "accident" (that is, Customary History). The old may be respected insofar as it is reasonable, and for prudential reasons it may even be accorded a measure of deference. But it was not an ultimate standard. As Publius asks: "Is it not the glory of the people of America, that, whilst they have paid a decent regard to the opinions of former times and other nations, they have not suffered a blind veneration for antiquity, for custom, or for names, to overrule the suggestions of their own good sense, the knowledge of their own situation, and the lessons of their own experience?"[29]

A final and quite different version of History, becoming known at the time of the Founding, was Philosophy of History. "Philosophy of History" (the term was coined by Voltaire) has been defined by Karl Löwith as a "systematic interpretation of universal history in accordance with a principle by which historical events and successions are unified and directed toward an ultimate meaning."[30] Philosophy of History was first developed in France by Jacques Turgot and the marquis de Condorcet and by a school known as the Physiocrats (or the Economists).[31] Its dominant form proclaimed a scientific "law of progress" which held that the movement of things in human history was a form of data continuous with other observable data in nature. Just as the natural sciences had discovered laws of motion respecting the properties of physical things—laws that, once known, could then be employed to humans' benefit—so there was, to cite Condorcet, "a science that can foresee the progress of humankind, direct it, and accelerate it."[32] The future is knowable; the philosopher of history could produce a unified account of the entire temporal process. The study of history now paradoxically focused more on the future than on the past.

Philosophy of History over the past two centuries has been observed to have two divergent political implications. In one, associated with Karl Marx, Auguste Comte, and the American Progressives, the objective is to make use of human intelligence in order to direct history in the path that it is destined to go—to "accelerate it," in Condorcet's language. This idea has generally favored rational control, planning, and a centralized state. In the other tendency, associated with Adam Smith and certain libertarians, the process of development takes place on its own, and planners and government officials ought not to interfere with it. Strong centralized authority will only create unjust privileges and thwart progress. In America, insofar as Philosophy of History had influence, it was this second view that held sway from the Founding until the end of the nineteenth century.

Philosophy of History appeared on the margins of debates over the Constitution. It was employed in some cases by Anti-Federalists to oppose a stronger national government. If a process immanent to History itself assured progress, if the great problems of domestic politics and security in international affairs were solving themselves, there was less need for discretionary governmental authority and for a powerful executive to cope with the challenges of a permanently chaotic world. History would take care of the major difficulties. Traces of this view were found in the proposal (of Jefferson) for a periodic rewriting of the Constitution and in the prognostications, drawn from Montesquieu, of a coming era of "perpetual peace." Defenders of the Constitution rejected Philosophy of History. The authors of *The Federalist* identify it as not just fanciful, but dangerous. The idea of a Historical law of progress was a foundational concept put forward by "speculators," "projectors," and "utopians" who sought to deny government the needed attributes of stability, power, and energy.[33] To the Founders, the political world was permanently unstable and contingent. Nothing inside the historical process assured an end to major difficulties, and political actors would always be faced with the task of managing and superintending an unpredictable environment.

It is easy to get trapped by the term "history" and to convey a false impression. Even though the major Founders downplayed History, understood as the attempt to locate an ultimate standard of right in the realm of time, they were by no means inattentive to history (with a small *h*). On the contrary, not only did they give history great weight, but they were instrumental in transforming American historiography. In concert with a new group of historians that included Jeremy Belknap, David Ramsay, and John Marshall, the authors of *The Federalist* sought to make history into a discipline in which change was explained by observable causes, events, and accidents. They helped to introduce what can be called "rationalist history."[34] The enormous significance that these authors assigned to the American Revolution and Founding, in which these events were depicted as being of such magnitude that they could change the course of the modern world, led some later to charge that this history was not as "rational" as it was claimed to be—that it was, in fact, a secularized version of Sacred History or a new form of Customary History replete with the creation of modern legends. But these historians had a response. A select few events are objectively world-shaping in their importance, and the American Founding, in the event that the experiment proved a success, could rightly be placed in this category. Furthermore, in the case of America, a recounting of the actual history, without embellishment, could produce a salutary effect. The best apology for the Founders is to tell the story exactly as it was.[35]

The most important step taken by the Founders, a step whose significance became more apparent as time went on, was the turn from History to nature. This shift in foundations marked a revolution in the realm of ideas that was as momentous as were the events at Lexington and Concord in the realm of politics. It was the thought heard around the world. Americans were the first to bring nature down from the realm of philosophy and introduce it into the political world as a foundation of a full nation. Not myth, mystery, or History, but philosophy or science—the two terms were then synonyms—could serve, perhaps in a simplified version, as a public foundational concept. There could be "public philosophy."

The decision to adopt the concept of nature was deeply controversial. Many doubted whether science could ever form a viable foundation for a political society, however much it might help in the short run to dissolve the connection with Britain. An appeal to nature was an appeal chiefly to reason, which was too tenuous and would lead over the long term to a questioning of authority and a weakening of the bonds of society. The response to these doubts was both pragmatic and theoretical. In the 1774 debate in the Continental Congress referred to earlier, both John Adams and John Jay stressed the practical reasons for embracing the new foundation. In the event of a full break from Britain, reliance on customary foundations of historical right would be insufficient, as they encouraged sympathy for Britain. Adams pleaded "very strenuously" for "insisting on it [the law of nature] as a resource to which we might be driven by Parliament much sooner than we are aware."[36] John Jay thought that it was "necessary to recur to the law of nature and the British constitution, to ascertain our rights."[37] Proponents of the concept of nature argued further that it was helpful not just in the "destructive" task of tearing down illegitimate authority, but also in the "constructive" task of building support for properly constituted governments.[38] Recourse to the principle of nature could cement popular support for a new system by reminding people of the legitimate purposes and ends of government. What people understood and consented to, they would willingly adhere to. This view was encapsulated in some of the state constitutions written during this period, which began with theoretical statements based on the concept of nature that set forth the criteria of legitimate government.

What did it mean to embrace nature as a foundation? Nature as it was understood at this time is a difficult concept for us to grasp today, less because of its complications (which are considerable) than because its original meaning has been distorted by successive intellectual campaigns directed against it, especially by the Progressives, who succeeded in labeling this concept "metaphysical," where "metaphysical" is regarded as a term of pure fantasy. In fact, however, at the time of the Founding the concept of nature widely regarded to be the product of a science, and a turn away from mythical, theological, or obscure cosmological thinking. For shorthand, this science can be referred to as "politicalized psychology" (a neologism that is necessary in order to distinguish it from the well-developed field of "political psychology"). This science rested on a body of knowledge that began from elements of what we today call psychology; the primary substance or matter of nature that was of concern in politics was human nature, or the psychological makeup of individual human beings. This "substance" was then treated within a form of logical or hypothetical reasoning that was related to the question of how to put together a stable political order. The most familiar version of this science derived from English philosophy of the seventeenth century. It held that by performing a certain mental experiment, individuals could see the logic of a reciprocal exchange of rights and obligations in order to form and maintain allegiance to a properly constituted political order.[39] The aim of this science was not to develop knowledge of pure psychology—"rights," for example, is not a term of psychology—but to use aspects of psychology in combination with political reasoning to show how a successful political community might be constituted.

Not all of the Founders, to be sure, understood the concept of nature in exactly this way. Nature and natural law had meanings that stretched back to the classical philosophers and to Christian sources, and these previous views influenced the thinking of many Founders. Elements of these other conceptions were woven together, sometimes uneasily, with the more recent one. Religious thinking about the concept of nature at the time was widespread; it was also highly diverse. In some instances religious thinkers embraced the idea of nature in much the same sense as it was articulated in the more recent scientific account: God was author of the laws of nature, and nature was just as recent philosophy had described it. Expressing this view in theological language nevertheless kept religious duties and concerns of faith closer at hand than in a purely secular account. In other instances religious thinkers adopted a different concept of nature, adding Christian themes such as man's sinful nature or the natural status of the community. These thinkers often proceeded by the same method as that used in prevailing philosophic accounts, constructing a political community by combining psychology and political reasoning. The religious ideas could be confirmed by reason, even if they were suggested by religious thought and revelation. Thus, while there were differences in the understanding of the concept of nature, there was broad support for seeking a rational source of guidance for the political world.[40] According to James Kloppenberg, Americans in this period "were confident that the exercise of reason would enable them to fulfill their divinely ordained mission...Rationalism and religion seemed fully compatible."[41]

There is another sense in which the concept of nature has been accused of being "metaphysical." A number of European political theorists in the next generation, reflecting mostly on the uses of the idea of nature in the European experience, complained that "laws of nature" were magically invoked in every context, with a claim that abstract and deductive reasoning from nature could resolve almost every major issue of governance and public policy. This was clearly not the case with the concept of nature that was used in *The Federalist*. The idea of nature derived from politicalized psychology was central in providing a standard of right, in offering instruction on the ends or purposes of government, and in fixing a few essential elements about the structure of government. But deductions from nature could not provide direct guidance on most issues of constitutional construction or most policies relating to governing. The determination of how to proceed in these areas could be assisted by a different body of knowledge—namely political science, which was not deductive, but rather derived from compilations based on experience and on the observation of political matters.[42]

The account of the adoption of the concept of nature in the Founding period illustrates how questions about the foundations of political right, which many contemporary academic thinkers like to treat as purely theoretical issues, often arise within the realm of political life. The fate of these ideas is partly decided by political actors who measure these questions according to political judgments using political criteria, taking into account not only what they think will achieve an immediate objective, but also what they estimate will promote political health and well-being over the longer term. Foundational concepts that are invoked as ultimate justifications for immediate political action cannot simply be set aside or discarded in the aftermath, but continue to exercise an influence. In their own way, therefore, political actors engage in calculations having great theoretical importance. These judgments, especially in the latter case, rely both on theories and on their own experience. Political actors, except in rare or accidental circumstances, do not invent foundational ideas; they take them first- or second-hand from major thinkers. But the political actors often make the concrete determinations of how and when to "recur" to foundational concepts. Their range of choice may also be much broader than is usually depicted by intellectual historians, who like to present these decisions as somehow explained or determined by a dominant idea of the time. Here, however, modern historiography of the Founding, taken as a whole, points to an opposite conclusion. So many different schools have each staked a claim to dominant ideas—from enlightenment liberalism, to Whig traditionalism, to classical and Gothic republicanism, to Protestant communitarianism—that none was perhaps quite as determinative as has been made out. Could it be that the statesman of this period had to choose?

## The Early Period, 1776–1830

Following the Revolution and the Founding, nature became the chief foundational concept of American political life. Moderate Whig Customary History dropped out because of its connection with Britain. Real Whig Customary History enjoyed a slightly better fate, hanging on at the margins, especially among a few Jeffersonian-republican writers, where the Gothic thesis justified a decentralized view of authority.[43] But it played an increasingly minor role. The two main foundational debates involved Philosophy of History and a disagreement on the interpretation of the meaning of nature. These debates help to define the conflict between the Jeffersonians and the Federalists.

Philosophy of History emerged as an important partisan issue in the 1790s. The source of the controversy was the French Revolution, which in America became the prism through which many political leaders and thinkers began to view much of political life. To its inveterate opponents, who were concentrated in the group that became the core of the Federalist Party, Philosophy of History was seen as the driving theoretical force of the Revolution and thus of the radicalism of modern philosophy. Philosophy of History appeared in France in the 1790s in a more advanced and systematic form that gave Historical laws priority over the laws of nature in directing society. History's laws were broader, bolder, and more compelling than nature's ahistorical laws. Most important, the law of progress actually denied the concept of nature by claiming that the core substance of nature (human nature) was not permanent, but changed and progressed—so that, in Condorcet's words, "the progress of the perfectibility of man is truly indefinite. . . . The progress of this perfectibility . . . has no other limit than the duration of the globe upon which nature has cast us."[44] This claim crossed a theoretical red line, which some of its proponents in America tried to elide or to hide. But for opponents of Philosophy of History, this issue always lay at or just beneath the surface of every controversy.

It is questionable in what measure Jeffersonian republicans actually adopted the advanced positions of Philosophy of History. But in that decade's caldron of overheated partisanship, in which thinkers on both sides often approached a state of paranoia, Federalists ascribed all of the elements of this philosophy to the Jeffersonians. Jefferson was targeted for being "a disciple of Turgot, a pupil of Condorcet" and was widely designated the apostle of the doctrine of progress.[45] And it is true that he subscribed to large parts of the doctrine, although he certainly did bring the whole of his party along. But the reaction of the Federalists was the more important point. After reading Condorcet's *History* in 1795, John Adams commented that Condorcet had "waged a more cruel war against truth than was ever attempted by priest or king."[46] This sentiment signaled the advent of an important political change in America. It meant the end of adherence to a common "party" of philosophy and enlightenment that was aligned against the alleged obscurantism of the old regime; there was now more than one enlightenment. Americans could now also feel free to form closer political alliances with monarchies, if this step was needed to defeat new and greater threats to liberty and civilization coming from parts of modern philosophy.

To understand the debate over Philosophy of History, not just in this period, we need to clarify the term "progress." Except for a few gloomy souls such as Henry Adams, who elaborated a theory of historical decline, almost no one dares to speak against progress. Since the Progressive era, "progress" has been widely understood in America to encapsulate a single theme in which those who preach the theoretical idea of progress are its only real advocates, and know best how to secure it, at a practical level. But this usage obscures the fact that what we think of as progress contains *two* ideas, which were once known to be distinct and which often used different words. One idea—attached to Philosophy of History—is the "law of progress," which holds that there is an immanent process at work in the temporal realm; History possesses its own agency.[47] The other idea speaks of "improvement" or "advancement." Advancement is a genuine possibility. Its history can be recorded and trends can be observed. But it is not tied to an intrinsic movement of History. Leaders of the Federalist and Whig Parties were proponents of advancement, even as they rejected the philosophical "idea of progress." Historians, who for a long time were entrapped in the Progressive understanding of progress, have woken up to discover that it was often the "conservative" parties that were the engines of development, while the self-proclaimed progressive parties could often lapse into nostalgia.[48]

Despite the charges and counter-charges about the status of Philosophy of History in the 1790s, leaders of both the major parties claimed to take their bearings from the concept of nature. But they developed significant differences in their understanding of what "nature" meant. Part of this debate fell within the boundaries of conflicting interpretations of what, looking back, we can now see as the same basic concept. The disputes here began with the question of how best to treat appeals to the concept of nature after the ratification of the Constitution, under an established and legitimate authority. Federalists argued that once a legitimate government had been instituted, it was best to be reticent about making direct political appeals to nature, for fear that they could destabilize government. Talk of nature in an active way should recede to the background. Jeffersonians, by contrast, continued to make appeals to nature, believing that this position served as a salutary check on governmental authority, which otherwise tended to expand. This difference reflected a related divergence on which of the two basic types of natural rights should be given greater emphasis: "collective rights" (the right of a people to alter or abolish its form of government) or individual rights (individual liberty and property). Federalists put more emphasis on the status of individual natural rights, especially after the establishment of the government, and regarded appeals to collective rights as dangerous and destabilizing. Jeffersonians put as much emphasis on collective as individual rights; this view led to their position on the need and even the wisdom of rewriting constitutions, which they abandoned after 1800 at the national level but maintained, with much success, at the state level. The emphasis on the collective right was eventually extended to the Jacksonian view of popular sovereignty and democracy as a kind of natural right.[49] As Daniel Rodgers has noted, well before slavery became a major issue of public discussion, for Democrats in the South "the hard core meaning of Natural Rights was a collective right: the revolutionary right to begin society over again," while in the North and especially among Federalists (and later Whigs), "natural rights inhered in the citizens as individual liberties."[50]

But it is clear that a major theoretical issue was at stake, although one in this case that the participants themselves had only begun to articulate. It went to the core of the meaning of "nature." Although both sides claimed to be interpreting the same concept, and probably thought they were, in retrospect it is evident that they began to articulate two very different ideas based on distinct sciences. The seeds of this difference can be traced to earlier debates between Anti-Federalists and Federalists about the extent of the use of nature in political life. Federalists, as noted, held that it supplied a general standard for the ends of political life, but it did not provide—and was not intended to provide—detailed assistance for writing constitutions, legislating, or conducting matters of policy. By contrast, some opponents of the Constitution invoked the concept of nature much more broadly, claiming that it meant, in a general sense, that which works "naturally" or easily on its own, or that which proceeds and sorts itself out according to a principle of spontaneous order. This issue emerged in the late 1780s in the context of constitutional discussions and the question of the merits of a unicameral versus a bicameral legislature. The deeper theme was that of the need for complexity in constitutional arrangements. Some Anti-Federalists sought help directly in the idea of nature. Thomas Paine stated this principle first: "I draw my idea of the form of government from a principle in nature which no art can overturn, viz. that the more simple any thing is, the less liable it is to be disordered and the easier repaired when disordered."[51]

The debate turned into an important transatlantic theoretical dispute that had a good deal to do with the formation of American political science. Turgot and Condorcet engaged in a famous exchange with John Adams and the Federalists, in which the French thinkers argued for the superiority of a unicameral legislature, as was found in Pennsylvania. Condorcet published an essay in America on this issue in 1787. Adams believed that the pamphlet marked the beginning of a campaign to redo all of America's state constitutions as well as the federal constitution.[52]

In this debate one begins to see that the two parties were no longer, in fact, interpreting the same concept of nature, but were speaking of different concepts that drew from different sciences. This was only the beginning. In what became the Jeffersonian-republican use of nature, thinkers went well beyond politicalized psychology and began to speak of the relations of all things—a notion of nature drawn principally from physics that posited a natural harmony and spontaneous order in matter as a whole. This idea came to Jeffersonians from the science of Physiocracy, or political economy. Physiocracy, which was the original name given to this school by its founder, François Quesnay, meant literally "the rule of nature," or, as Quesnay once put it, the "order of the laws of physics that govern the universe."[53] The principle of spontaneous order that governed the universe became the guiding idea for economics as well as politics. Things should be arranged so as to allow this principle to operate. Under the aegis of this view, the wisdom of the Jeffersonian legislator consists in establishing laws and norms that remove impediments to the spontaneous operation of nature. The famous expression that captured this strategy, a term which has been attributed to the Physiocrats, is *laissez faire*, meaning "allow to do," or, embellishing a bit, "allow nature to follow its course."[54] The version of this doctrine that is better known to us today was formulated by Adam Smith, a disciple of the Physiocrats, under the label "the system of natural liberty" or, more simply, "the invisible hand."

Followers of this understanding of nature among the Jeffersonian-republicans applied it to a broad range of political policies. One of the earliest and most important was in the area of economic policy, where Hamilton's plans for political and economic development became the central domestic issue around which the political parties formed. The Jeffersonians selected George Logan to be one of the chief theoretical respondents to the Federalist program. Logan's articles, published in the *National Gazette,* relied on the new science of "political economy," which Logan thought was "the best system of promoting the happiness of men united in society."[55] Its foundational principle was the idea of spontaneous order drawn from natural law: "The same Great Being who created man for the purposes of his own glory has also appointed an order of conduct calculated to conciliate the interests of men united in society."[56] The policy of noninterference, as the correct normative and regulative idea, applied not just to economic matters, but to other realms of policy as well. Remove special discretionary actions by government, and the underlying harmony at work in nature will come to the surface. This view of nature bordered on merging with a progressive Philosophy of History; if humans would allow the workings of nature to operate uninhibited, steady progress would result.

For Federalists, the concept of nature in relation to political life remained anchored in the science of politicalized psychology. There was no reason to think that the laws of spontaneous order that governed physical matters also governed human matters in the political realm. In fact, experience showed the opposite. In the political realm, chaos and force were often the prevailing facts of reality, requiring constant superintendence. Even activities in the human realm had to be divided. The "laws" that often seemed to apply in one area (economics) did not govern in another (politics).[57] The attempt to impute a general rule of spontaneous order to political affairs represented an unwarranted extension of the natural sciences into the political realm. It would eliminate the distinctness of political science, conflating it with the natural or physical sciences and making it subordinate to them.

This theoretical error—the error of the overextension or imperialism of the physical sciences—is one of the few genuinely philosophical themes that Federalists discussed in their political writings, a fact which is an indication of its significance. The treatment began in *The Federalist,* erasing in this case any distinction, until later, of the Founders and the Federalists. The error resulted in part from the ignorance of speculative thinkers, who knew little if anything about practical affairs and accordingly transported principles from one realm to another, seeking in effect one undifferentiated science of all of nature. If something was true in one area, they concluded, it must be true in another. The error also came from the ambition of these thinkers. If a homogeneous principle governed all matter, then philosophers, not political actors, were the best suited to understand it and could rightly claim a larger sharer of governing; scientific or philosophical expertise should hold sway over political judgment. The Federalists rejected this approach. The laws of nature in political life—because they involve humans in a political setting—are different in kind from the laws of nature in the physical realm.[58] There is no single meta-science, but different sciences applicable to different spheres.

On the basis of this understanding, the Founders and then the Federalists argued for a distinct political science. It supported, in their view, complexity in constitutional arrangements; broad discretion in the conduct of political affairs, especially in international relations; and, in what became the impetus for partisan division, significant interventions in economic matters to promote conditions of prosperity. Federalist economic policies rested on their own view of the field of "political economy," according to which a "political" logic took precedence over an "economic" logic, even when it came to more purely economic issues such as economic growth.

## Whigs and Democrats, 1830–1850

The period from the 1830s to the 1850s—sometimes known as the period of the second-party system—is notable for the introduction of History as a foundation in American politics. By the middle of the 1830s, the two major political parties had each embraced an idea of History in a synthesis with nature. The Whig Party relied on the Historical School while the Democratic Party adopted a version of Philosophy of History. To borrow a formulation from Emerson, the Whigs were the "Party of Memory," the Democrats the "Party of Hope."[59]

The recourse to History cannot be understood without going back to the reactions in Europe to the French Revolution. An entire apparatus of thought that developed in the first decades of the nineteenth century was brought over and introduced into American partisan controversy. Opponents of the French Revolution faced a crucial decision. One option was to wall off the dangerous parts of philosophy, branding them as pseudo-philosophy, while continuing to defend philosophy rightly understood. A second option was to raise suspicions about philosophy itself as a political foundation. This position rested on a judgment that the radical emanations of philosophy were either its logical conclusion or the likely consequence of any effort to make philosophy public. Conservative thinkers in Europe increasingly embraced the latter option. In an attempt to counteract the ills of philosophy, they turned to the particular histories of their different nations. If people would give up their fascination with abstractions (nature) and look instead to the accumulated wisdom of their traditions, the door would be opened to a safer and better standard of right. A turn to History, in the form of tradition, could be the cure for the "metaphysical madness" introduced by the French Revolution.

In Germany, which became the primary source for American historical thinking, this theoretical position quickly became the basis for the new academic discipline of history. It was to be a discipline based on empirical inquiry and conscious methods of documentary and archival research. These historians claimed to have discovered the principle of organic growth of distinct communities as the salient fact of history itself. Some drew the conclusion from this discovery that the historian had a vital political and social function to perform: to bring this great historical truth, already intuitively sensed by each people, to the surface of its consciousness. The historian should evoke and cultivate a community's "experience of history" or its "historical sense."[60] This approach is what scholars now generally refer to as the "Historical

School." Meanwhile, a second cluster of German thinkers, while endorsing the general premise of the organic growth of communities, objected to the unwillingness of the historians to go beyond individual cases. It was possible, these thinkers said, to combine the insights of the Historical School with the idea of a general Philosophy of History. Each nation or culture possessed its own character, or its "idiosyncrasy of spirit" as Hegel said, but in the succession of empires, nations, and cultures, one could still detect a universal account of the advancement of humankind.[61] At each stage of development, one nation or culture carried forward the universal movement of History. A nonrevolutionary, Idealist Philosophy of History emerged in Germany that was distinct in tone from the version associated with the French school of Condorcet, although still fully committed to the idea of progress.

These two views of history were introduced into American politics in the 1830s and 1840s. The Whigs, as the party of memory, emphasized tradition as the source of identity, praising the Founders as "Fathers." Since the Founders themselves had relied on the foundation of nature, the Whigs treated the concept as genuine in its own right and as an integral part of the American tradition. Unlike European conservative parties, American Whigs did not initially oppose tradition to nature. They sought a synthesis. Their appeal to tradition was nevertheless intended to supplement, perhaps even to moderate, the concept of nature, at least in the way that they claimed it was understood in their day. The concept of nature referred to a mechanist and materialist understanding of human beings, which Whigs attributed not to the Founders, but to John Locke, whose name was widely evoked, in this case by intellectuals of all stripes, as a symbol of materialist rationalism. In the Whigs' view, the appeal to tradition could save the American system. It could prevent the concept of nature from being appropriated entirely by Lockean rationalism, allowing it to be connected to the more moderate thought of the Founding; it could encourage certain moral and political qualities, such as duty and nobility, that were undervalued in the philosophy of nature; it could ensure that political rhetoric spoke to the whole person, the heart as well as the head, sentiment as well as reason; and finally, it could make Americans understand themselves as a naturally occurring whole, or "people," rather than as a collection of disparate individuals or states bound together in a merely contractual arrangement.

Fostering national unity was a major theoretical concern of the thinkers of the Historical School in Europe. And it was of uppermost importance to the Whigs, who also had to consider the political situation in America. The heated controversy over Missouri's application for admittance to the Union as a slave state in 1819 and 1820, which Jefferson referred to as a "fire bell in the night," revealed the depth of sectional feeling that was present in the country. The immediate crisis was resolved by the Missouri Compromise, which balanced Missouri's admission with that of Maine as a free state. But sectional feelings again boiled to the surface in 1828 with the passage of what John Calhoun, then vice-president, called the "Tariff of Abominations" and the ensuing attempts by the state of South Carolina to nullify this law. In response to the threat of disintegration, political leaders in both parties sought to find a basis for restoring national unity. The Whigs preached a "thicker" or more substantive version of cohesion than the Democrats; in their approach, there needed to be common beliefs, common feelings, and a common sense of history. One of the Whigs' primary criticisms of the Lockean concept of nature was that it did not recognize or reflect seriously enough on the character of the community. The idea of nature was predicated on the individual (and all individuals—that is, humanity or mankind), not on peoples or nations. If nature was to serve as the standard, then how could the most important element of politics—a people or nation—be denied the status or dignity of being a full natural entity? Because of this defect, Whigs sought to endow the historical process itself with the status of being part of nature in its own right, so that the nation or community could be seen as a product of natural organic growth. Implicit in this view was a new and different understanding of nature that had loose connections to biology. But neither the American Whigs, nor those of the Historical School in Europe, succeeded at this time in making this idea of nature part of a full positive science; it was nature by analogy, akin to what was seen in the growth of mighty trees or beautiful English gardens.[62]

The Whigs were self-consciously a "conservative" party. Conserving the existing political system (and the Union) depended on developing an appreciation for the "experience of history," meaning the inclination of a people to see itself as linked to its past and as finding its identity in common chords of memory. Cultivating this experience was the chief function of the historical writer, as well as one of the highest obligations of the statesman. In the words of one of their ablest spokesmen, Senator Rufus Choate, the study of history

> holds up to our emulation and love great models of patriotism and virtue. It introduces us into the presence of venerated ancestors, "of whom the world was not worthy." It teaches us to appreciate and cherish this good land, these forms of government . . . by reminding us through how much tribulation, not our own, but others', these best gifts of God to man have been secured to us. It corrects cold selfishness which would regard ourselves, our day, our generation, as a separate and insulated portion of man and time; and, awakening our sympathies for those who have gone before, it makes us mindful, also, of those who are to follow, and thus binds us to our posterity by a lengthening and golden cord. It helps us to realize the serene and august presence and paramount claims of our country, and swells the deep and full flood of American feeling.[63]

Whigs intended the historical sense to influence not just *what* people thought, but more importantly *how* they went about thinking. It would discourage viewing the world as a *tabula rasa* or an arena for willful remaking, which were central charges leveled against Jacobinism and Jacksonian Democracy. The cultivation of the historical sense would serve as an antidote to an expanding pragmatic mode of thinking, identified at the time by Tocqueville, wherein "tradition is taken only as information" and individuals are "constantly led back toward their own reason as the most visible and closest source of truth."[64]

Having elevated tradition to so high a status, Whigs had to determine its content. New England Whigs initially emphasized the "rediscovery" of the Pilgrims and the Puritans, creating the thesis of the two foundings—a thesis embraced in a qualified way by Tocqueville—that declared the Puritans to be our "first Fathers," who were set alongside the "Fathers" of 1776–1789 as the creators of America. America had two originary moments. The two-foundings thesis solidified the Whigs' theoretical synthesis of nature and History; the elements emphasized in the Puritan founding were those that were needed to correct the inadequacies of the concept of nature. In his oration "The Age of the Pilgrims, Our Heroic Period" (1843), Choate commended the Puritans for having "blended harmoniously into living systems . . . the ancient prudence and the modern, the noble free genius of the old Paganism and the Christianity of the Reformation, law and liberty."[65]

As a harbinger of the instability that eventually undermined this synthesis, one strand of Whig thought revived the Gothic thesis to the virtual exclusion of the concept of nature. America's first important environmentalist, George Marsh, delivered an oration, "The Goths of New England," in which the Founders almost drop out and the Puritans, described as the heirs of the Saxons and Goths, become the source of American liberties. These liberties are ascribed to the mores acquired in the forests of Germany, rather than to any philosophical doctrine. "Gothicism," a term Marsh coined, was the source of "true moral grandeur" and "higher intellectual power," while philosophy, especially the Lockean variant, leads to "grasping ambition," "material energies," and "selfishness."[66] This was a pure expression of political

Romanticism that broke in theory, if not yet in name, from the Founding.

The Whigs developed a new way of conducting discussions of national political theory. The approach consists of theorizing through historical interpretation, or what has since been labeled, in a phrase adapted from Choate, as the creation of a "usable history."[67] A historical moment, deemed originary, is selected and receives special emphasis, in part for its pure historical importance, but also because it contains ideas that support a current political position. A helpful account of the past, as Choate noted, "tells the truth, to be sure . . . but does not tell the whole truth."[68] The Whigs sensed that it was simpler and more effective to promote certain ideas by locating their origin within a widely respected political tradition rather than by advocating them solely as abstract propositions. Theoretical argumentation cannot generate the same authority and legitimacy as that which is conveyed by appeals to tradition.

Although New England Whigs intended the two-foundings thesis to be the basis for a *national* history, it predictably encountered resistance from other parts of the country, causing Whig leaders to search for themes having no regional color. The better course became the celebration of the work of one set of founders (Founderism) and the dignity of the original constitutions (Constitutionalism). Choate memorialized this theme in a famous address delivered at Harvard Law School in 1845: "To interpret these constitutions, to administer and maintain them, this is the office of our age of the profession. Herein have we somewhat wherein we glory; hereby we come into the class and share in the dignity of founders of the States, of restorers of States, of preservers of States."[69] This theme is far better known to us today from a speech given by the young Whig Abraham Lincoln, in which he intensified the call for developing a national historical consciousness by advocating a "political religion": "Let reverence for the laws be breathed by every American mother, to the lisping babe, that prattles on her lap—let it be taught in schools, in seminaries, and in colleges; let it be written in Primers, spelling books, and in Almanacs; let it be preached from the pulpit, proclaimed in legislative halls, and enforced in courts of justice. And, in short, let it become the *political religion* of the nation."[70]

The Democratic Party, in its dominant "Jacksonian" strand, introduced an American version of Idealist Philosophy of History. American Idealism was built on the theme of progress understood as the spread of democracy. In contrast to the original version of Condorcet, which countenanced revolutions, the emphasis for American Idealists was on steady organic growth. America, in their view, was born with the germ of democracy already implanted—a germ that originated in Germany and that has been unfolding ever since. Idealism assigned roles in the unfolding of universal history to particular nations, with America in our age, the last age, being the leader. This historical mission was wrapped up as well in a pantheistic form of Sacred History, with Providence seconding Spirit in pushing Democracy forward.

Like the Whigs, Democrats professed support for the concept of nature and initially promoted both foundations in a loose synthesis. Democrats had reasons of their own for seeking to qualify or supplement the concept of nature. They worried that it was not a thoroughly democratic concept, especially as interpreted by conservative forces. It also favored the idea of rational construction in political life, which undermined the view that there was an automatic process in History that was responsible for progress.

The great American spokesman for this position was George Bancroft. Bancroft was not only the most renowned American historian of the age, but he was also an advisor to many Democratic presidents and politicians and was a cabinet member under President James K. Polk. He was a "public intellectual" before the term existed, a role he played with greater deftness and less sycophancy than many of our self-proclaimed public intellectuals today. Many of the great statements of Jacksonian Democracy have Bancroft's intellectual fingerprints all over them. It was the historian's function to speak to the public, since History was meant to be the foundation of political life. The historian traces events to their causes, but, not stopping there, looks for "the place they occupy in the progress of humanity, . . . and when history is viewed from this point, it is found that humanism is steadily advancing, that the advance of liberty and justice is certain."[71]

Bancroft equated liberty and justice with the Democratic idea (with either a big or a small *d*). As he declared before a state Democratic Party convention: "The voice of the people is the voice of pure Reason. . . . Give power to the whole people and you get the nearest expression of the law of God, the voice of conscience, the oracle of universal reason."[72] America moved forward by incorporating and building on its past, not by turning away from it. But Bancroft ridiculed the posture of reverence adopted by the Whigs. He favored a bias for change, on the grounds that the present was always better than the past: "Everything is in motion for the better. The last system of philosophy is always the best. . . . The last political state of the world likewise is ever more excellent than the old."[73]

As an advocate of Philosophy of History, Bancroft could never lend his full faith or credit to the idea of a conscious making, or a rational founding, of a political regime. The assumption of History is that an immanent process, and not human agency, ultimately determines the movement of things inside the temporal process. Despite his many eloquent praises of the Founding Fathers, Bancroft sought to discredit the idea of the rational legislator: "The formation of political institutions in the United States was not effected by giant minds. . . . There can be no such thing as a creation of laws; for laws are but the arrangement of men in society."[74] The colonies' development into a great nation was not "the offspring of deliberate forethought; they were not planted by the hand of man; they grew like the lilies, which neither toil nor spin."[75] As an alternative to conscious making, Bancroft described a process that worked through the unplanned and unconscious instincts of the mass of the people. The more democratic a society is, the more natural it is—"natural," now, in the sense of spontaneously felt and organically developing. Rationality is to be found not in the individual mind grasping reality, but in the invisible hand of History. The historical process is identified with democracy, because the race or species is greater than the individual. In one of Bancroft's best-known passages he says:

> The people can discern right. Individuals are but shadows, too often engrossed by the pursuit of shadows; the race is immortal: individuals are of limited sagacity; the common mind is infinite in its experience: individuals are languid and blind; the many are ever wakeful: individuals are corrupt: the race has been redeemed; individuals are time-serving; the masses are fearless: individuals may be false; the masses are ingenuous and sincere: individuals claim the divine sanction of truth for the deceitful conceptions of their own fancies; the Spirit of God breathes through the combined intelligence of the people.[76]

Manifest Destiny, a doctrine that Bancroft helped to formulate, was the supreme practical expression of this foundational concept. The term was coined in 1845 by John O'Sullivan, who, with help from President Martin Van Buren, founded the *Democratic Review*. O'Sullivan was a leading light of the Democratic intellectual movement known as Young America. It was egalitarian, opposed to the stuffy Whigism ("Old Fogery") of New England thinkers, and favorable to the expansion of the democratic idea. O'Sullivan was a great admirer of Bancroft, whom he frequently consulted, and many of his editorials read like glosses on Bancroft's early orations:

> The expansive future is our arena, and for our history. . . . We are the nation of human progress, and who will, what can, set limits to our onward march? . . . The far-reaching, the boundless future will be the era of American greatness. . . . There is

an immense field open to us, if we would but enter it boldly and cultivate it as our own. All history has to be re-written; political science and the whole scope of all moral truth have to be considered and illustrated in the light of the democratic principle. All old subjects of thought and all new questions arising, connected more or less directly with human existence, have to be taken up again and re-examined in this point of view.[77]

A few years later, Stephen Douglas, another political leader who consulted George Bancroft, became a leading voice of Young America and one of the principal figures in the Northern Democratic Party. The character of the Democratic Party in the 1850s is entirely misread if it is viewed as the defender of old ways. Douglas was the supreme advocate of Manifest Destiny and progress, which were the major positive themes he developed in his Senate race against Abraham Lincoln in 1858. He objected to the Republican Party on the grounds that the divisiveness it introduced on the question of slavery would be an impediment to territorial expansion and thus to genuine democratic progress. He announced that "whenever it becomes necessary in our growth and progress to acquire more territory, I am in favor of it without reference to the question of slavery. . . . Just as fast as our interests and our destiny require additional territory in the North, in the South, or on the Islands of the ocean, I am for it."[78]

From a theoretical point of view, the period of the 1830s and 1840s is arguably the richest era of foundational thinking in American history. Public intellectuals and political actors considered almost all of the theoretical options of American politics and indeed of modern political theory. No question was left unstudied, but none perhaps was considered in an entirely satisfactory way. It was also a period in which the choices political actors made about foundational concepts seemed at times to be only marginally related to the realities of American political life. The memory of the crisis of the French Revolution, and of European reactions to it, held sway out of all proportion to its relevance to American life. The emergence of new and powerful political events in the next decade broke this spell and forced a reassessment in foundational thinking.

## The Struggle over Union, 1850–1865

The decade of the 1850s provides the clearest case in American history in which the political debate of the day focused directly on foundational concepts. Republicans often insisted on a dialogue of this kind, with Lincoln taking the lead. The view is expressed in his statement cited earlier: "No policy that does not rest upon some philosophical public opinion can be permanently maintained." Republicans were not alone in stressing foundational ideas. Abolitionists, Southern Democrats, and elements of the Northern Whig Party took part as well. The political controversies of this decade serve as a textbook example, if ever one were needed, refuting the skeptical view that foundational concepts are merely epiphenomenal.

For Republicans the national crisis was prepared by the open rejection of the original concept of nature. The moving force in denying natural right came chiefly from thinkers in the South. John C. Calhoun, in a famous Senate speech in 1848, labeled natural equality "the most false and dangerous of all political errors."[79] In place of nature, Southern thinkers relied on two alternative foundational principles: a version of the Historical School and the science of ethnology as the basis for a new standard of natural right. These foundations undergirded the Southern movement of secession and helped to form the ideational basis for the Confederacy.

Proponents of the Southern Historical School, as exemplified by the South Carolinians John Calhoun and James Hammond, adopted the same theoretical position on History as the Whigs. In this view, the standard of right is found in the tradition of each particular people or culture. Just as some Whigs had once concentrated on the local (New England) as the genuine or authentic source of tradition, and of who "we" are, so these Southerners appealed to their community of the heart, the South, which antedated the Founding and which included the institution of slavery. Hammond, the governor of South Carolina, conceded that Southerners had mistakenly embraced the Founders' concept of the law of nature after the Revolution. Only recently had they become aware of their error, when the radical policies advocated by the abolitionists and Republicans forced them to take stock of their situation. Echoing an argument made by the rump of the Northern Whig Party, these Southerners equated the Founder's concept of nature with the same kind of principles that produced the French Revolution. In Hammond's words, "Abolitionism had shown the face of fanaticism, and this fanaticism showed the same spirit—indeed was the historical legacy—of the Jacobinism of the French revolution."[80] For emphasis, the proponents of the Historical School also tried to argue that culture was an expression of nature, though without offering a full scientific explanation. In Calhoun words, "men's natural state is social and political. . . . [Instead of] being born free and equal, [men] are born subject, not only to parental authority, but to the laws and institutions of the country where born, and under whose protection they draw their first breath."[81]

The Southerners' other challenge to the Founders' understanding of nature derived from a science of man that was different from politicalized psychology—the science known as ethnology or natural history. In the original eighteenth-century statement of this science, Linnaeus and Buffon began by classifying living creatures into their different natural groupings or species. Of particular interest was the study of differences among subgroups of the same species—for example, the different types or varieties of dogs. This analysis was then applied to the study of human beings, where natural differences were connected with morphological attributes, chiefly those of the different races. The conclusion commonly drawn was that the races differed markedly not only in physical appearance, but also in intellectual and moral qualities.[82] This science began without any concern for politics, but was imported into the political realm. If nature was to be the standard for modern society, then this science, which studied man in a scientific way, should have a place alongside politicized psychology.

The political consequences derived from ethnology were disputed, but a frequent inference was that the different varieties of men (races) should not live together in the same political community. Amalgamating the races was somehow against nature and would have the unhappy consequence of lowering the superior races in an averaging process with the inferior ones. Thomas Jefferson introduced this science into America in his *Notes on the State of Virginia*, a work in which he attempted systematically to combine and make consistent the two sciences of politicized psychology and natural history. From politicized psychology he concluded that because all men, by virtue of being men, were equal, they enjoyed a claim to natural rights, while from natural history he concluded that because of the differences between blacks and whites, the two races should live in different communities. His solution, consistent with ending slavery, was to recommend two nations on the North American continent, one white and the other black. By the 1830s this tenuous attempt to combine the two sciences was unraveling. To many, natural history with its extensive body of empirical research was considered to be the more genuine science. Southerners began to draw on it in a new way to deny outright the science of the Founders and to justify slavery as a natural relation. According to Alexander Stephens, vice-president of the Confederacy, the American Founding "rested upon the assumption of the equality of the races. This was an error. . . . Our new government is founded upon exactly the opposite idea; its cornerstone rests upon the great truth that the negro is not the equal of the white man; that slavery—subordination to the superior race—is his natural and normal condition."[83]

For Republicans the immediate practical controversy was not with Southerners, where the Republican Party had no following, but with its Northern competitors, the remnant of the Whigs that did not join the Republicans and the Northern Democrats. Lincoln's debate was chiefly with the leaders of the sections of these parties—with Rufus Choate and Stephen Douglas. Each became the explicit target of Lincoln's criticisms—Choate for trivializing the Declaration by referring to its "glittering generalities," and Douglas for restricting it to "white Europeans" only. These criticisms showed what had had happened to their parties over the past decade. Going back to the 1830s, each national party had adopted a foundational concept of History while attempting to tie it, in a loose synthesis, with the Founders' concept of natural right. As time went on, History played an increasingly larger role, diminishing the purchase of the Founders' view of nature.

The conflict between the Republicans and those who remained Whigs is best summarized in the Lincoln-Choate debates. Republicans insisted on the primacy of nature over History, while the Whigs chose History over nature. Most Republicans, of course, had been Whigs, and they showed the influence of their origins by continually invoking the tradition of the Founding. But that tradition now was of the Founders who had gloriously "discovered" the concept of natural right. There was no doubt about the supremacy of nature over tradition in Republican thinking. The "Republican Fathers" whom Republicans venerated in their first party platform were celebrated because of their invocation of the "self-evident truths of the Declaration."[84]

Choate attacked the Republicans as rationalist Jacobins responsible for introducing abstract principles at the expense of the concrete good. While he continued to speak of natural right, he did so without according it any real effect. He characterized the Republican Party as a dangerous "Geographical party," and described its "constitution" to be "the glittering and sounding generalities of natural right which make up the Declaration of Independence."[85] His sole active foundation now was History. Lincoln famously singled out Choate for trivializing the concept of nature. In his address to the first Republican state convention of Illinois, he is quoted as saying, "Choate, from our side of the house, dares to fritter away the birthday promise of liberty, by proclaiming the Declaration to be 'a string of glittering generalities'; and the Southern Whigs, working hand in hand with proslavery Democrats, are making Choate's theories practical."[86]

Given Choate's fervent opposition to the Republican Party, it is not surprising that he made the pragmatic decision to support the Democrat James Buchanan in 1856 rather than the Whig Millard Fillmore. Buchanan, he believed, was the candidate most likely to prevail, and he sought to rally the remaining Whigs to the Democratic banner. Besides his arguments against the Republican Party, Choate found a way to defend the Democratic Party, praising it because it burned "with that great master passion this hour demands—a youthful, vehement, exultant, and progressive nationality."[87] This endorsement was striking because it showed the leader of the party of tradition supporting the party of progress. The two variants of History—the Historical School and Philosophy of History—were not as far apart as the public intellectuals of the Whig and Democratic parties had previously thought. Both of the foundational concepts derived from History, and each, in the end, was closer to the other than either was to the concept of nature. A large part of the Democratic Party, favorable to the law of progress, and remnants of the Whig Party, devoted to tradition, joined together in condemning the Republican Party's recourse to nature.[88]

The conflict between Republicans and Northern Democrats, featured in the Lincoln-Douglas debates, focused on the Democrats' direct denial, or their acquiescence in the denial, of the Founders' foundation of nature. The basis for this denial was never perfectly clear. In the Declaration, as noted, Democrats had attached the argument of popular sovereignty to the natural right of consent of the governed, but by the 1850s, to satisfy the Southern wing, they stopped referring to the original standard of nature. The most important foundation for the Democrats, however, was Philosophy of History. The idea of progress did not demand accepting Douglas' "don't care" policy, as seen by the fact that a number of Northern Democrats who subscribed to progress deserted the party. But there is no doubt what Douglas thought. In his estimation, the Republican Party's staunch opposition to slavery would block territorial expansion and close the door to the spread of democracy. The Republican Party was an impediment to progress.

Lincoln did not make Philosophy of History a major issue in his debate with Douglas, but it did attract his interest. In an uncharacteristically theoretical analysis of the Democratic Party, Lincoln singled out the Young America movement for examination, portraying the "Young Democrat," with more than a touch of irony, as someone who believes himself to be "the inventor and owner of the *present*, and the sole hope of the *future*." The "soul" of the typical Young Democrat he continued, is filled with "a great passion—a perfect rage—for the '*new*.' . . . He knows all that can possibly be known; inclines to believe in spiritual rappings, and is the unquestioned inventor of 'Manifest Destiny.'" Lincoln criticized the philosophical idea of progress, which did not produce real advancement. The engine of genuine development—practical progress—lay in a rational spirit of "observation and reflection" that produced "discoveries, inventions, and improvements."[89]

Northern Democrats were also at least partly influenced by arguments that derived from ethnology. Lincoln's response to those arguments reveals much about the epistemological character of the Founders' concept of nature. Lincoln never engaged in a direct quarrel with the empirical findings of ethnology, a matter on which he possessed no scientific competence. State-of-the-art science at the time had established that there were important differences among the types of man (the races), a view that remained in effect until the early twentieth century. What Lincoln did was to restate, in various ways, the logic and evidence of the original science of politicalized psychology, using it to reject any inferences from natural history that were at odds with the established facts of equality in rights and a common human nature. On this basis, whatever ethnology might have proven about differences among groups, it remained that the basic rights deriving from equality apply to all, not just to the "superior races," and that slavery was "a gross outrage on the law of nature."[90]

Lincoln did not use politicalized psychology to claim that there were no differences between races or groups. This science had never spoken directly about this issue. To attempt to extend the concept of nature to deny the possibility of group differences would be to change it from a science into what so many later criticized it for being: mere ideology or sentimental moral posturing. Lincoln did, however, point out an important contradiction in how Democrats made use of ethnology. Their case for slavery drew on the biological argument against amalgamation, which was the point in this science that enjoyed the widest support. Yet from this very argument, according to Lincoln, the opposite conclusion followed. The institution of slavery, which involved forced sexual relations ("concubinage") as well as forced labor, increased the rate of intermixing. Slavery "is the greatest source of amalgamation."[91]

Lincoln's treatment of foundational concepts should be looked at as a source of instruction on the general theme itself. Lincoln went through three phases of foundational thinking that were different, although not contradictory. He began as a Whig, affirming a general Whig synthesis of nature and tradition while speaking infrequently of the concept of nature. In his second phase, as a Republican in the 1850s, the center of his thinking flowed from restating the concept of nature. In a third and final phase, evident only in the last year of his life, he added the dimension of a new version of Sacred History that became the framework for his Second Inaugural Address.

The third phase never succeeded in shaping the thought of the Republican Party or the nation, as Lincoln's life was cut short well before he could articulate this account in full, if in fact this had ever been his intention. The Second Inaugural nevertheless looms sublimely over all subsequent American political thought. Lincoln's understanding of Sacred History was of a different order altogether from either the old Puritan version or the newer Idealist (and pantheistic) version of Bancroft and others. Lincoln's invocation of the "providence of God" did not offer Sacred History as a direct guide to action. On the contrary, his understanding of Providence expressly denies the possibility of any sort of ultimate knowledge of the course of affairs in human history. This view is closer to the Founders' conception of rationalist history (with a small *h*) than it is to the Puritans. But Providence does add one element that is not present in rationalist history: it provides a sense of consolation that all will work out in the end. It helps to avoid despair and sustain resolve. Instead of fostering an attitude of resignation, it promotes the view that human action, however difficult it might be to discern its immediate effects, still has ultimate meaning. Lincoln's articulation of an idea of Sacred History seemed designed to serve as an antidote to the previous Idealist (and pantheistic) views of Bancroft and others. In light of the awful experience through which the nation was passing, a foundational concept proclaiming a law of progress could only appear empty and absurd. Second, the theme of Providence or Sacred History never denied or detracted from the concept of nature as the human standard of right. But Lincoln's Sacred History was clearly meant to speak to parts of the human experience—to themes of suffering and redemption—that scientific reasoning cannot address. There is no "tragic dimension" to the philosophical concept of nature.

Lincoln's "evolutions" suggest that while intuitions or convictions of the right foundation may not change, the tasks of political action in different contexts may demand alterations of emphasis and presentation. Lincoln was never overly concerned about proving his consistency when he shifted from the Whig to the Republican Party in 1856, but he did offer a clear reason for the change. The Whig Party's loose synthesis of nature and History, which worked well enough in the 1830s and 1840s, had been destroyed by shifts in the elite's and the public's foundational views. By the 1850s, support for natural right was in danger of collapsing: "The spirit of seventy-six and the spirit of Nebraska are utter antagonisms; and the former is being rapidly displaced by the latter."[92] Under this circumstance, not to insist openly on natural right would be to acquiesce in its burial, which would be a betrayal of the original Whig position. Lincoln claimed the sanction of the founder of the Whig Party, Henry Clay.[93] In the move from natural right to Sacred History, Lincoln sought to connect the natural-right teaching of the Founding to a view that made sense of the enormous sacrifice that the nation had endured in the Civil War. In all three phases, Lincoln dwelt on the problem of how it is possible in political life to secure a measure of resolve, beyond that provided by mere preference, to sustain a difficult course of action. The need in politics for an underlying foundation—or, as he put it, a common "philosophical public opinion"—was never in doubt.

## The Late Nineteenth Century, 1870–1900

The concept of nature was central to the political position of the Republican Party immediately following 1865. It served as a theoretical justification for the three Civil War Constitutional Amendments, as well as for the major Civil Rights legislation of the period. It is nevertheless a striking fact that after little more than a decade, the status of the original concept of nature as a full-fledged foundation began to decline precipitously. Republican Party rhetoric still paid deference to it, and it remained a formal or official principle. But many Republicans concluded that the staunchest proponents of the concept of nature in their own party —known, significantly, as Radicals—had extended the principle far beyond its original theoretical scope, using it as an ideological doctrine to push for full social equality. They had untethered the Declaration from the Constitution and pursued a moral postulate without regard to law. As for Democrats, most of them never fully embraced the concept of nature in the first place. Many remained proponents of the idea of progress, and their hope now was that with the slavery question resolved the party could return and reassume its status as the majority force in American politics. In brief, many in the nation were exhausted with or exasperated by "principle"—meaning, in this case, natural right. Lincoln's stature grew even as his influence diminished.

A parallel development was taking place in the theoretical realm. The concept of nature was widely regarded, perhaps even during the Civil War itself, more as a moral postulate or a tenet of "philosophy" than as a conclusion grounded in science. By the 1870s, "real" thought was no longer to be found in philosophy but was the domain of science, and "science" meant natural science. Within natural science, the dominant view of what constituted nature favored an evolutionary biological idea of progressive development, the shorthand name for which became "Darwinism." (The exact relationship of this view to Charles Darwin's scientific writings, which was always disputed, is of little significance.) The principle of evolutionary development was taken to be the cardinal fact of reality, or of nature, and it was quickly applied to the realm of human things. Nature in this sense became the template for human history. The two foundations—nature and History—now became virtually one and the same. Developmental biology and developmental History pervaded most fields of human knowledge.

There are many statements of this position. Perhaps none captures it better than a retrospective pronounced by Charles Francis Adams, a notable historian, who helped to establish the professional discipline of history in America:

On the first day of October, 1859 [the publication date of Darwin's *Origin of Species*], the Mosaic cosmogony finally gave place to the Darwinian theory of evolution. Under the new dispensation, based not on chance or an assumption of supernatural revelation, but on a patient study of biology, that record of mankind known as history . . . has become a unified whole—a vast scheme developing to some result as yet not understood. . . . History, ceasing to be a mere narrative made up of disconnected episodes having little or no bearing on each other, [became] a connected whole.[94]

The theoretical change to Darwinism had a momentum of its own, independent of the decisions of any political actors. But many political actors elected to acquiesce in it, seeing practical implications that they favored. Opponents of Reconstruction began to sense that it might provide help for their position not only by denying the scientific standing of the concept of nature, but also by dampening enthusiasm for reform. Reforms, in this view, could not work because members of an inferior race could not compete. According to the intellectual historian George Fredrickson, during Reconstruction "Social Darwinism, if not fully formulated or accepted as a popular creed, was nevertheless in the air, and some applied it explicitly to Reconstruction and the Negro."[95] Later on, other interpretations of Darwinism were used to justify a withdrawal of government from society (to allow the natural struggle to proceed) and even to reestablish and strengthen the racialist conclusions of ethnology, only now on a developmental foundation.

As in most attempts to combine nature and History, the dominant partner in the synthesis turned out to be History. Darwinism in this period was "Philosophy of History," except that no one dared to use this label out of embarrassment over the word "philosophy." This account was science, and some Darwinians referred to it as "scientific history." The prejudice in favor of natural science was so great that thinkers of the previous period, like George Bancroft, were compelled to recant their "metaphysical" approach and poetical style as the price for remaining members in good standing of the newly formed American Historical Association. But the disputes between the Darwinians and the older proponents of Philosophy of History seem in retrospect much less significant than they did at the time. The new scientific view favored the same idea of a law of progress as found in Idealist Philosophy of History, only it presented in a less sentimental way and without reference to terms like "Spirit" or "God." It was tough progress, born of struggle, but it was progress nonetheless. Its tone fit the sense of pathos many felt following the Civil War, when those who had witnessed the horrors of the period saw life at the individual level as governed by blind chance or fate. Progress there was, but it was progress compatible with a universe that was indifferent to man.[96]

The discipline that had the greatest influence in introducing History into political life was actually sociology, not history. Historical sociology (drawing on Darwinian biology, but in many cases foreshadowing it) applied evolutionary theory either directly, by referring to man's evolution as a species, or analogically, by arguing that social phenomena (institutions, languages, cultures) followed the same laws of movement as governed living beings. The leading early figure in this movement was the British sociologist Herbert Spencer, who enjoyed near-cult status in America. Spencerians were one of many schools in the "Darwinian" camp. They explained the mechanism of progress by a decentralized model in which nonintentional action produces a harmonious effect. Rationality was the blind result of a process, not a consequence of planned makings or constructions. Applied to the economic realm, Spencerians considered the *individual* human being as the primary unit, with progress coming through competition. The old Physiocratic principle of laissez-faire was now placed on the more solid ground of a biological idea of nature. In social policy, the Spencerians favored the same method of decentralized efforts and piecemeal trial-and-error mechanisms, not government interventions. As William Graham Sumner, a leading American social theorist of Spencerianism, observed: "The social order is fixed by laws of nature precisely analogous to those of the physical order. . . . The law of the survival of the fittest was not made by man and cannot be abrogated by man. We can only, by interfering with it, produce survival of the unfittest."[97] These Darwinists found a way to combine the necessity of Philosophy of History with free choice. Man possessed just enough agency to prevent progress: "The most that man can do is by ignorance and self-conceit to mar the operation of social laws."[98]

There is no question of the importance of this variant of Darwinism during this period, which Theodore Lowi described as the era's "public philosophy." It is customary in making this claim to catalogue the actions of the "captains of industry" or "robber barons," one of the most famous of whom was Andrew Carnegie, an individual of remarkable frankness. In his essay "The Gospel of Wealth," Carnegie defended the law of competition as "best for the race because it insures the survival of the fittest in every department."[99] His view seemed to differ from Lowi's only in his doubt that this harsh doctrine of nature could ever become a "popular" or "public" philosophy. It is not clear that its opponents ever thought so either, since they frequently charged that laissez-faire systems operated through the elite influence of wealthy industrialists and the courts. Spencerianism was a "nonpublic philosophy"; in the words of the Progressive platform of 1912, it was "an invisible government owing no allegiance and acknowledging no responsibility to the people."[100] The Progressives' main target of criticism in the American political system was the undemocratic exercise of excessive power of the courts, supported by the even more undemocratic authority of the Constitution.

Lowi's characterization of Spencerian or laissez-faire thinking as the dominant set of ideas of this period followed the lead of most progressive historians. They often designated the period from the 1870s until 1912 (or 1934) as the "Lochner era," named for the Supreme Court case of *Lochner v. New York* (1905). This case, which struck down a law limiting the working hours of bakers, was regarded as the quintessential symbol of laissez-faire thinking, and in Progressive writings it generally replaced the *Dred Scott* decision as the most infamous case in the annals of

Supreme Court history. It was in this decision that Justice Oliver Wendell Holmes, in dissent, issued a rebuke to his fellow justices, forever branding Herbert Spencer's name into America's historical consciousness: "The Fourteenth Amendment does not enact Mr. Herbert Spencer's *Social Statics*."[101]

The idea that Spencerianism was the sole claimant to Darwinist thought is, however, a clear exaggeration, born of the political passions of Progressive polemicists. There were other variants of Darwinism that rivaled Spencerianism in influence and importance. These differences found expression in competing factions in the Republican Party, since few Republicans in this era ever considered switching to the Democratic Party, which was still widely viewed as treasonous. All of the Darwinist factions stressed the biological idea of struggle that ended in progress, but they identified different entities as the primary "natural unit" or substance that constituted political reality. Against the Spencerians' emphasis on the *individual* human being, other currents stressed the collectivity, such as the "race" or the "nation." The practical effects resulting from these changes were often substantial. Shifting the primary natural unit could cause or justify different positions relating to the role of government or to the nation's place in the world. If the nation or the race was the natural unit involved in the struggle, then group solidarity or strong national action took precedence over laissez-faire. Theodore Roosevelt's initial brand of Progressivism relied on this line of reasoning, as did his view of world affairs. Whereas Spencerian proponents of laissez-faire, among them Sumner and Carnegie, opposed the Spanish-American War, in part because of its reliance on collectivist measures and political projects to direct the course of human affairs, Roosevelt took the opposite stance, attacking the Spencerians for being the "same types" who "stood against the cause of national growth, of national greatness, at the end of the century as at the beginning."[102]

Darwinian Philosophy of History also influenced the religious realm. A religiously oriented strand of Sacred History, known as the "Social Gospel," sought to marry evolutionary history to the coming of the Kingdom of God. It developed a substantial intellectual following. According to James Kloppenberg, "the Social Gospel moved gradually from the periphery to the center of American Protestantism."[103] Together with secular nationalist forms of Darwinism, elements of the Social Gospel movement helped to underwrite a new phase of American involvement in the world, in which the Anglo-Saxon race, now lodged chiefly in America, was seen as the instrument of progress. It was Manifest Destiny writ large. The best-known proponent of this position was Josiah Strong, whose works were among the most widely read of the period. Providence again became a source of particular guidance, enjoining a divine commission on America—"that God, with infinite wisdom and skill, is training the Anglo-Saxon race for an hour sure to come in the world's future. . . . The time is coming when . . . the world [will] enter upon a new stage of its history—the *final competition of races, for which the Anglo-Saxon is being schooled.*"[104] In Strong's theory, America had the sanction not only of God, but of the next-highest authority, Charles Darwin: "Mr. Darwin is not only disposed to see, in the superior vigor of our people, an illustration of his favorite theory of natural selection, but even intimates that the world's history thus far has been simply preparatory for our future, and tributary to it."[105]

No matter what the particular version of Darwinism, however, the concept of nature underlying it is clearly at odds with that presented at the time of the Founding. In the Darwinian view, the core of nature is a *process* that works in or through individuals or groups ("competition is the law of nature"), whereas under the Founders' concept, "nature" refers to the permanent and unchanging character of things. Yet even with this huge difference, most Darwinists in this period refrained from publicly emphasizing a break with the original idea of nature. They preferred to maintain an ambiguous alliance. For the conservative Darwinists, who wished to preserve the existing system of law and property, the Constitution was regarded as a bulwark of their position. Since progress came piecemeal, the Constitution and Founding were seen as parts of a developing heritage. Finally, for the Spencerians the claim of a natural right to property, although clearly fictitious, served as a convenient myth that supported the conditions for achieving progress.

The period from Reconstruction to the twentieth century is the Dark Ages of American politics, except that most Americans probably recognize the names of more of the Holy Roman Emperors than presidents of the United States. Scouring this period for statesmen who were able to command knowledge of the full breadth and depth of theoretical developments, and to shape it for any bold and constructive practical purpose, is a difficult if not futile endeavor. For many, this may have been precisely the point. They wished to avoid the influence of any strong foundation. Darwinian theoretical ideas were allowed to seep into politics, with the line of causality moving mostly from thinkers to politicians. One thing, however, is certain. The original idea of natural right lost ground, and with it any plan for securing for the rights of all citizens.

## *The Progressive-Liberal Era, 1900–1960*

Progressivism was a cross-party political movement of the early twentieth century that dramatically recast foundational thinking in America. Insofar as Progressivism had a common practical concern, it was rooted in a broad judgment that the new industrial order in America could not sustain civilization or its development. The nation and the world were in crisis. America had reached the end of an era, and only wholesale changes could now ensure its survival. A new and bolder course of action was required, in which government would have more authority and discretion to arrange or rationalize social processes.

This judgment emanated originally from intellectuals more than political actors, and it was supported from the outset by theoretical doctrines. No political movement in American history was more influenced by philosophical thought, even if much of that thought, under the label of pragmatism, was designed to clear away the influence of past philosophy and open the way to a new reign of social sciences. Political leaders like Theodore Roosevelt and Woodrow Wilson signed on, looking to win a margin for maneuver and a license to support much-needed political action and reform. But the influence of political leaders was minimized by a simple fact: Progressivism as a movement operating under its own name lasted a very brief time. It achieved dominance for only a few years (1913–1918) before being temporarily set aside. Progressivism came to live in America not in its original or pure form, but in the shape of the dimmer copy of Liberalism, which did not come to the forefront until the 1930s. By this time, however, the lines of foundational thought had been sketched and hardened by almost thirty years of previous thought. Liberals made significant changes on the other levels of ideas, but they merely tinkered and adjusted with the Progressives' foundational thinking.

Progressives—the name does not deceive—subscribed to the idea of progress. Like the Darwinists of the late nineteenth century, they took Philosophy of History as their foundational concept. While many remained Darwinists and subscribed to what they sometimes called "naturalism," they never subscribed to the notion of direct guidance from biological models of growth in which progress comes about on its own through individual competition.[106] They emphasized instead the need for conscious collective planning under the guidance of new and more advanced forms of social science. Since the past did not supply the answers, Progressives sought to liberate Americans from their servitude to tradition. They were directly critical of the original concept of nature, making Progressivism the first major national movement to offer the concept of History as the nation's primary foundational idea.

The Progressives' view of History developed more from the academic disciplines of sociology and philosophy than from history itself. The most important figure in launching Progressivism was the father of American sociology, Lester Ward, a declared disciple of Condorcet and Comte. Ward understood the function of sociology to be exactly that which Condorcet had claimed was the function of Philosophy of History: to discover the underlying principles of what causes social action, so that mankind could then make use of these principles to foresee and direct matters on the path of progress. Ward called this "intelligent control by society itself in its own interest."[107] John Dewey, the great Progressive philosopher, was less taken with sociology. Dewey called himself a Darwinian, but he made it clear that he was not following a strict biological model of automatic struggle. Mankind's distinctive tool for dealing with the world and for meeting the challenge of survival was human intelligence, or what Dewey called the "social conception of intelligence," to distinguish it from purely individual planning.[108] Until now, mankind had been able to progress without the need for much rational social planning, but the end of the nineteenth century was a critical turning point, not only in American history but also in world history. Social planning was an evolutionary necessity. In order to begin the task of reconstructing all fields of human knowledge, especially in the areas of morals and politics where science lagged so far behind, mankind would need the new instruments of pragmatic philosophy and a new social science.

Many prominent historians also joined the cause of Progressivism, lending the weight of academic history to this position. For the Progressive historians, the idea of progress was seen, at least initially, not as a postulate or a theory but simply as the objective reality of what history actually was.[109] The historians' greatest contribution, however, was not in the realm of original theorizing about the foundation of History, where they followed the lead of others, but in combating the sentiment of reverence for the Founders, in particular for the Constitutional Founders. Charles Beard, who wrote the most widely read academic work of the era,

*An Economic Interpretation of the Constitution of the United States* (1913), set the tone for these studies. An avalanche of such works followed, and even today, when advanced historical interpretations have gone in other directions, the Progressive view still informs many high school history texts. The result of the Progressives' professional historical writing was summed up by the Progressive intellectual historian Vernon Parrington: "Considered historically perhaps the chief contribution of the Progressive movement to American political thought was its discovery of the essentially undemocratic nature of the federal Constitution."[110] Herbert Croly, although not himself a professional historian, wrote works of American intellectual history assailing any sentiment that could be construed as cultivating reverence for the Founding and the Constitution. To honor the Constitution was to enslave one's mind and submit to an ancient authority that had become an instrument of repression. The Constitution was the functional equivalent of what it claimed to replace: "monarchy." "The Law in the shape of the Federal Constitution really came to be a monarchy of the Word."[111] Croly enjoyed considerable influence at the time as the founder and editor of *The New Republic*. Political leaders read his works—or claimed to—and insisted on consulting him. No wonder so many public intellectuals today appear to suffer from acute Croly envy.

In a curious way, the Progressives—led here by John Dewey—helped to "resuscitate" the Founders' concept of nature. They did so by insisting that the Founders' idea of nature was still the dominant foundational idea of American politics, notwithstanding their steady polemics against the Spencerians. As Darwinists themselves, they sought to protect that way of thinking, attributing the real problem of property rights more to the original concept of nature, with its notion of "timeless truths." Progressives accordingly set up a battle of the Titans between the Founders' philosophy of natural right and their own new philosophy of pragmatism. The outcome was never in doubt. Arguing that the concept of nature was "located in the clouds," Dewey declared that it was "a theory whose falsity may easily be demonstrated both philosophically and historically."[112] While it had served a constructive and progressive purpose in its day, it was now a retrograde doctrine that was being used to defend an absolutist right of property.

On a higher theoretical level, Progressives presented the argument that the concept of natural right was pure fiction. There were no permanent or trans-historical truths. "To ask whether the natural rights philosophy of the Declaration of Independence is true or false," the historian Carl Becker wrote, "is essentially a meaningless question."[113] Modern thinking did not work in this way. Mankind had grown up and passed beyond the metaphysical age. As Charles Beard remarked, "Efforts have been made to give force to rights by calling them natural [but] that was an eighteenth century custom."[114] John Dewey then took the next step, more important for philosophy in our time than in his day, of denying not only the reality of any idea of permanent nature, but also its utility as a standard for political life. Any view of permanent nature ("foundationalism," as it is referred to today) has an undemocratic effect. This charge may sound strange in light of the influence many believe has been exerted by the foundational claim that "all men are created equal"; but Dewey contended that, as a general philosophical proposition, any position that implies a theoretical hierarchy supports a principle of authoritarian political rule. A view that is "committed to a notion that inherently some realities are superior to others, are better than others, . . . inevitably works on behalf of a regime of authority, for it is only right that the superior should lord it over the inferior."[115] True democracy is foundation-less. Hidden in this position is an implicit "metaphysical" position of its own: only if the cosmos is seen as egalitarian is democracy safe.

Most Progressive intellectuals probably never expected that political leaders would engage in an open confrontation against the Founders. Their theoretical positions were not intended literally as "public philosophy"; they were meant as ideas that would slowly—and "progressively"—begin to weaken reliance on the Founders' doctrines. Parts of the Founders' practical work could be praised, up to a point at least, but the concept of natural right would be permitted to die a slow and painless death, never to be appealed to again in any significant cause.

Despite the Progressives' attacks on the Founders, it has been noted that their emphasis on science and reason, as well as their rejection of tradition, possesses certain similarities to the Founders' approach. Both were seeking to carve out a space for free action guided by human rationality in order to rescue liberal democracy from crisis. But in the end, it is the contrast between the two views that stands out; for although both endorsed political science, their conceptions of the discipline were at odds. Political science, for the Founders, was one of many distinct sciences that explored a realm possessing its own principles and logic. Investigation of political phenomena showed, for example, that while the application of collective reason to human affairs was possible and justified (as at the Founding itself), good judgment also dictated that it was wise to instill veneration for a functioning order: "The most rational government will not find it a superfluous advantage to have the prejudices of the community on its side."[116] Political science, for the Progressives, was part of general social science, which in turn emulated the natural sciences. By this understanding, an attitude of veneration of past authority, which stood in the way of progress in the natural sciences, was likewise of no benefit in the political world. For the Founders, political science had much to do with assigning and limiting powers and establishing political institutions within which civil servants would operate. In the tasks of governing and dealing with specific issues and problems, the Founders placed enormous weight on the discretion of political actors, whose decisions, for good or ill, would determine the outcome of political affairs. For the Progressives, social science itself could be relied on to determine the best policies, and social science expertise all but replaced the prudence of the statesman. Finally, the Founders' ordinary political science was encased within their understanding of nature, which instructed on the permanence of human nature. This foundational principle led to political conclusions that made the protection of rights a central aim of government and that placed limits and checks on political power. Rejecting a foundation in nature, the Progressives evidenced no such fear of political power. Their foundation in History, in which rational control assumes responsibility for guiding progress, had the consequence of adding to the power of the state.

A great deal has been written on Progressive theory, much of it laudatory. Its highest praise comes from those who hold that it supplied the dominant framework of thought for much of the twentieth century up to the 1970s. This position assumes a virtual identity between Progressivism and modern political Liberalism, which can be seen above all in their common advocacy of "positive government." This interpretation has recently been challenged, in particular by Michael Sandel, who has emphasized the conception of citizenship, rather than views of the scope of government, as the determining factor in defining a "public philosophy." Here is an instance where a failure to distinguish among the different levels of ideas leaves analysts talking past each other. Progressivism and Liberalism are at one on certain matters, but at odds on others. On the level of foundational concepts, it is the continuity between Progressivism and Liberalism that stands out. In regard to the concept of nature, Liberals, unlike Progressives, frequently invoke claims of rights, but following Progressives they rarely anchor them in a permanent idea of nature. (Or where they have done so, as in the opening phases of the Civil Rights Movement in the 1950s and 1960s, the practice has not continued.) The greatest Liberal expressions of the theme of rights are found in Franklin Roosevelt's speech on the "four essential freedoms" (1941)[117] and his allusion to a "second Bill of Rights" (State of the Union Address, 1944). Roosevelt appropriated the language of rights, but the basis of rights—at least of the new ones—lay in an evolving consensus:

This republic had its beginning and grew to its present strength under the protection of certain inalienable political rights. . . . They were our rights to life and liberty. As our nation has grown in size and stature, however—as our industrial economy expanded—these political rights proved inadequate to assure us equality in the pursuit of happiness. We have come to a clear realization of the fact that true individual freedom cannot exist without economic security and independence. . . . In our day these economic truths have become accepted as self-evident. We have accepted, so to speak, a second Bill of Rights under which a new basis of security and prosperity can be established for all—regardless of station, race, or creed.[118]

On the foundational concept of History, Liberalism, like Progressivism, was initially wedded to the idea of progress. Liberals minimized open attacks on the Founding and the Constitution, but their view of the Constitution shows an underlying continuity with Progressivism. Liberalism adopted the idea of the "living constitution"—an idea that is doubly progressive, first in its conception of fundamental law as an evolving body of doctrine, and second in its belief in measures favoring "social justice" (equality) and "evolving norms of human dignity."[119] During the New Deal, the "living constitution" referred to a method of judicial interpretation that deferred to Liberal legislative enactments—i.e., judicial restraint. In a second phase, which began in the 1950s, the "living constitution" referred to a method that promoted Progressive-Liberal interpretations, if need be *against* legislative measures—i.e., judicial activism. If ever the "living constitution" ceases to function in favor of promoting Progressive-Liberal goals, the doctrine is certain to become a dead letter.

The combination of Progressivism and Liberalism into a single bloc helps to account for the emergence of the original definition of the "public philosophy" as a set of ideas that "dominates" the formation of public policy. For if there was ever any set of policy ideas in American history that has met the criterion of becoming a decisive winner and of routing its foes, at least among the intellectual segments of society, it is modern Liberalism. Lionel Trilling opened his book *The Liberal Imagination* (1950) with the observation that "in the United States at this time Liberalism is not only the dominant but even the sole intellectual tradition."[120] His point was not that there was no conservative opposition, but rather that most of it was instinctual, without a coherent theoretical framework or a set of foundational concepts.

There were nevertheless two significant alternatives to Liberalism offered during this period. Their immediate political weight was small, since Liberalism was then so powerful, but they have managed to persist and now appear as important currents within the Republican Party. The first position is traditionalism; the second, libertarianism. Both rely on a foundation of History, one in the Historical School and the other in a form of Philosophy of History.

Traditionalists today trace their origin to the Southern Agrarian movement of the late 1920s. The leaders of this movement, which included such notable literary figures as John Crowe Ransom (its chief spokesperson), Allen Tate, and Robert Penn Warren, published a controversial tract, *I'll Take My Stand*, in 1930 that was intended to overthrow the foundation of American life based on a progressive Philosophy of History. The book opened by proclaiming "support of a Southern way of life against what may be called the American or prevailing way of life."[121] The American way of life was one devoted to the "Gospel of Progress," the evangelists of which were those on the Darwinian Right (laissez-faire capitalism) and the Progressives. To the Agrarians these two groups were essentially the same, differing only on the means of how to achieve their end. The Agrarians offered the Southern tradition—a loose Jeffersonian-Jacksonian view, but without any philosophy of nature—as the alternative to a progressive Philosophy of History. To broaden the movement, they appealed to all regionalisms—not just that of the South—insofar as these held out against the thin materialism and homogenizing effects of modern progressive mass culture.

The Agrarian movement was stillborn, but it helped to inspire the next generation of traditionalist intellectuals, led by Russell Kirk, who re-introduced the more general framework of the Historical School based on Edmund Burke's analysis. For Kirk, the conservative mind believes that the old ways are typically the right ones and that change best occurs through a slow organic process. Joining the "European" traditionalist position, Kirk attacked any abstract concept of nature, including the American form found in the Declaration, which he essentially equated with the rationalism of the French Revolution. His stance left him in the curious position of defending an American tradition while rejecting what most considered to be its cardinal elements: a revolutionary break with Britain and a founding based on the concept of natural right. Kirk resolved this problem in an innovative way by claiming that natural-rights philosophy had very little to do with America's origins and that the real American Revolution consisted in maintaining the traditional historical rights of Englishmen. The Founders were essentially moderate British Whigs who made a revolution on behalf of the old English Charters, not on behalf of natural rights. "Respect for precedent and prescription governed the minds of the Founders and the Republic. We appealed to the prescriptive liberties of Englishmen, not to liberté, égalité, fraternité."[122] This was pure English Customary History.

Yet Kirk and other traditionalists always seemed more devoted to their theoretical position opposing natural rights than to their historical arguments. If the American Founding was not in fact completely based on Whig Customary History, then in Kirk's view it should have been: "Until 1776, protesting Americans had pleaded that they were entitled to the rights of Englishmen as expressed in the British constitution. But Jefferson's Declaration of Independence had abandoned this tack . . . and carried the American cause into the misty debatable land of an abstract liberty, equality, fraternity."[123] In this account of Revolutionary thought, the Golden Age occurred just before the official proclamation of the American Revolution in the Declaration of Independence. The American experiment began to go astray the moment the concept of right based in nature was introduced as a public doctrine. Traditionalism in this respect, while never widely popular in America, enjoyed some influence, especially for a time within the Southern wing of the Democratic Party. It has had an ambivalent relation not only to the American Founding, but also to the founding period of the Republican Party, which sought to resuscitate the abstract principle of natural right.

Setting aside this particular line of historical argument, traditionalist thinking overall introduced a more intellectual dimension into American conservatism. It connected conservatism with many of the great thinkers and ideas of the past, and it discovered largely ignored elements of conservative thinking within American history. It promoted skepticism about Philosophy of History and warned of the dangers of central rational planning. It is the first source for a revival of conservative thought in America, and still occupies one of the major "seats" inside intellectual circles in the Republican Party today.

The other challenge to the Progressives came in the 1940s in the form of a revival of classical economic thinking, led by Friedrich von Hayek. From this position has evolved the modern school of economics (the "Chicago School") and libertarianism. Unlike traditionalists, libertarians defend a form of rationalism. In some cases, this view stops with a simple affirmation of natural rights, but in most cases it embraces an idea of progress. For libertarians, rationality is found in the "invisible hand" of the market—a principle that is extended to developments in all other realms. Libertarianism in many formulations is based on the principle of a spontaneous order at work throughout all of nature. Social life, including economics and politics, is governed by this same principle. History is subject to an evolutionary process in which the more viable practices are selected, producing a series of growing successes. Progress is only impeded or thwarted by overall plans that interfere with this process and try to determine the outcome by rational design. As Hayek observed: "We owe all of our success, not to our intelligence having chosen our culture as the right thing, but to having been selected, as it were, for doing the right thing without knowing why it was better."[124]

Insofar as traditionalists respect the notion of organic historical growth, economists and libertarians can willingly join together with them. According to Hayek, it is to the traditionalists' "loving and reverential study of the value of grown institutions [that] we owe (at least outside the field of economics) some profound insights which are real contributions to our understanding of a free society." But traditionalists failed to extract the principle of limited government and noninterference as the appropriate guide to policy. Traditionalism may "succeed by its resistance to current tendencies in slowing down undesirable developments, but, since it does not indicate a direction, it cannot prevent their continuance."[125] The economists have been prepared to call, if necessary, for radical departures from existing practices. They have had a huge impact on modern conservatism and on the Republican Party, especially in their critique of "Big Government," which refers not just to a government that is large in scope, but to one that is animated by the idea of rational social planning as the best way to resolve problems. The critique of Big Government comes from many economists who make no foundational arguments, but treat economics as a science with competence to judge matters of economics and public policy. Libertarians take a further step, claiming that the principle of spontaneous order that is found throughout all of biological nature also governs processes not only in economics but in politics as well. This claim supports a law of progress.

## The Present Era

When we study developments in our time, analysis is complicated by the fact that we are living in the midst of the phenomenon and do not know how things will turn out. All explanations are therefore more speculative and must be advanced with greater caution. In addition, with so many important matters now under dispute, there is a powerful temptation, often unconscious, to bend the treatment of issues to bolster a favored current position. Partisanship is hard to avoid. A difficulty of another kind is that political actors today relate to foundational ideas in a less direct way than their predecessors did. More than a century ago, James Bryce called attention to the fact that "the busy life of the modern statesman leaves no time for reflection." The hectic pace of politics in our day lends even more weight to the veracity of this observation.[126] Our educational systems are much more specialized, and few political leaders, even those who are highly educated, encounter theoretical ideas in a serious way during their university studies. Foundational ideas can have a fuzzy relationship to the political order, arriving after being laundered by think tanks and neatly packaged by speechwriters. Yet somehow or other, foundational ideas do manage to make their way into political life. Controversy over these ideas has been at the center of discussion by public intellectuals in the past few years, especially in the huge outpouring of articles and books that have spoken, either favorably or critically, of a revival within the Republican Party of an active concept of natural right.

To understand the contemporary era, we must start by noting developments that occurred in the purely theoretical realm, once removed from politics. The most important was the collapse of the theoretical underpinning of Progressivism in the 1950s, a collapse that was first analyzed by Leo Strauss and Walter Lippmann. Both men called attention to a sea change that had taken place in philosophy and that cast doubt on all claims of the objectiveness or truth of existing foundations. Not only had it become impossible to accept an account of nature as true, because there was no truth to permanence, but it was also said that there was no objective structure to history. The idea of progress, only recently considered an objective scientific fact, was no more than an opinion. Strauss and Lippmann labeled this position "historicism," defined as the view that there can be no objective or true perspective, but only the arbitrary claims of each age (or perhaps each individual). A more radical version of historicism, then found chiefly in Europe, was also preparing a transatlantic crossing. It went beyond the apparent neutrality of the first version and contended that the entire scientific or philosophic view that undergirded the Western project, dating back to the Enlightenment or perhaps even to the dawn of philosophy in Greece, was predicated on human beings' control of the world around them and on the exploitation of all things for human use. This view separated Western individuals from their deeper moorings and "authentic" existence. The Western project was now in crisis and in danger of coming to an end, a prospect many saw as a strange opportunity to retrieve the authenticity that had been obscured by the rationalist or scientific mindset.

Although Strauss and Lippmann found these intellectual developments to apply at the moment only in the intellectual realm, both men noted the connection of these ideas to politics and foresaw that they must soon be transferred, in some way, to the political realm. Progressive Liberalism in its current form would not be able to survive the assault by historicism. Both thinkers concluded that this situation portended a crisis for America. A nation that had lived with rationally grounded foundations could not endure—or endure forcefully—in the absence of such a belief.

The first indication of the validity of this analysis occurred with the emergence of the New Left within the Democratic Party. In a well-known article in 1977 surveying the history of Liberalism in the twentieth century, Samuel Beer traced the standard line of Progressive-Liberal development from Herbert Croly to Lyndon Johnson, citing excerpts from Johnson's speeches that read like grammar school versions of Croly's idea of progress.[127] Yet Beer paused at the end to take note of a huge interloper in the Democratic Party that, to him, seemed to come almost from another world. Inside what had been the Progressive-Liberal Party appeared a movement that rejected the idea of progress. Reflecting the analysis of radical historicism, the New Left argued that America—even Western civilization itself—was heading in the wrong direction, away from authenticity. It was not just the Founding and natural right that were responsible for this decline, but Progressive Liberalism as well. Progressivism was part of the problem, not part of the solution. The Founding and Progressivism were essentially one in their obedience to rationality. According to the New Left's most important manifesto, the Port Huron Statement: "What we had originally seen as the American Golden Age was actually the decline of an era."[128]

This decline was so fundamental and so interwoven with the fabric of American life that only a revolution—one that was cultural as much as political—could reverse it. The New Left account married objective pessimism (the decline of the West) to outlandish optimism (the transforming power of the Revolution). The hopes for revolutionary change regularly included aspirations that, to the more sober judgments of today, seem almost inconceivable. It was not only the political order that would change. Norman O. Brown, a leading American theorist in the movement, argued that human fulfillment was to be found in "erotic exuberance . . . based on the polymorphously perverse body."[129] This was hardly the same movement of Lester Ward, John Dewey, or Woodrow Wilson.

Many political leaders in the Democratic Party felt pressured by the "spirit" of these arguments, although most have since taken pains to distance themselves from its fundamental pessimism and anti-Americanism. These ideas still survive, absent the romantic hope tied to a Revolution, in what is variously labeled the Cultural Left or the "multiculturalist" movement, which has redoubts in many American universities. For political actors in the Democratic Party, this movement remains too important to be completely neglected, but too dangerous to be fully embraced.

A second indication of the collapse of the Progressive foundation was found in the innovative effort to recreate a new form of

Customary History that linked the Left to a foundation in tradition, rather than to Philosophy of History. This position was first outlined by Hannah Arendt, who claimed to have discovered a new kind of republican or communitarian view at the core of the American Revolution, including in the Declaration of Independence. Republicanism excluded any recourse to nature. The Declaration's greatness "owes nothing to its natural-law philosophy. . . . [Its] grandeur consists not in its philosophy and not even so much in its being an argument in support of an action as in its being the perfect way for an action to appear in words."[130]

A similar position has since been advanced by a school known as communitarianism. Communitarians look for support for their position in the past—not, to be sure, with the Goths or the Puritans, but with the American Founders, rebaptized as republicans. Communitarians are traditional almost to the point of orthodoxy, finding a correspondence between the original and the good and treating the most important deviation from our roots, in the form of Liberalism (a later development), as the source of America's woes. We have sinned, and now we should return. This school rejects a foundation in nature and has turned to experience. In the words of Michael Walzer, communitarians value an approach that is "more historical than philosophical" and that rests on "a reflection on experience rather than a reflection on ideas."[131] Fortunately for the communitarians, American academic historians at this time began to discover a republican character to the Founding, allowing the communitarians to root their preferred views in a new historical consensus. The communitarians' new Founderism represents a clear break with Progressivism, which adopted a position adversarial to the Founding.

A final acknowledgment of the collapse of Progressivism is found in a program on the Left, sometimes referred to as neopragmatism or anti-foundationalism, that seeks to revive the substance of the Progressive view, but without grounding it in any foundational concept. Anti-foundationalists speak of shared ideals—the values of the Left, which include social justice or equality and alleviation of suffering—but link these to nothing deeper than what have been called "narratives of hope" and to the consensus that exists among the most enlightened thinkers. If enough intellectuals keep telling themselves (and all those who follow them) that something is "true," then it must be so.

Among the most prominent theoretical proponents of idealistic anti-foundationalism is the philosopher Richard Rorty, who has continued John Dewey's attack on nature and metaphysics, arguing that foundations lead to rigid or absolutist politics. No one is more iconoclastic in his theoretical views than Richard Rorty, and no one comes close to him in the disarming frankness with which he expresses his position. Agreeing completely with historicism, Rorty insists that, by the tenets of advanced philosophy today, there are no foundations; there is no such thing as nature and no such thing as a structure to history. Indeed, there is not even a possibility of objective history; there are only diverse interpretations, which he calls "narratives." A narrative can be written almost any way one chooses, since "there is no nonmythological . . . way of telling a country's story. . . . Nobody knows what it would be like to try to be objective when attempting to decide what one's country really is, what its history really means."[132] To distinguish the new academic discipline that produces such accounts, we can speak of "narrativity" rather than history and refer to its practitioners as "narrativicians," not historians. Narrativicians are important to public life, maybe even necessary, because they foster solidarity and nudge things along in the preferred direction. Narratives sound a bit like foundations; but unlike full foundations, they involve no claims of being tied to deeper structures of reality, as found in Philosophy of History. They are "stories," no more and no less. People may be strongly invested in a foundational concept, but who would sacrifice for a narrative? And this is exactly the point: narratives are adaptable and do not lead to rigid or absolutist politics. The well-being of American democracy depends on eliminating once and for all the vestiges of foundational concepts.

It may seem an error, or at any rate an exaggeration, to consider anti-foundationalism to be a view that has influenced the modern political Left, so much does it resemble an "academic" development. No sane politician would ever go around and directly repeat the provocative skepticisms of this school, much less dismiss truth or question that "What is, is." But once the more extreme rhetoric is set aside, a strong case can be made that idealistic anti-foundationalism, or something like it, already exercises a sway in American politics and has a solid grip on large parts of the Left today. We must bear in mind that the purpose of anti-foundationalism is not to supply a doctrine that will be publicly proclaimed in its bald form; rather, it aims to "work" in a much more indirect way, sanctioning a draining of belief in the authority of all foundational concepts, which is a development that some believe is in any case happening on its own. Anti-foundationalism does its job when intellectuals and political leaders treat the old and prized foundations as mere shibboleths, to be used mostly for ritualistic purposes. There is evidence that this view is effective: the plain fact is that many leading thinkers on the Left today deny the possibility or advisability of proclaiming any kind of foundation. Concurrently, many political actors on the Left are at least visibly uncomfortable with invoking foundations in a serious way.

These three responses both reflect and acknowledge the collapse on the Left of the progressive concept of History, as well as any other kind of foundation. This development has been of more immediate concern within the Democratic Party, which had previously been the chief home of the progressive view. Initially, Republicans seemed less affected by or even oblivious to these theoretical developments, which many considered the problem of "intellectuals," of which there were precious few in the party. Traditionalists in the Republican Party felt vindicated, since they had long opposed a progressive Philosophy of History and mistrusted abstract statements about nature. (Traditionalists have never considered their own position of finding right in tradition to be a "foundation" in the full sense.) Libertarians in the 1950s believed that their views had the support of objective science, and some feel this even more strongly today, as increasing numbers of people today look to evolutionary biology as a true science capable of supplying political foundations.

Yet looking at the Republican Party today, we can clearly see that a further development has taken place. While traditionalism and libertarianism are important parts of the conservative position, they no longer suffice to define the whole conservative movement. A new element has been introduced into American politics: a restoration of the foundational concept of nature. It has been introduced not as myth or convenient fiction—something to be believed just because it is salutary—but as something intelligible based on an account of the nature of human beings and of the political order. Leo Strauss and Walter Lippmann proposed this position in the 1950s for both political parties, but today most of its supporters are housed chiefly within the Republican Party, where they enjoy considerable influence despite the obvious tensions between their position and other currents of modern conservatism.[133] Strauss and Lippmann emphasized the centrality of the foundational concept of nature in the context of the struggle of the Cold War. Natural right served to draw a clear line between liberal democracy and Communism, and it offered a basis to combat the skepticism and relativism of many in the West who were unwilling to condemn Communism. Ronald Reagan, who managed to blend so many of the different elements of conservatism, echoed this foundational idea in his foreign policy pronouncements of the Soviet Union as an "evil empire," which drew on his earlier analysis of Communism as "a temporary aberration which will one day disappear from the earth because it is contrary to human nature."[134]

Recourse to the concept of natural right was also revived in the battle against quota policies and affirmative action. The appeal to this foundation has been a central theoretical element in the legal thinking in court cases that were brought against these policies, and it has been even more important in the public referenda campaigns fought on this question. Ward Connerly, the chief spokes-man for this movement during the campaign in California to pass Proposition 209 in 1996, continually evoked a version of natural right and has carried the same message to national audiences: "Moral principles do not change with the seasons. That is precisely why the founders proclaimed that certain truths are 'self-evident' and 'endowed by our Creator.' They are not meant to change or to be bargained away. Our inalienable rights are the centerpiece of that moral system, and the principle of equality is central to our system of rights."[135] The debate on natural right in the context of affirmative action policies has taken what many might consider a paradoxical turn in light of the history of civil rights issues, but it is one that accords today with the underlying theoretical division between Left and Right. The "civil rights community," which invoked natural right in the first phase of the struggle over civil rights legislation in 1964 and 1965, has since backed away from this position and now bases the defense of its policies of group rights on nonfoundational ideas of social justice. Theoretical defenders of multiculturalism, who advocate quota policies in order to promote cultural "diversity," have taken a further step based on the position of radical historicism. They have attacked the concept of nature as an emanation of rationalist thought that is said to be responsible for the oppression of submerged groups in liberal societies. Only as America moves away from a foundation in nature can there be hope of just policies for minorities and women.[136]

The foundation of natural right has become much more prominent in American politics since 2001, in the wake of the "war on terrorism." In explaining and justifying this war, President George W. Bush has recurred to the principle of natural right, which has come to occupy a central place not only in his articulation of the goals of American foreign policy, but also in his understanding of the broader purpose of the American experiment. What he has called the "challenge of our time" awakened for him a new way of thinking and talking. Addressing the National Endowment for

Democracy in 2003, for example, he argued that "liberty is the design of nature and [that] freedom—the freedom we prize—is not for us alone, it is the right and the capacity of all mankind."[137] Bush's Second Inaugural was an extended elaboration of this theme. Statements of this kind might be found in the speeches of many presidents, and in themselves these words might have little significance. But in this instance, the importance that the opponents of the president placed on this theme helped to elevate the question of natural right to the status of a fundamental issue in American politics. The president clearly joined the battle, appealing to this foundation with more frequency and emphasis as time went by. Critics began to attack the administration's assertion of a universalism that was attached to a firm foundation; the main target was "neo-conservative" thinkers, who were said, with little analysis and much exaggeration, to be dictating administration policy.[138] But it was certainly appropriate to claim, as Mark Lilla argued, that "neo-conservatism, [which] began as an intellectual movement, is now an essential part of Republican politics, and therefore of American life."[139] The hope of the critics of neo-natural right was to make the 2004 American election into a referendum in which the concept would go down to defeat and be discredited among elite segments of the electorate. This project is now the work for another day.

The introduction of the concept of nature into American politics, especially since 2001, has been met with alarm from many quarters, where it is seen as absolutist and ideological. Intellectuals attempting to discredit it often refer to the influence of "Straussianism," employed as a pejorative label. Bowing to current linguistic practice, I will use the term here, but only in accord with the strictest canons of modern social science, as a purely value-free word designating a position of neo-natural right. Evoking "Straussianism" is relevant, since Leo Strauss was one of the first to call attention to the collapse of foundations and to suggest the possibility of recapturing the intelligibility of the concept of natural right in modern thought. He coupled this suggestion with an argument against History as a foundation. This step has proven to be the most important element of his "practical" legacy, especially within the conservative camp. Although it is an unhelpful exercise to attempt to connect a philosopher like Leo Strauss with the practical application of a general set of principles or with any particular policy, it is appropriate to consider his influence on foundational thinking.

Strauss argued that the two Historical foundations—Philosophy of History and the Historical School—although for a long time at odds with each other on the plane of practical politics, often defining the modern Left and the modern Right, were at a deeper level expressions of the same premise. This premise is that History, not nature, is the true foundation. For Strauss, the fundamental theoretical alternative was never between these two variants of History; rather, it was between History and nature. On this point, he broke with the dominant view found within conservative thought since Burke and located conservatism—if one wishes to call him a conservative—closer to the American Founders and to Lincoln than to Burke and his traditionalist heirs. Strauss supported his theoretical argument about History with an analysis of its consequences. Whatever success the turn to Historical School might have had in combating radical ideas in the nineteenth century, its political benefits have long since come to an end. By the early twentieth century, the effect of relying on History as a foundation had led to the emergence of historicism, including its final manifestations in Europe of support for irrational regimes, and what we know today as postmodernism. Its major impact was no longer conservative. For Strauss, the turn to History constituted the great idol of modern thought. The Classics, he wrote, did not "dream of a fulfillment in History and hence not of a meaning of History."[140] Mankind could live without this foundation.

To avoid confusion, it is important to reiterate that the discussion here is in reference to History *as a foundation,* meaning the use of temporal accounts as the source of right. To abandon a reliance on History obviously does not mean to ignore history in its ordinary sense as a discipline that provides knowledge of the past, with all the instruction which that knowledge can supply; nor does it mean dispensing with helpful or edifying recitations of history in public rhetoric. Neither the original nor the modern proponents of the concept of natural right have ever advocated ignoring history. Just the contrary. They have argued that abandoning History as a foundation opens the possibility of using history in a more modest, but more reasonable, way. Large numbers of historians have long objected to History's elevation to the status of a foundation, contending that such claims have only distorted history's true character. Part of the intellectual movement today directed against History *as a foundation* has been associated with a resurgence of rationalist historical scholarship, especially of the Founding period.[141]

Foundationalism has become an issue of contemporary partisan dispute. In the Republican Party, variants of all of the major foundational concepts are arrayed against each other in an internal theoretical battle; but the foundational concept of nature has now emerged as the prominent face of the party. On the Democratic side, nearly all advanced intellectual elements now oppose the concept of natural right, and the leading strains of thought in the party seem to favor one version or other of idealistic antifoundationalism.

## The Role of Foundational Ideas in Modern Political Life

What can be concluded from this account of foundational concepts? I offer three points of reflection. The first relates to the purpose of this inquiry. The field of American political development has devoted itself largely to explaining historical causality, focusing on how an antecedent factor $A$ contributes to an outcome $B$. In the case of the study of foundational ideas, $A$ would refer to a foundational concept (or to the general class of foundational concepts), while *B* would designate the formation of ideas on other levels, shifts in policy regimes, or the occurrence of events. Pursuing an investigation of this sort, an analyst might try to prove strong causal links between foundational ideas and major events that closely followed: no concept of nature, no Revolution; no Southern Historical School, no secession; no revival of nature, no end to slavery; no Progressive Philosophy of History, no New Deal; no revival of nature, no collapse of Communism. Alternatively, downplaying a direct causal connection to immediate events, the analyst might consider foundational concepts more as justifications that sum up a position, with a causal impact coming afterward. In this scenario, for example, a turn to the concept of nature did not cause the Revolution, but the strength of the concept grew in the wake of the Revolution and in turn altered much of American politics and the history of the West.

Studies of this kind, which attempt to determine causality, are surely both worthwhile and necessary. But no one should be surprised if a point of diminishing intellectual returns is quickly reached. Major historical events are usually the result of many factors interacting with one another, making the determination of the weight of any single factor difficult to assess. In addition, although the individual foundational concepts identified are sufficiently similar to merit being referred to by a common label ("foundational concepts"), they hardly constitute a homogeneous "class" in the strong sense of sharing major properties. Individual foundational concepts are extremely varied, making it unlikely that one could deduce from them a general law about how much causal impact they have; different foundational concepts will have different effects. A fair analysis of studies of specific cases nevertheless indicates that foundational ideas have often had a major influence on events and on subsequent thought—sometimes, as noted, more powerfully after the immediate event than before it. Prima facie "evidence" of the significance of foundational concepts also comes from the fact that political actors themselves often consider these concepts to be highly important. Surely their judgment, in the absence of proof to the contrary, should be accorded some probative value.

There is, however, another purpose to political inquiry besides APD's noble obsession with historical causality. Suppose, as seems reasonable, that foundational concepts surpass some minimal threshold of importance in their causal effect; it then makes sense to fix attention on another purpose of our discipline. Political science exists to supply a body of knowledge that can assist political actors in performing their functions. In the area of political ideas, one set of actors consists, oddly enough, of thinkers who engage in formulating ideas in an effort to influence political life. To perform their task better, these actors would benefit greatly from a framework to help guide their reflections. Unfortunately, what passes for "public philosophy thinking" today is a haphazard mix of musings, undisciplined by an overall concept of what constitutes the relevant field of ideas. Political science has yet to supply an account of the categories that need to be addressed and the major options that exist within each category. Until public philosophers become political scientists or political scientists become public philosophers, there will be no end to our troubles.

My second reflection concerns the cause of the cause—that is, who creates foundational concepts and sets them in motion? Here, unfortunately, the long intellectual battle noted earlier between "idealists" and "materialists" led both sides over time to adopt ever more extravagant assertions. For idealists, the maximal position became not only that ideas are the primary cause of events, but also that the course of the development of ideas could be accounted for by trends inside theoretical life. Ideational causality now came to include the corollary assertion of the dominance of the world of action by philosophers: stronger ideas will eventually win the day. A doctrine of ideational determinism grew up to rival that of materialistic determinism. History, as one idealist put it, is "a continuous succession of political actions guided more or less directly by the evolution of *philosophy.*"[142] The political world is no more than a stage for the unfolding of great ideas, with political actors reading the script.

Although no one doubts that the preparation of foundational ideas derives ultimately from great thinkers, an examination of political activity casts doubt on the claim that theorists rule the world. The relationship between theory and political activity may be divided, under a simplistic distinction, into two types. First, there are political actors who serve as virtual conveyor belts for theoretical ideas, engaging in political activity in an effort to maximize a theoretical view. These actors sometimes form movements or parties that represent different philosophical schools. They are labeled "ideologues," or persons who seek to define all practical political issues in terms of theories.

Second, there are political actors—we can call them practical politicians, or statesmen—who, while they operate loosely under a theoretical framework, are engaged chiefly in the task of handling affairs for the good of their community. So long as the political situation remains within ordinary boundaries, these actors are often content to leave questions about foundational concepts to operate in the background, invoking them only vaguely. Their attitude toward questions of this kind is apt to be one of benign neglect: if theoretical ideas are not troubling the political community, they see no reason to trouble the community with theoretical ideas. But in political life, on occasions when pressing circumstances arise, statesmen may find themselves in situations in which they need to actively engage foundational concepts—either to defeat a concept that threatens the community or to enlist or revise one that can promote its well-being. The practical political activity of tending to the good of the community comes, in the course of human affairs, to include theoretical matters. While the statesman's selection of foundational concepts comes from a catalogue derived from the realm of theory, his choices may depend on

84

an assessment of the value and effect of these concepts as they are measured in the crucible of real political activity. This assessment involves considerations of both the immediate and long-term consequences of foundational concepts.

On the broader question of who is responsible for making history, it now turns out that foundational concepts that are chosen by political actors, and that prove to be significant in the political world thereafter, subsequently become subjects of inquiry by philosophers. Causality flows in two directions: not only from the theoretical world down to the political world, but also from the political world up to the theoretical world.

My third and final reflection has to do with the deeper functions of foundational concepts. Discussion of this question is made more delicate by the fact that it is now being raised inside political life as a partisan issue. The position referred to earlier as anti-foundationalism has developed a full set of arguments about the role of foundations and has made it a major theme of modern theoretical inquiry. Perhaps to assuage fears of the radical character of this position, anti-foundationalists have sought to minimize its significance by arguing that foundations have never been all that consequential for American politics. Richard Rorty has written: "The idea that liberal societies are bound together by philosophical beliefs seems to me to be ludicrous. . . . Philosophy is not that important for politics."[143] No harm, no foul. But as antifoundational thinkers, Rorty included, have devoted pages—nay, volumes—to arguing against foundations, the claim of negligible significance seems to be no more than a ploy to disarm their critics. The real core of the anti-foundationalist argument is not that foundations are inconsequential, but, on the contrary, that they do enormous harm. By claiming knowledge of standards beyond community opinion, those who call for authoritative foundations promote dogmatic and rigid thinking. Their approach to political life has authoritarian and undemocratic overtones. By contrast, anti-foundationalism would be a boon to our society, "chiming

. . . with the spirit of tolerance that has made constitutional democracy possible."[144] Chiming is the replacement for "philosophical public opinion."

Anti-foundationalism has proven a remarkably appealing doctrine, especially to contemporary intellectuals. Already disposed to disbelieve in the notion of truth in their own fields of study, many thinkers today are pleased to be informed that such claims can be dispensed with in politics as well, and without any cost to the realization of their dearly held values. Furthermore, because anti-foundationalism draws on some of the most advanced philosophical arguments of our age, its proponents can take a certain pleasure in regarding those who still cling to foundations as theoretical primitives, likely to lose out in the end as practical politics finally catches up with advanced thought. Perhaps the greatest source of this doctrine's appeal, however, derives from how it has framed the question, dividing all thought into the binary categories of foundationalism and anti-foundationalism, as if all foundations somehow fit into a genuine class. Once this way of defining the issue takes hold, the disastrous properties of some foundations can subtly be imputed to all of them; for example, although the position of natural right is not the same thing as Marxism, both, after all, are "foundations" and therefore partake of the same fundamental problems. This neat binary division also holds out the hope of inaugurating a new age in politics, in which all of the difficulties relating to foundations will be resolved by one simple theoretical step. If people cease to promote foundations of any kind, the political world will be a safer and saner place. Democracy will have achieved its maturity. Anti-foundationalism thus contains its very own "narrative of hope." It divides history into two parts, with the anti-foundationalist millennium just around the corner.

The actual consequences of an experiment with anti-foundationalism can only be guessed at. Some have wondered whether its effect would be to leave a vacuum at the center of political life that might eventually be filled by a dangerous alternative, as once occurred when ideologies replaced the skepticism that came to prevail in many of the new democracies of Europe in the 1920s and 1930s. Alternatively, others argue that the real problem with anti-foundationalism would become apparent if it actually managed to take hold of public life; the result might be a nation that is listless, apathetic, and lacking in resolve. Observations of other democratic nations in the world today that are arguably trending toward anti-foundationalism might provide a firmer basis on which to make such judgments.

Past political theorists have asked *why* political societies have relied on foundational concepts of one kind or another. A common response has been that, from a purely functional perspective, they provide an important source of unity. A fundamental problem in political life is that everything is potentially a matter of opinion; in order to form a community, there must be something a group of people considers beyond mere opinion. As Tocqueville observed, "Without common ideas there is no common action, and without common action men still exist, but a social body does not."[145] The alternatives that have performed this function have included myth (which only works insofar as it is not widely considered as myth), revelation (which functions for those who believe), and a claim of truth of some kind that can be widely grasped and understood. Any one of these foundations might help to create a bond of unity as well as a reservoir of commitment and resolve.

If stating the functions of foundations suggests why a foundation may be necessary or important, it also acknowledges the dangers that such ideas sometimes pose to society. This point was never doubted by thinkers in the past; but never imagining, like anti-foundationalists, that society could do without a foundation, they proceeded to the next logical question, which was what kind of foundation could be most effective for supporting a healthy political order. At the time of the Enlightenment, many attacked the nonrational foundations for their obscurity and for the authority they gave to cult and mystery. A great hope emerged that a turn to rational foundations resting on philosophy (science) could guarantee political stability and happiness. Yet the briefest survey of the foundations proffered on the basis of a serious claim to rationality (and that have been taken seriously by intelligent people) shows that this hope, in its simple form, was never realized. Who needs to be reminded of the millions who were sacrificed on the altar of a science of History? Nor have many of the attempts to establish foundations on the basis of a science of nature fared well either. Difficulties have appeared on all sides. If one aim of a foundation in nature is to provide a solid and indisputable standard, based on something objective, a strong temptation exists to turn away from the more difficult and less evident sciences of human things in favor of sciences that treat physical things; these sciences seem to rest on much firmer ground, so that transferring their understanding of nature to the political realm is thought to assure indisputability. Moreover, the human mind in its quest for rationality seems to have an affinity for the simple idea of applying one principle of explanation to all things ("matter"), in preference to the more complex idea of applying different principles to qualitatively different kinds of things in distinct realms. The consequence of succumbing to these temptations—illustrated in the attempts to draw political foundations from natural history, physics, and biology—has been to adopt foundational concepts wholly unsuited to the world of politics and to extend their formulas beyond the domain in which foundational ideas of any kind could possibly claim competence.

The search for a sound foundational concept cannot therefore be conducted under a broad slogan that calls for rational ideas. A mere call for rationalism is insufficient. There is no alternative to the investigation of the characteristics of different alternatives. A foundation needs to be true, which is a matter for philosophers or scientists to consider, but it also needs to meet certain political requirements, which is a matter on which political scientists have something to contribute. At a minimum, a useful foundational concept is one that remains within proper boundaries, allowing most political matters to be determined by political means. It must also be sufficiently simple and direct to form the basis of a public doctrine that can be understood and acknowledged. Yet because any simple formula of right is likely to be incomplete, leading to inevitable distortions, even the best practical statement of it will need to be qualified and supplemented to meet the shifting requirements of different eras. The task of reformulating and refining a nation's foundation is never-ending.

# 2

---

# CAN WE KNOW A FOUNDATIONAL IDEA WHEN WE SEE ONE?

*Jack N. Rakove*

## Disciplinary Perspectives

Early in his paper, James Ceaser interjects a cautionary aside that seems to encode my name and professional address. Introducing the first of his two "foundational concepts" of nature and history, he observes that the latter does not refer "to accounts generated under auspices of the intellectual discipline of history"; rather, it alludes to "temporal accounts that are designed to establish a fundamental purpose or a standard of right. Such accounts are premised on the notion that something occurring in time is the source of ultimate meaning and of guidance for human life and for politics." And then Ceaser adds, parenthetically: "Most academic historians . . . do not aspire to provide accounts of this kind, nor do they think that history properly understood is capable of applying such foundations." If this caution is correct, I can only wonder whether I should comment on this extended essay at all. On the one hand, regarding myself as a very traditional kind of historian,[1] I might be expected to question Ceaser's entire enterprise. If we historians proper disdain such exercises, I should predictably object, what hope can we have that poachers from cognate disciplines can pull them off? On the other hand, having happily and without mental reservation joined my own university's Department of Political Science, I might have been easily marked as a fellow traveler. So perhaps I have been enlisted to combine a measure of historical criticism with an open-minded appreciation of Ceaser's quest.

If so, I find the first element of Ceaser's parenthetical remark more persuasive than the second. We historians are notorious for happily confessing the limits of our competence and expertise. Our favorite disclaimer—as useful in casual encounters with inquisitive strangers as in fending off tough questions from students—is "Sorry, that's before [or 'after'] my period." And "period," for most historians (especially Americanists), is often measured in bare decades. True, some historians boldly go where none of their colleagues have gone before. One wonders, for example, how many of us first got hooked on politics by reading the essays in Richard Hofstadter's book *The American Political Tradition and the Men Who Made It* or the bold hypotheses of *The Age of Reform*. But among working historians, Hofstadter remains the exception who proved the rule. He was, if truth be told, not a research-oriented historian, intent on exhausting the sources before committing pen to paper, but a scholar who had his eyes on grander prizes. In his own way, he was a pioneer of APD *avant le fait* (and a noted "public intellectual" before that term existed, much less acquired its debased current meaning).

Yet Hofstadter could not have attempted to write as he did, had other historians not been busy doing the scut work of monographic scholarship. And this in turn leads me to question the second element of Ceaser's parenthetical aside: the observation that historians would deny that their discipline can provide the foundation for a foundational account. Philosophers, poets, even sociologists can all do a better job, Ceaser suggests, presumably because they purvey the big-ticket items (whether aesthetic or theoretical) from which "temporal accounts"—which can range from mythic renderings of the American past to neo-Tocquevillean interpretations of our democratic civilization—can be put forward

94

as "political foundations." Be that as it may, a *scholarly* explanation of *how* such accounts have varied and functioned over time would still be necessarily "historical" in the academic or disciplinary sense of the term. That is, generalizations about which foundational concepts have fared well or ill at particular moments would have to be sustained on historical grounds. And whether or not historians lack the imaginative breadth of their colleagues, their work would still be essential to Ceaser's project. The fact that some academic historians would remain naturally skeptical about such projects does not obviate the extent to which the broader generalizations of APD have to build upon the more bounded writings of political historians.

One can wonder as well whether historians really look askance at the uses to which their work can be put in a closely related field. The rise of APD has in fact offered a consolation of sorts to lift the gloom darkening the breast of many political historians who worry that our field, once preeminent within the discipline, has never been less fashionable; that the fluff of cultural studies is steadily corrupting an empirical discipline with the subjectivist heresies of the literati; and that the useful corrective of trying to do history from the bottom up has given way to the allure of doing it from the margins out. So to echo Thomas Paine, there are those historians who wonder whether departments of political science might yet heed our plaintive cry: "O! receive the fugitive; and prepare in time an asylum for mankind"—or at least for those of us who believe that politics matters most, even in a society where populist and other suspicions of our elected leaders run so deep.[2]

So let us not belabor these disciplinary distinctions any further. If Ceaser's project makes sense for political scientists, it should also work for historians. For both, the essential question would remain: Does the hitherto neglected search for foundational concepts provide us with better means of explaining the role of ideas in our national political discourse and decision making? Whether that question is posed in terms of identifying recurring motifs in

American political history, or as a device for explaining particular episodes or passages within that history, should not affect our assessment of its merits. We should expect to encounter ideas that are truly "foundational" operating at both the macro and micro levels of analysis, over both the long run and the short term.

The search for foundational concepts, however, is necessarily only one element, or a single specification, of a much larger problem, all the more vexatious because it seems so familiar. That problem is simply to understand the role of ideas in political life: how they are generated and used, transmitted and transformed. Calling attention to a peculiar subset of ideas labeled "foundational" may help to clarify and focus our own thinking about these questions, but it cannot by itself solve all the problems with which historians and political scientists continue to wrestle. Indeed, our capacity to assess the particular character and function of foundational ideas would seem to depend on the prior elaboration and acceptance of some larger model or analytic framework for thinking about the genesis and deployment of political ideas more generally. If, for example, foundational ideas (as described by Ceaser) reside at the base of some pyramid (something I very much doubt), it would be helpful to know more about the stratigraphy of what lies above.

In his paper, Ceaser occasionally refers to this broader problem in passing, but naturally focuses quickly on his specific project. In my comment, I propose to do the reverse. I will begin with a discussion of what might be meant by "foundational," and then ask how well Ceaser's approach to foundational ideas illuminates the larger set of questions under which it may be subsumed.

## Some Problems of Definition

What makes an idea or concept "foundational"? How do we distinguish foundational concepts from other political ideas? Are foundational ideas important because they shape or influence the formation of positions on "real" issues—that is, the stuff of elections, legislative actions, policy determinations, and the like? Or are they better understood as the source of rhetorical tropes, instrumental devices for advancing interests and legitimating positions adopted for other reasons? Are differences in the attractive and repulsive power of rival foundational ideas a manifest source of division within the body politic or among its elite? Or do they merely reflect latent intellectual tendencies and dispositions that would have been hard to detect at the time—phenomena more evident to scholars than to political actors? (For example, what does it mean to say of the different ways in which Federalists and Democratic-Republicans appealed to the authority of nature that, in Ceaser's words, "a major theoretical issue was at stake, although one in this case that the participants themselves had only begun to articulate"? At stake for whom?) Finally, and perhaps most important for present purposes, how do we know that ideas of "nature" and "history"—or "religion," which is introduced as the third element of a trinity but regrettably neglected in the ensuing analysis—are the right foundational concepts to emphasize?

To begin to answer these questions requires almost thinking aloud as one makes one's way through the opening pages of Ceaser's essay, which could do more to articulate both the rationale for the inquiry and the underlying conception it explores. A foundational concept, Ceaser argues, is one that can be "offered as a first cause or ultimate justification for a general political position or orientation." Such a concept "is usually presented as requiring no further argument, since it is thought to contain within itself its first premise."[3] Ceaser then announces that "nature" and "history" both meet this definition. He does not say whether they are the only concepts to do so, or the most important—a point to which I will shortly return—but the clear implication is that the number of foundational ideas any polity can possess must be small and limited.

But what does it mean to describe a foundational idea as an explicitly political entity? Here the introductory section of the paper provides a handful of brief illustrations that leave the general definition of the phenomenon it proposes to study still a bit elusive. Ceaser first evokes an example I know well, since I first wrote about it thirty years ago: the opening debate in the First Continental Congress of 1774 on the sources of colonial rights. That debate was not about defining what those rights were; on this the delegates were already in general agreement. Rather, it was about choosing the best "foundation" on which to ground claims of colonial rights: on the law of nature, on one hand, or such historical sources as common law, colonial charters, and the rights of Englishmen, on the other. The choice of a foundation thus appears to be rhetorical and strategic, representing a way of advancing and confirming those substantive rights the colonists already knew they wished to claim. Or as the legal historian John Phillip Reid has observed, the rights that the colonists had claimed for themselves, throughout the imperial controversy, "were British rights and well known. Why Americans were entitled to them was more controversial and more complicated."[4]

Ceaser's other illustrations are quotations from three presidents (Wilson, Lincoln, and Jefferson), each appealing to nature or history as dichotomous alternatives. But the brief conclusion he then draws introduces a qualification: "In the practice of politics," Ceaser notes, "foundational statements are not always so 'pure' or exclusive. . . . [M]atters are often blurred or obfuscated, as political actors discover reasons for seeking syntheses, genuine or contrived," presumably by appealing to both foundational concepts as convenient, and muddying or muddling the distinction for rhetorical advantage. Ceaser then goes on to suggest that foundational concepts should interest political scientists because "they constitute a potential variable—if not an independent one, then at any rate an intervening one"—and all variables are presumably grist for the political scientist's mill.

To say they are a phenomenon worth classifying does not explain what deeper function their analysis would serve. Ceaser offers his project as a superior alternative to two other broad-gauge efforts to classify other clusters of fundamental political ideas.

One (echoing Hofstadter?) is the notion of shared "political traditions," conceived as "prefabricated essences" that impose an imported order on the "disparate ideas of American political life." The other is the notion of an accepted "public philosophy," which no well-ordered polity can purportedly do without. Both conceptions appear to have hegemonic aspirations; to historians, as to other social scientists, both sound like the shopworn idea of consensus that was the object of so much scholarly angst in the 1960s and 1970s. Both seem to offer little in the way of a concrete research project or agenda that scholars could readily apply.[5] One can therefore readily concede that Ceaser's project to trace the complex interplay of concepts of nature and history offers a more sophisticated, arguably less vacuous, set of analytic possibilities.

Even so, one has to walk one's way through these introductory pages because they do not seem to offer a wholly adequate account of the rationale for the project. They do not even justify the choice of "nature" and "history" as the foundational concepts most meriting examination. Nor do they explain the omission of Ceaser's third category of analysis, religion, which arguably has provided the most obvious and fruitful examples of foundational ideas at play in the polity. At first glance, after all, it is much easier to credit the idea that religious values and differences have materially affected the course of American politics and the character of political debate than it is to assume that the competition between claims grounded in nature and history exposes a deeper fault line in the structure of our public life. While one would not want to exclude the possibility that, at some deep level, attitudes toward the authority of nature and history do indeed distinguish our understanding of political goods in some fundamental way—and therefore even operate as an independent variable in terms of shaping our political preferences—that assumption itself would seem to demand serious testing. One would want to identify an issue where this would plausibly be the case, and devise a rigorous strategy for testing the salience of these ideas and attitudes in forming both the positions that political actors take and the rhetorical strategies they adopt. The modern debate over affirmative action would be one obvious candidate, but perhaps attitudes toward the welfare state more generally would work just as well.

I remain skeptical, moreover, that this trinity of history, nature, and religion exhausts the realm of potential foundational concepts. Consider the rival claims that could be made on behalf of an alternative set of concepts: liberty and equality. Ceaser mentions both in passing, as examples of "ideas that refer to the ends of government and society" that properly belong, in his categorization, to the "public philosophy studies" he now finds inadequate. But, he then adds, there is "another kind of idea, higher in the scale of abstraction, [that is] present in American life, influencing the course of development," and this higher level is where appeals to nature, history, and religion operate. But this begs the question: Why is rank on the "scale of abstraction" the best measure of what is and is not properly regarded as "foundational"? True, as values, notions of liberty and equality might not operate as a "first cause." But they would certainly seem to qualify as an "ultimate justification," if our definition is elastic enough to embrace values that ostensibly embody fundamental commitments of the polity. Liberty, after all, was the great public good whose enjoyment distinguished eighteenth-century Britons and their American cousins from other regimes. As no less an authority than the celebrated Montesquieu famously noted, "One nation there is also in the world that has for the direct end of its constitution political liberty."[6] There was no mystery about the identity of this nation, and no ambivalence in the American colonists' insistence that they fully shared in that identity. The fact that the reigning Anglo-American conception of liberty was flabby—best defined, Reid has suggested, in contradistinction to its evilly winsome opposite, licentiousness—did not weaken its political authority.[7] We could certainly trace how a prior concept of liberty and property as fundamental values evolved into the language of rights that now, by some accounts, pervades our politics.[8]

A similar inquiry could be pursued by taking equality as a

foundational concept. For an Americanist, it would be easy to begin with the Declaration of Independence, with its creedal statement "that all men are created equal." In its original formulation, this principle was not primarily advanced to support an equality of political and civil rights among individuals. Its true political purpose was to sustain the claim that Americans, as a *people,* or even as a collection of *peoples* organized within their provincial polities, were collectively entitled to exercise the same rights and liberties as their estranged former countrymen across the water in England. It was in this sense that the author of the Declaration later argued that emancipated African Americans were entitled to live as "a free and independent people"–only somewhere else, at a place whose location in Thomas Jefferson's geographic imagination continually grew more and more distant from their captive homeland in the southeastern United States.[9] But in the nineteenth century, this original commitment to an equality among collectively self-governing *peoples* was transformed into a belief in the legal and social equality of *individuals.* The Declaration's terse statement of equality became easy to reinterpret and appropriate in the next century, for the obvious purpose of attacking slavery, and just as important to rebut.[10] And each of the three categories of foundational ideas that Ceaser posits was summoned in the ensuing debates.

In designing the pyramid of various political ideas that Ceaser wants us to construct, we could thus reasonably ask whether equality is a more or less foundational concept than nature or history. After all, when ideas of nature and history have been summoned into political and rhetorical battle, they have often been invoked to assert or defend one concept of equality (or inequality) against another. The belief in subsisting and persisting inequality between ostensibly distinct racial or ethnic groups has often been defended as the consequence of (in Jefferson's language) "the real differences that nature has made,"[11] and just as often criticized as the product of specific historical circumstances that have conspired to maintain existing hierarchies of status and power. It may be that how one thinks about equality depends on prior views of the respective force of nature and history. But it is more plausible to assume that divergent ideas of equality come first, and arguments from nature and history are simply deployed for rhetorical or strategic effect. It is hard to credit the notion that attitudes toward the authority of nature or history are the primary sources of our political judgments.

It is entirely possible that I have misunderstood (though not misunderestimated) the very concept of a foundational idea, which may be too abstract a concept for a working historian to grasp. At the very least, if Ceaser's appeal to give such ideas their due is to be heeded, then more work remains to be done to clarify the fundamental idea and definition of a foundational idea itself. Ceaser's working definition appears as yet inadequate to the task. One would still want to know why appeals to the distinctive authority of nature, history, and religion define the realm of the foundational, while other, more explicitly political values—such as liberty, equality, or (in a post–September 11 world), the fundamental Hobbesian right of self-preservation—do not.

## An Agenda and an Example

To say this is not to deny that appeals to nature and history have often informed and even constituted rival modes of political discourse. Teaching the middle (Columbus to Jefferson) segment of a big freshman history course back in the mid-1990s, I found this distinction a useful way of explaining why Hobbes and Locke departed so strikingly from the dominant modes of political discourse in the seventeenth century. It was to move beyond endless and ultimately unresolvable appeals to the evidence of either medieval charters or Scripture—as expressed in the controversy over the ancient constitution or the sudden popularity of Sir Robert Filmer's *Patriarcha*[12]—that both writers grounded their great political works on ideas about the state of nature. To encourage the students to understand why Hobbes and Locke could have been drawn to this device, I asked them to consider why appeals to the inherently ambiguous evidence of either history or religious authority would seem inadequate, and why the two writers whose works we study most closely were therefore driven to do political philosophy in the proper sense, to teach not us, their later and arguably more expert readers, but the contemporaries whom they sought to influence. An argument like this, oversimplified as it doubtless was for heuristic purposes and the tyranny of the fifty-minute lecture, nevertheless makes a strong claim about how foundational concepts might operate in explicitly political contexts. It provides a plausible hypothesis about why these two potent political thinkers were driven to resort to foundational concepts, at a time when most political argumentation took strikingly different forms. And with *Leviathan* and the *Two Treatises, Patriarcha,* and *Eikon Basilike* all in the mix, seventeenth-century England clearly offers as fair a field for applying the concept of foundational ideas as nineteenth-century America.

Yet when Ceaser moves on to his substantive analysis, his argument takes an ironic turn, at least from this historian's perspective. What it presents is less an analysis of how foundational concepts have operated *politically,* than an intellectual history of the waxing, waning, and occasionally promiscuous intermingling of nature and history, generally detached from the concrete description of real political phenomena. Ceaser's attempt to trace surges in the alternating currents of these appeals over two centuries is certainly impressive in its ambition. It is also, for the same reason, rather frustrating, precisely because its rapid pace leads to the repeated substitution of assertion and generalization for texture and demonstration. Ceaser provides ample reason for agreeing that such a history could indeed be written. But it is less certain whether such a history would truly mark a fresh contribution to APD, opening up avenues for reexamining the relation between the realms of political ideas and political action, or simply identify a fresh if previously neglected topic in the history of American political thinking (or APT). In his opening pages, Ceaser suggests that he wants to locate his project within the larger problem of classifying and ordering different kinds of political ideas. He rightly notes that different kinds of ideas have different valences and uses, and cannot be crudely lumped together. Yet when Ceaser turns to discussing the deployment of nature and history as foundational concepts, the analysis reverts to a fairly conventional foray into intellectual history. On closer examination, its claims for novelty prove to be not methodological but topical. Another historian, one more intimate with nineteenth- and twentieth-century sources than the present critic can pretend to be, might be able to demonstrate that these findings are in fact misguided. (Recall that my own professional trump card says: "After my period.") But that colleague would also recognize Ceaser's mode of analyzing ideas and debates as a familiar exercise in intellectual history.

Once past his extended survey, however, Ceaser concludes on a different note. Perhaps worrying that his historical dabbling has carried him along too far, he offers three "points of reflection" on the value of his inquiry. The first, presented rather lukewarmly, is exactly the one that a historian proper would be most expected to appreciate: identifying "causal links" between the formulation or expression of foundational ideas and specific political outcomes. Here, as a good social scientist, he realizes that exercises in causality are densely multivariate, and the probability that any good scheme of multiple regression will return a high value for the intermediate "foundational concept" variable is not high. The third reflection (we will return to the second shortly) pivots on a self-reflexive observation about the contemporary moment in which Ceaser's project is itself situated. Ceaser worries about the consequences of the anti-foundationalist tendencies of the modern academy and the larger culture—as best represented, perhaps, by Richard Rorty. Just as a polity may not need a genuine public philosophy, so there are "dangers" inherent in grounding all of its political commitments on a single foundational concept. But accepting the interplay of multiple such ideas may be essential,

Ceaser concludes, because "the task of reformulating and refining a nation's foundation is never-ending."

Between these two reflections, however, Ceaser interjects a third which lies closer to my own interests. This "concerns the cause of the cause—that is, who creates foundational concepts and sets them in motion?" Ceaser begins his brief discussion of this point by reminding us of the long-standing division between "materialists," who believe that ideas derive from and are driven by "physical and economic factors," and "idealists," who hold that "ideas have consequences."[13] But rather than resolve this sterile debate, Ceaser raises a more intriguing question by imagining situations in which "political actors" who ordinarily are preoccupied with the "task of handling affairs" find themselves having to "engage foundational concepts—either to defeat a concept that threatens the community or to enlist or revise one that can promote its well-being." Under such circumstances, statesmen will have to depend on some existing "catalogue [of concepts] derived from the realm of theory," but their choice will depend on how those concepts will be perceived to operate "in the crucible of real political activity." Such choices will in turn promote further theoretical inquiry beyond that crucible and back in the academy or some other sphere of intellection.

This situational account of how political ideas are generated or deployed is very different from the hackneyed choice between materialist and idealist explanations (which arguably represent foundationalist modes of thinking as well). It also identifies, I believe, one of the most important and least adequately conceived problems in writing the history of political ideas. Despite all the volumes and essays and commentaries that have been written on this subject; despite all the methodological debates that rage over the hermeneutics of reading texts or tracing unit ideas; and despite all the scholarly energy that has been spent locating and classifying ideologies, traditions, public philosophies, and plain old isms—notwithstanding all these, it still seems to me that we lack adequate accounts or theories of how ideas are generated and deployed within explicitly political contexts. We know much more about what has been thought than about thinking, and more about the content of political ideas than about their formation.

To generalize broadly, and no doubt simplistically, the vast bulk of this prodigious literature can be reduced to attempts to answer three main questions. First, how do we best read, understand, interpret, and critically assess political texts? Second, how are ideas transmitted and absorbed, such that texts written in one time or place "influence" later writers or those acting in other political spaces? Third, how do we describe and measure the dynamics of political debates in which ideas are not merely instrumental means of legitimating and advancing positions taken for other reasons, but themselves active objects of political controversy?

On all of these subjects, it is easy to identify and discuss rich bodies of scholarly work. On the matter of how to read a text, or define the appropriate context within which it can be read, no one could claim that we are all Straussians, we are all Skinnerians— but we know full well what is at stake in casting one's lot with this side or that. On the vexatious question of influence, there are simple explanations of how prior authors inspire later ones (Madison stumbles upon the solution to the problem of republican government by recalling or returning to the essays of David Hume)[14] and complicated stories of the transmission of ideas from one generation or place to another, often quite distant in time and space (the recovery of classical republicanism by Machiavelli and his contemporaries; the absorption of their writings on the subject first by seventeenth-century English radicals and then by their provincial American cousins a century later).[15] Sometimes this belief that we are what we read can take an especially determinative form. Passages of Forrest McDonald's book on the intellectual origins of the Constitution make it appear as if the Framers came to Philadelphia less as delegates from individual states than as subscribers to correspondence schools featuring celebrity authors from James Harrington to Bernard Mandeville.[16] And of course any of a number of major American political debates, from the pre-Revolutionary quarrel with Britain and the struggle over the ratification of the Constitution down to the present, have been reconstructed in elaborate scholarly detail, with close attention paid to the rival views of the different sides.

What remains rare, I believe, and strangely neglected, are studies of *how* political ideas are generated, or self-conscious scholarly efforts to identify and delineate the varieties of ways in which political controversy or uncertainty inspires the formation of new ideas and the refinement of old ones. Not that the subject has been wholly neglected. William Riker's efforts to formulate his theory of heresthetics (no novelty to practitioners of APD) constituted one such effort.[17] So, arguably, did the authors who contributed to the bicentennial volume on conceptual change and the Constitution.[18] I have tried to formulate my own tentative notions on this subject in a recent paper, "Thinking Like a Constitution," in which the pun on James Scott's well-known book introduces a brief exploration of various innovations in modes of political thinking both inspired and necessitated by the American project of adopting written constitutions of government and then realizing that these were conceived to operate as supreme fundamental law.[19]

Observant readers will have noted that these illustrations are all drawn from a single period of political history: the epoch of remarkable creativity we label the Revolutionary era. Herein lies a problem. Studies of this era almost invariably, perhaps inevitably, emphasize just how innovative it was. That, after all, is what revolutions are about: innovation, transformation, readjustment to and retrenchment against the brave new world that visionary enthusiasts have tried to create. The study of what happens to political ideas amid such turbulence may, in the end, have little relevance to the questions that Ceaser poses about how foundational concepts operate in more stable times. Perhaps the dualist notion of politics that Bruce Ackerman deploys in his *We the People* volumes is apposite here.[20] There are forms and norms of political discourse that operate more or less routinely in ordinary times, and others that come into play only during extraordinary moments of constitutional change (like 1787).

Yet by the same token, it is also during the latter transitions—whether conceived, as Ackerman sees them, as highly compressed, momentary episodes, or as the longer blocks of time with which historians are more comfortable—that we are most likely to encounter the broadest array of uses for political ideas, or the conditions under which new ideas are most likely to be generated. Having spent the past three decades trying to understand the generation of new constitutional ideas during the Revolutionary era, without feeling the potential of the subject is exhausted, I also remain convinced that such periods offer the most challenging and rewarding, though not always the most representative, "sites" for the systematic study of the underlying problem. And so, by way of pondering the larger set of problems for which Ceaser's foundational quest specifies only one application, I close by considering the one work I know that best illustrates what the requisite self-consciousness about explaining the development and deployment of different kinds of political ideas would entail.

That work is (not surprisingly) also the one that made me into a student of early American history when I first came to Cambridge: Bernard Bailyn's *Ideological Origins of the American Revolution,* which remains for me not only the most important book written about this (or any other) era of American history, but also a remarkable illustration of the multiple problems that anyone who wants to work in the history of political ideas has to confront. This declaration may surprise uncritical readers, who believe that the book primarily couples proof of the early presence in America of Richard Hofstadter's "paranoid style" with an account of the origins of the political tradition known as "republicanism." In fact, in analyzing the multiple forms and uses of political ideas and accounting for sources of conceptual invention and transformation, the book is a far richer text.[21]

Careful readers will discover that *Ideological Origins* makes at least five distinct arguments about the nature of political ideas, their influence, deployment, motivating power, and evolution or transformation. Bailyn begins by distinguishing the respective influence of various "sources and traditions," or modes of thought, that were present in eighteenth-century American political discourse, recognizing, in effect, that any modern polity is likely to be host to a variety of political ideas. This initial survey concludes, however, that not all such traditions were equally influential. One, associated with the radical Whig critics of the post-Walpole British constitution, is discovered to have resonated with particular strength among eighteenth-century Americans.[22] From the problem of assessing the respective strength of different "sources" of American political thinking, Bailyn then turns to a description of this radical Whig tradition, and in particular to its obsession with the intertwined themes of "power and liberty." Analytically, the chapter that takes this phrase as its title is the most conventional in the book, a rendering of the contents and animating spirit of a body of writings that can reasonably be said to constitute a school of thought.

That conventional chapter, however, is also fundamental to the ensuing explication of the "logic of rebellion"; the chapter on this topic is the one that most directly plots the American Revolution's ideological origins. Here Bailyn draws the legacy of these radical Whig ideas about liberty and power to their explicitly political conclusion. It was the colonists' absorption of these ideas *prior to* the imperial crisis that ended with independence, he argues, that best explains why their reaction to the new departures in British policy after 1765 took an increasingly radical and militant turn. There were other ways to explain British miscues than a belief that holders and wielders of power in London were bent on depriving Americans of their traditional rights and liberties, the better to turn them into "slaves," in the era's political use of that term. But in a political culture predisposed to assume purposefulness behind every action,[23] this way of thinking about public events inclined American radicals, and over time growing numbers of their countrymen, to interpret British actions in the worst light possible, as evidence not of misinformation or incompetence or misjudgment but of a systematic design. This provides an ideological interpretation in a sense rather different from the passing reference to ideology in Ceaser's paper. Here ideology is important less as a body of beliefs per se than as a filter through which those imbued with its power view and interpret events—and thus act in response to them.

Yet the logic of rebellion alone does not explain why Americans rejected British authority in 1776. Having reached the decision for independence in his narrative, Bailyn doubles back to 1765 to review the constitutional origins of the controversy between Britain and its colonies. Here the analysis of political ideas takes a different form still. Now it involves not the application of an ideological filter or prism to a course of political action, but the "transformation" of the fundamental concepts of eighteenth-century Anglo-American constitutionalism "in the course of a decade of pounding controversy." In this story of "conceptual change," the initial dispute over taxation escalated unpredictably but inexorably into further discussions of the sources of colonial rights, the nature of the imperial constitution, and finally the location of sovereignty. Starting from familiar premises, the colonists found themselves reaching a host of novel conclusions, all of which subsequently proved foundational to the evolution of American political thinking.

All of the ideas undergoing this transformation were part of the manifest issues of the imperial controversy. But these ideas—or the deeper attitudes they reflected—had an unintended infectious effect as well, producing a "contagion of liberty" that spilled over to inflame other questions (slavery, religion, social hierarchy, and the politics of deference) that the dispute with Britain had never implicated. As I previously suggested in discussing the changing meaning of Jefferson's statement of equality, political ideas—and especially ideas of equality—can be only propounded, not copyrighted. Once introduced into discussion, they are always there for someone else's manipulative or earnest expropriation, always susceptible to the iron law of unintended consequences, always capable of taking a provocative turn within the issue space, or setting off along some new dimension altogether.

Here the original version of *Ideological Origins* ended, posing a great question about the foundational concept of equality that the Revolution had unleashed. "How else could it end?" Bailyn asked in conclusion. "What reasonable social and political order could be built where authority was questioned before it was obeyed?" Or where, we might add, no authority could determine whether appeals to nature, history, or religion should have the final say?[24] In the epilogue to the expanded edition covering the constitutional debates of 1787–1788, Bailyn introduced a further refinement yet. His account of the quarrel between Federalists and Anti-Federalists takes the form of a contest, less between the partisans of nature and history than between two readings of history, one faithfully adhering to the lessons of the past discovered before 1776, the other embracing those learned since. More fundamentally, Bailyn poses the conflict between those who were still thinking ideologically—men not of too little faith in the promise of the Constitution but of too much loyalty to what they already knew—and those who had begun reasoning pragmatically, who were no longer acting on the dictates of established authority but who now begged to know why old beliefs should continue to command uncritical adherence.

The genius of *Ideological Origins,* then, transcends its many observations about the substantive content of American political ideas during this formative founding epoch. As an inquiry into the nature of political ideas, into their generation, transmission, and transformation, it offers a multifaceted approach to issues that remain all too poorly formulated or conceptualized in the disciplines of political history and science alike. This claim may be incautious, brash, and even wrong, yet it points to a deeper concern that James Ceaser's provocative paper raises but does not resolve. The larger problem, I believe, is that we do not have an adequate account or theory about how political ideas are generated or refined, especially when the source of this generation and refinement is not the "ingenious theorist" conjured in James Madison's *Federalist* 37, working alone "in his closet or in his imagination," but (as Ceaser observes) political actors forced to dabble and more in foundational concepts. Ceaser's particular concern makes an interesting contribution to this larger project, but there is a more ambitious agenda out there waiting to be defined as well as pursued.

# 3

---

# REPLACING FOUNDATIONS WITH STAGING

## "Second-Story" Concepts and American Political Development

*Nancy L. Rosenblum*

D ANGEROUS IDEAS, FIRST COOKED IN THE HEADS of philosophers, "find a welcome among the masses and acquire the driving force of a political passion," Alexis de Tocqueville remarked.[1] Karl Mannheim brought the point home to scholars when he observed that "philosophers have too long concerned themselves with their own thinking."[2] In a similar spirit, James Ceaser reminds us that politically consequential ideas are not the exclusive creation or study of philosophy. He is right, and absorption in philosophy is a particular peril for political theorists, whether what exhausts their attention consists of canonical texts or contemporary analytic arguments. We do not have to agree with Ceaser that "Americans were the first to bring nature down from the realm of philosophy and introduce it into the political world as a foundation" to get his point. Ideas that originate in the minds of philosophers or poets or some broader intelligentsia "move out." They are adopted, adapted, and used in politics by thoughtful (and—a point that Ceaser should acknowledge—thoughtless) political actors. Politicians articulate, amplify, and exploit important ideas in their ceaseless efforts to win, persuade, bargain, lobby, reform, destroy, oppress, and build. They give philosophy life. In other words, these ideas gain autonomy;

they escape their origins; they are not just adjectively "political" articulations of philosophy. They move out from philosophy and take on independent political life, as political actors forge alliances, create agendas, and fashion institutional and policy change. Political deliberation and persuasion entail more than theoretical argument, and, for better or worse, political actors find ideas for penetrating and altering their world.

Ideas in the minds and hands of political leaders facing specific problems deserve the same close study that Cambridge political theorists pay to the surrounding intellectual milieu, reading lists, conceptual toolkits, and persuasive purposes of the authors of canonical texts. Of course, in his schematic overview of nature and history in American political thought, Ceaser could not possibly do what he recommends; his paper is a promissory note. Still, even in outline Ceaser fails to follow his own prescription. He identifies certain concepts in the speeches and writings of partisans, pundits, and statesmen, and then he stops. Mannheim's point, and Ceaser's promise, was to try to understand *how* ideas make their way from philosophy into political thought and practice in specific instances, *how* they are used by political actors to support institutions, policies, or ideologies—in short, *how* they "are encountered as tangible political phenomena that are in play in the practical political world." More specifically, American political development is the frame for our discussion, and we could reasonably expect Ceaser to show whether or how certain ideas shape the periods and provide the dynamic of political development.

My commentary addresses Ceaser's paper, but it should be read as a broader reflection by a political theorist on the theme of foundational concepts. I begin by exploring the interpretive and evaluative faces of Ceaser's project, and what I take to be his political motivation. I go on to explore two elements of the project in some detail.

One comprises periods and dynamic. By asserting the importance of foundational concepts for American political development, we expect them to play an identifiable role in periodization and in the dynamic of political change. Ceaser shows that political appeals to concepts of nature and history may illuminate periods already defined by historians and political scientists in other terms, but he fails to show that foundational concepts are the exclusive or even most important concepts at work, much less that they actually shape these periods. I will also try to fill in what I take to be a central gap in Ceaser's thesis, and suggest a potential dynamic by which philosophical ideas move out and affect political life.

The second theme I explore in some detail is at the heart of political theory: what a foundational concept is, how such concepts are used in political life, and why Ceaser's case for the political necessity of foundational concepts is at odds with a leading strain of democratic theory. I conclude by proposing an alternative to foundational concepts in the study of American political development: "staging," or "second-story," second-order ideas derived from political theory, not philosophy, and tied more directly to actual political conflict and institutional design.

## Interpretation and Evaluation

Ceaser's project has two faces. The first is interpretive but it is not, as we might expect, the argument that certain identifiable concepts are the foundation of American political development. His title is not "The Conceptual Foundations *of* American Political Development" but "Foundational Concepts *and* American Political Development." This deserves attention, for it circumscribes his study in two important respects.

For one thing, it means that the project aims at something more modest than the foundations of American political development. Instead, what Ceaser calls foundational concepts of nature and history are in some respect—short of forming the foundations of American politics—important to political development. This interpretive face should contain an argument that even if foundational concepts are not foundational exactly, they are uniquely important.[3] To be meaningful, foundational concepts must compel and constrain what is experienced, what is intended, and what can be done. If foundational concepts are, as Ceaser says at one point, of only "minimal threshold importance," the project is diminished from the start. I will return to this point shortly.

The title "Foundational Concepts and American Political Development" circumscribes Ceaser's interpretive purpose in a second respect. The subject is not politically efficacious ideas per se, though we know that ideas can be an important, even determining political variable in American political development even if they are not foundational. Ceaser's concern is one specific class of ideas. His subject is not popular political opinion, recently acquired impressions, vulnerable to media effects and advertising. It is not diffuse political culture, or its producers and consumers. The ideas that concern him are also distinct from ideology. At least, Ceaser wants to avoid the thought often implicit in ideology that individuals and groups are so interest-bound in their thinking as to be simply unable to see certain facts. His foundational concepts are intelligible to and manipulated by political actors without any suggestion of distortion, false consciousness, or unwitting deception.[4] Just what counts as a foundational concept, distinct and separate from all other ideas, becomes a central concern, as I show below.

The second face of Ceaser's essay is evaluative. His project is infused with the judgment that American democracy needs foundational concepts in forms suitable for political discourse. But if foundational concepts are necessary, they are not always available, and Ceaser warns us not to assume that these ideas arise naturally or spontaneously in political life, or that they move out from philosophy and are recognized as political resources as a matter of course. The fact that Ceaser casts foundational concepts as imperative for democracy but that political actors do not always have access to them may explain why in the end he pays relatively little attention to the role foundational concepts play in political life, attending mainly to capturing the moments when political actors invoke philosophical ideas. An example would be the Whig conservatives who deliberately cultivated historical experience as a touchstone, choosing the Pilgrims as the central element of a "usable past" and inventing the two-founding thesis.

Foundational concepts are necessary, Ceaser advises, but their discovery and use are not guaranteed. Why should it be a crisis if there is, as he claims, a near-vacuum of foundational concepts at the heart of political life? If the necessity for a public philosophy grounded in nature or history is not an empty imprecation, what is the imperative? Ceaser does not give the analytic philosopher's answer: the appeal to foundational concepts just *is* what it is to make a reasoned political argument. More interestingly, for Ceaser the necessity for a public philosophy is not a *moral* necessity. The nature he commends as a guide may be amoral, and the imperative that nature sets for us may be a matter of acquiescing in or exploiting inescapable constraints. This is famously the case with natural right understood as the drive to self-preservation, and its corollary imperative: judging for ourselves the conditions of safety.

Instead, the necessity for foundational concepts that drives Ceaser's search is political, and I think he means to say that it is also distinctively democratic. Democracy is peculiarly vulnerable to the chaos of fluid public opinion, and is therefore peculiarly in need of foundational ideas that compel and constrain action over the political long term. The danger of an absence of foundational concepts (and what of multiple, competing foundations?) is arrant flux. Foundational concepts provide a "general political orientation," Ceaser advises—meaning, I take it, that certain ideas have coherence and staying power. Foundational concepts have persuasive power, with lasting effect beyond the immediate political purpose at hand. In this way, foundational concepts differ from appeals to momentary expedience or mutual advantageousness or the fugitive consensus of public opinion, which may be nothing more than a response to polling. Ceaser's concern is the effectiveness of foundations for "ensuring political stability over the long term."

Ceaser goes farther down this evaluative path to suggest a hierarchy of foundational concepts: nature is better than history, and both are better than religion.[5] In fact, early in this essay, and without explanation, religious foundations drop entirely from view. Writing from the standpoint of the present, Ceaser records the complex back-and-forth of variations on the concepts of nature and history, but also an overall slide from strong foundations in nature to weaker history to debilitating nihilism. History overtakes nature, and anti-foundationalism threatens to eclipse both.

We recognize Ceaser's pair of foundational concepts—nature and history—as the guiding threads of Leo Strauss's *Natural Right and History,* and Ceaser acknowledges the affinity between his sense of crisis and Strauss's. Many writers have identified modernity (and America) with liberalism,[6] and see liberalism as decline: a lowering of sights from the good life to mere life, selfish materialism, atomism, and so on. What distinguishes Strauss's jeremiad is the specific charge that liberals are responsible for abandoning natural right, and the judgment that "the need for natural right is as evident today as it has been for centuries and millennia. . . . The rejection of natural right is bound to lead to disastrous consequences."[7] Ceaser echoes both the judgment and the charge. The difference is that when Strauss writes, "The issue of natural right presents itself today as a matter of party allegiance," the two camps he conjures have world historical sweep: liberals from the seventeenth century to the present on the one side and disciples of Thomas Aquinas on the other.[8] Ceaser substitutes the New Left, which he unaccountably identifies with the philosopher Norman O. Brown, and the Republican Party. Within an overarching drama of modern decline is Ceaser's local drama of American political development, with its fall from already dispirited Progressivism and modern liberalism into arrant anti-foundationalism. Moreover, in Ceaser's hands this drama is a partisan political story: the contemporary Republican Party is the keeper of vestigial strains of foundationalism, including, most importantly, a re-vived natural right, while "nearly all advanced intellectual ele-ments" of the Democratic Party favor anti-foundationalism.

The interpretive and evaluative facets of Ceaser's essay are in-tertwined. He anticipates that by recapturing foundational con-cepts in APD, he can supply a body of knowledge to guide the re-flection of political actors. Ceaser has frankly set out on a search for foundational concepts for American democracy, and the stakes for him are not purely academic.[9]

## Periodization

I've said that Ceaser's subject is not the conceptual foundations of American political development but something different: the place of foundational concepts in American political develop-ment. APD is the name for a field of study, and Ceaser aligns him-self with two of the field's key elements. One is appreciation for the complexity of American political history, as evidenced by at-tention to unsuccessful ideas, alternative visions, submerged "multiple traditions." Thus, Ceaser resurrects the various "na-tures" that figure in public philosophy: the "original" nature of political psychology, ethnography, evolutionary biology, and their diverse incarnations.

The other alignment between Ceaser's project and APD is pe-riodization—that is, the claim that on certain dimensions, mea-sured by certain facts, any particular period differs decisively from those that preceded it. Development is not necessarily im-provement, but it is intelligible continuity such that the change from one state to the next can be explained with reference to the earlier one. "Critical elections" are perhaps the best-known basis for periodization in political science. According to Bruce Acker-man's account of dualist democracy, to take another example, pe-riods are marked by either normal politics or higher-lawmaking, initiated by the exercise of popular sovereignty.[10] Ceaser does not spell out whether or how his periodization differs from others, and in fact the moments he points to correspond to political eras made familiar by historians and political scientists (with one exception—namely, the breakpoint he sets between 1960, the end of what he calls the Progressive-Liberal era, and the present; this period is peculiarly tied to Ceaser's own political narrative).

For the most part, the foundational concepts he associates with each period are familiar, too. If the uses of nature and history correspond to continuities and breakpoints identified in other terms, then Ceaser's claim for the importance of investigating "foundational concepts and American political development" is relatively weak. Ceaser locates appeals to nature and history in the public speeches and writings of political actors, and undeniably there is added value to accenting these bits of intellectual history. But nothing in Ceaser's account shows that foundational concepts define or alter these periods. To make his project a compelling alternative to other studies of American political thought and history, Ceaser would have to show that the foundational concepts he identifies are defining, or in some way uniquely important.

Ceaser's position on this essential matter is elusive. He explicitly rejects APD's "noble obsession with causality." Study of this kind has "diminishing intellectual returns," he says, because major events are the result of multiple factors. Scholars of APD recognize this, of course. What is wanted is not a knock-down counterfactual argument that if a particular foundational concept had been unavailable or had not been articulated by an influential political actor, specific political outcomes would not have occurred, or would have occurred differently. But to be meaningful, foundational concepts must compel and constrain what is intended and what can be done. It is one thing to say that foundational concepts do not drive policies, that there are intervening constraints. But identifying and showing in some detail how certain foundational ideas are used to support specific institutions and policies and why they are effective is the heart of the matter. How do foundational concepts make their way into public discourse? And then, under certain social conditions and in certain institutional settings, how do they propel and constrain action? If Ceaser does not enter the causal fray to this extent, how can he show what work foundational concepts do that cannot be adequately understood by institutional or materialist histories, or by other cultural approaches to APD, or by intellectual histories in which the most important ideas for politics are not foundational at all? If the most that we get is identifying invocations of nature and history in the speeches and writings of political actors, the conjunction in Ceaser's title—"foundational concepts *and* American political development"—begs the crucial questions.

Here is an example of the difficulty I have in assessing the political effect of foundational concepts. Ceaser tells us: "Federalists held that it [the concept of nature] supplied a general standard for the ends of political life, but it did not provide—and was not intended to provide—detailed assistance for writing constitutions, legislating, or conducting matters of policy." He goes on to say that the Jeffersonians claimed nature *could* supply active guidance on how constitutions should be written and on policies in the economic realm. Now, it is fair enough to say that prima facie evidence of the significance of specific ideas shows that political actors themselves consider them to be important. It is another thing to demonstrate whether and how these beliefs about foundational ideas work directly or indirectly to shape or motivate or constrain political action. Were the Federalists and Jeffersonians faithful to their respective notions of the use of foundational ideas? Were they correct in their statements about how these foundations could be politically employed? Whose notion of the use of "nature" was borne out in practice, and how would we know? The move from philosophy to public discourse and from there to political action, institutions, and policy is not spelled out; indeed, sometimes Ceaser loses sight of it entirely. "If there was ever any set of ideas in American history that met the criterion of becoming a decisive winner and routing its foes, at least among the intellectual segments of society, it was the liberal bloc," he insists. Maybe so, but the promise was to show how those ideas *move out from the preserve of intellectuals,* and to what political effect.

## What Happened to Religion?

If foundational concepts define, shape, or at least affect distinct periods, then we must be convinced that the conceptual tools Ceaser identifies with these periods are the chief ones at work. If not, the periods would look different; indeed, the result might be an altered periodization. The obvious omission here is religion. Except for one mention of "social gospel" in the late nineteenth century, Ceaser leaves religion behind with the sacred history of the Puritans. Why? After all, religion cannot be wholly identified with sacred history; its forms and conventions are much broader than that. Perhaps he thinks that religion is mainly operative insofar as it is intertwined with nature or history. Or perhaps religion drops out because it is dangerous, profitless, or untrue and so cannot meet the political requirements of foundational concepts. In any case, the absence of religion in this discussion is striking; every period that Ceaser discusses—most strikingly, perhaps, Progressivism—grappled with faith and its authority in the political realm. Appeals to faith and religious authority continue to play a part in politics today. Conor Cruise O'Brien is only one of many foreigners to remark on American religiosity, to take the National Prayer Breakfast seriously, and to call America "God land."[11] Today, religious narratives and appeals to faith are ubiquitous and eclipse nature, history, and certainly anti-foundationalism in political discourse. In the United States, religion has been and remains indisputably central to political organization, mobilization, and partisanship, as well as to public philosophy.

To take just one current example, key political actors today represent September 11, 2001, as a point not only in historical time but also in sacred time. The events of that day are said to have provided Americans with an opportunity for spiritual revival as well as the necessity for military self-defense. We hear echoes of the famous claim: "In the exception, the power of real life breaks through the crust of a mechanism that has become torpid by repetition."[12] An emergency is a testing moment, an occasion for revivification. Our banal and corrupt personal lives and crass collective culture (hostile, on this view, to faith) can be redeemed by the exception. In the presidential campaign of 2004, George W. Bush credited his faith with inspiring firm decision making and steadfastness, and he linked religion with his understanding of America's purpose in the world and his ability to understand the nature of the terrorist threat. He fused faith and the cause of human freedom: "Freedom is on the march, and America and the world are more secure because of it. I believe in my heart of hearts that every person in the world wants to live in a free society. I believe this because I understand that freedom is not America's gift to the world; freedom is the Almighty God's gift to each man and woman of this world."[13] Moreover, the political efficacy of appeals to faith is connected to specific institutions, among them the current U.S. presidency, the configuration of politically mobilizable social groups, and the distinctive back-and-forth between denominational competition and interdenominational alliance that marks religious voices in American political life.

Something else is lost when religion drops out of Ceaser's account of foundational concepts. Religion might have served as an exemplary case of foundational ideas "moving out" so that they are useful to political actors and resonate with democratic audiences. We know that the translation from theology or doctrine to political orientation is indirect, and that it typically proceeds through several distinct steps. Religion makes its way from organized religious establishments via specially formed social and political offshoots of churches, led by secular as well as clerical authorities. The second step is the creation of religious political identity, of the sort we point to when we speak of the general political orientation (liberal or conservative, say) of religious denominations or of traditionalist or modernist factions within denominations. It requires a third step to get from religious political identity to faith-based justifications for political participation in support of parties or candidates or concrete policies.[14] I mention this progression in order to suggest the social and organizational conditions that underlie the effective political invocation of religious ideas. Something like this sort of movement would also point up the need to explain the dynamic by which ideas influence American political development.

## Political Dynamic and Political Parties

American political development is not a matter of chronology ("and then, and then") or of periodization, though that is how it appears in Ceaser's essay. The heart of studies of political development is a dynamic of stability versus change. Karl Mannheim, in his book *Ideology and Utopia* (quoted earlier), argued that consequential ideas are brought into politics by carrier groups. Ideas that drive politics are attached to classes, on his view, and the challenge is to explain the elective affinity between groups and a set of ideas. The idea of *correspondence,* of which individuals may not be fully aware, plays a part here. There is a correspondence between a given social situation, characterized by great interests, and a perspective, which Mannheim calls "ideology." The agents in Ceaser's story are not social classes, and correspondence is not obviously rooted in great social interests. His agents are mainly statesmen, who adopt and shape foundational concepts in public discourse and forge connections between these ideas and their political commitments.

But politicians are not alone, floating in the thin ether of what philosophers refer to as "public spaces." The carriers of public discourse are political parties, and, at least implicitly, parties are always there in the background of Ceaser's story. The effective agents of political development are parties, rather than social movements, interest groups, or creators and propagators of popular culture. Party politics might provide a portion of the dynamic missing from Ceaser's argument. Foundational concepts come into the world from philosophy—they don't come into the world as partisan. But partisans make them central to politics, and employ these ideas (and others) in party conflict within specific institutions and electoral frameworks. Public philosophy has its origin and traction in partisan politics. Again, Ceaser does not name parties or partisans as the agents who move foundational concepts out into public life, but they are prominent in his examples. These include philosophy of history as an aspect of party conflict in the 1790s; Whigs and Democrats in the 1830s and 1840s; competing "Darwinian" factions within the Republican party in the late nineteenth century; and contemporary Democratic and Republican partisans.

How might we construct a dynamic of American political development from these materials? At defining moments—or, more modestly, at those moments when public philosophy is defining—parties play a creative role. They are not centrist and undifferentiated; they are not public utilities, or support mechanisms for teams of competitors. They do not just reflect social cleavages or other lines of division. Rather, armed with policy purposes and with public philosophies, parties "divide political power into categories not found in uninstructed political practice."[15] They articulate, organize, and even create these differences as they appeal for support. Maurice Duverger resorted to a host of metaphors to capture parties' creative force: they crystallize, coagulate, synthesize, smooth down, and mold.[16] They use all sorts of ideas and narrative frameworks to do this work. Here are at least the rudiments of a dynamic that goes some way toward explaining the relation among concepts, public discourse, and political activity and policy.

There are good reasons to explore more closely and to argue more robustly for parties as the carriers of foundational concepts and other kinds of ideas in American political life. Very simply, elections are the defining institution of democracy, and competitive parties mobilizing voters are the heart of meaningful elections. Parties give content and shape to rival political orientations as well as to passing issues. Party competition commands attention; that is, parties are "public" in a way that other organized political groups are not. Parties may also help to explain why, as Ceaser says, foundational concepts invoked strategically for immediate political action "cannot simply be set aside or discarded in the aftermath, but continue to exercise an influence." If foundational concepts have staying power beyond the moment of use, one reason may be that they become identified with parties and partisans. In the United States, parties are good candidates for Mannheim's "carrier groups."

Notice that my critical discussion of periodization and dynamics could apply to any set of consequential ideas in American political development, not just to foundational concepts. As I pointed out at the start, Ceaser focuses on this specific class of ideas and argues that they are politically necessary. The notion of "foundational concepts" speaks directly to my business as a political theorist, and in the next two sections I want to ask what foundational concepts are, and why contemporary democratic theory is directly at odds with Ceaser over their political necessity.

## Foundations, Justification, and Persuasion

Ceaser offers the image of a pyramid of idea types, with foundational concepts at the base. The architectural image is inapt. After all, Ceaser's concern is not formal logic—the working out of premises. Political orientations, institutions, and policies do not follow deductively from these concepts. Often enough, they do not seem to follow from these concepts with any necessity at all. Public philosophy is not a systematic construct.

Another more promising route to conceptualizing foundations is mapped out in social and political theory. On this view, certain ideas stand in a "constitutive" relation to our selves and our experience. They shape moral and political identity. They circumscribe insights because they powerfully inform our experience. Deeply embedded, they set limits to what we can adopt or repudiate. Concepts of history or nature or religion fix who we are. Authentic political action, then, reflects what is ours (our history) or what is necessary or right (nature) or what faith commands. The character of a political society and its people is shaped by the principle (in teleological accounts, by the form and stage of the principle) embodied in it.[17] We recognize this as the "holist" view of culture and society, which can take many different forms: it can be organic or constructivist; it can hark back to the movement of Idealist spirit or to Marxist correspondence between base and superstructure. In every version, holism says that there is a structure to our experience, an intelligible interconnection that gives it identity and meaning despite apparent diversity. On this account, public philosophy and politics are expressive, and the task of interpreters is not just to conceive a correspondence or tension between, say, base and superstructure, but to give an acceptable account of how the base—in this case, the foundational concept—is able to exert this power of generating awareness of a specific social and political reality, institutions, and so on.

Ceaser does not formulate foundationalism in this way, and in the end, as I have said, he fails to speak to the question of the expressivism or the shaping power of foundational concepts for politics. I conjecture that the reason the constitutive relation between ideas and political experience does not make an appearance in Ceaser's essay is that holism and hermeneutic interpretation fail to capture the deliberate election of foundational ideas. Ceaser wants to claim autonomy for these ideas, and to accent the agency of political leaders who find themselves in situations in which they "need to actively engage foundational concepts." Foundational concepts, in his account, are chosen by political actors for strategic purposes. Ceaser turns out to be interested less in the sociology of knowledge than simply in the fact that concepts of nature and history are used by political actors. The statesman's challenge, he writes, is to assess the value of a particular foundational idea "as measured in the crucible of real political activity." Thus,

Ceaser writes that participants in the debates in the Continental Congress focused on "the effectiveness of different foundations in generating support for impending action and on their effect in ensuring political stability over time." In another example, the Whigs "sensed that it was simpler and more effective to promote certain ideas by locating their origin within a widely respected political tradition rather than by advocating them solely as abstract propositions." Ceaser explains the shifts in Lincoln's appeals to foundational ideas by adducing the specific political context and tasks at hand—Lincoln's strategic political needs.

This should caution us to question the positive normative status Ceaser assigns foundational concepts, their regulative power. After all, a lot of political questions are obscured by invoking who we are or what nature commands. Appeals to history or religion can serve to obfuscate and avoid: characterizing America as a "city on a hill" (Matthew 5:14) does not speak to foreign policy costs and who bears them; to consequences, and for whom; to efficiency; to institutional capacity; to the existence of actual policies reasonably capable of addressing problems. Notice too that foundational concepts can be invoked rhetorically. They are floridly aesthetic, simply sonorous, decorous, ritualistic. The image of America as a beacon is an expected element in just about every declaration of interventionist foreign policy. Foundational ideas are often routine "frozen accidents" that do no serious work. We want to allow for the possibility that they do not add substantively to motivations or reasons. The effectiveness of these concepts may be their familiarity and their capacity to arouse predictable public responses. When Ceaser associates natural right with Republican anti-Communism, we have to ask what force if any this had for decision makers during the Cold War. Public philosophy can be speechifying. I won't disparage rhetoric by saying these ideas are *merely rhetorical* or raise the issue of sincerity. But the plausibility of sheer display today is underscored by Ceaser's observation that political leaders today, given their education and the demands of political life, encounter theoretical ideas indirectly via think tanks and speechwriters. In fact, the ideas they are likely to get first hand are religious ideas, not concepts of history or nature.

The theoretical point here is that invocations of foundational concepts may serve purposes of political persuasion without serving the purposes of justification. Plainly, Ceaser's interest in foundational concepts is their political use, and he repeatedly points to one use in particular: justification. As an account of the use of foundational concepts, I argue, justification is both too weak and too strong. Too weak, because if we take foundational concepts seriously they are better characterized as causal or constitutive in the way I described earlier. They act as constraints on what is conceivable; they define possibilities and constitute experience. Too strong, because as the examples I cited suggest, something less than justification is going on when political actors invoke nature or history or religion. For justification is defined by a distinctive style of reasoning and argument that is typically precluded by invocations of nature or history.

In democratic politics, justification is "discursive," or deliberative. It is the back-and-forth of reasons, constrained by generally agreed-upon norms of argument and evidence, and shaped by institutional settings. What foundational concepts do—the reason they are foundational—is not justification in this sense. Nature, history, and religion are rarely invitations to deliberation. The whole point of foundational ideas in the form of public philosophy or persuasive narrative is to dictate the terms of argument, ideally to put an end to argument. As Ceaser himself observes, a foundational concept "is an idea presented as requiring no further argument, since it is thought to contain within itself its first premise. It supplies the answer to the question 'Why,' beyond which any further response is thought unnecessary." Foundationalism achieves a cognitive and affective coming to rest. The work of foundational concepts is to provide a ground and a horizon—to

131

enclose us in a close and ideally impenetrable bubble of meaning, a perspective without which we become morally and politically disoriented.

As J. L. Austin famously showed, what words do is as important as what they mean. The performative act of invoking history or nature (or religion) in support of political action is not justification but something else. I think the dynamic is best described as reconciliation. Foundational concepts are invoked to give policy the aura of necessity. That is the political requirement foundationalism must address, in Ceaser's account; that is why these ideas are supposed to stiffen resolve and produce stable public support. With persuasion in mind we see why Ceaser's examples include so many presidents, who address (and can get the attention of) the nation. As Keith Whittington and Daniel Carpenter have shown, the president's distinctive concern is not deliberation but strength and effectiveness[18]—persuasion, not justification.

## Democracy and Justification

Before I leave off probing foundational concepts and their political uses, I want to elaborate on the question of justification by bringing in contemporary political philosophy. Justification is central to perhaps the leading strand of political theory today, deliberative democratic theory, and this theory directly contradicts Ceaser's claim that foundational concepts are necessary for political stability.

Ceaser adopts a misleading characterization of philosophy as being divided between foundationalists and anti-foundationalists. Moreover, it is sheer hyperbole to suggest, as he does, that anti-foundationalism in any of its forms dominates philosophy, much less political theory, or that it is a real force in the thinking of political actors. It is strange to hear Ceaser suggest that "no major Democratic political leader would ever openly embrace" these ideas (the implication being that they embrace them covertly), or that "anti-foundationalism or something like it already exercises a sway in American politics and has a solid grip on large parts of the Left." Most progressive liberal and democratic theorists regularly avow foundationalism: consider how often Kantian autonomy, Millian perfectionism, and the appeal to Aristotelian natural capabilities appear in leading accounts of justice. Discussions of human rights inside and outside political theory are sometimes grounded in natural right, sometimes in the summum malum of fear, sometimes in sober reflection on historical experience. Contra Ceaser's suggestion, in political philosophy (including liberal political thought) foundationalism is rife and plural. My point is not just that Ceaser misdescribes the state of political philosophy, but that getting it wrong bears directly on his project.

The key division within political philosophy today is not between foundationalism and anti-foundationalism, but between foundationalism and anti-foundationalism on the one side and political justification on the other. Democratic theory focuses on the question: What should be the coin of the realm in justifying coercive laws and policies? This is *the* question of legitimacy in democracy under conditions of pluralism, which assumes not only diverse political values but also a multiplicity of distinct and sometimes conflicting foundational concepts of nature, history, and faith. Anti-foundationalism is one element of this pluralism. Against this background, democratic theorists argue that *neither* arguments grounded in foundationalism *nor* assumptions of anti-foundationalism should serve as the sole or principal justification for political authority, law, or policy. The main business of justification should be assigned to political concepts such as political equality, fairness, liberty, and reciprocity. These provide distinct, autonomous "public reasons" for political action. These reasons are powerful in addressing questions of justice and providing justifications to the extent that they *do not* rest solely on private or nonpublic interests, beliefs, and values—no matter that these are not naked preferences or selfish economic interests, but meaningful philosophical or religious notions of what is right and true. Rawlsian "political liberalism," with its idea of "public reason," is one incarnation of this focus on justification. Indeed, Rawls argues that the form and content of public reason "are part of the idea of democracy itself."[19] That is, democratic norms like political equality and respect demand that we reason in politics by employing generally accessible reasons. By doing so, by not relying solely or mainly on contested foundational ideas, we make political equality manifest.[20]

Of course, not all theorists of public reason urge "epistemological abstinence"; most admit that political justification does include appeals to comprehensive moral doctrines based on theology, history, or nature. They argue that disparate foundational concepts of nature or history or religion are compatible with *political agreement* about constitutional essentials and elements of basic justice, as captured by the idea of "overlapping consensus." Democratic theorists agree with Ceaser that on many political matters we need justifications that go beyond the contingent and mutually advantageous; we need public philosophy. But under conditions of pluralism and conflicting notions of foundations, public reason forms the most respectful, and most stable, basis of justification. This argument for justification in terms of public reasons independent of foundational concepts of nature, history, and religion (and independent of anti-foundational claims) is relevant because it too is tied to the value of stability. Recall that Ceaser looks to foundational ideas for stability; contemporary democratic theory argues against this position.

My point is not to endorse this way of framing the question of democratic justification, but to show that wariness about appeals to comprehensive accounts of nature or history or religious authority is not the same as anti-foundationalism. To tame foundationalism for the purposes of public philosophy, to be self-conscious about how appeals to particular foundational concepts of nature or faith are received, is not to renounce it. Simply, we are a political culture of subcultures, there are a lot of spooks running around in the dark of the foundational basement, and my "nature" may be positively ghoulish to you. In sum, what troubles this main stream of democratic theory is how to tame foundationalism, how to make it safe for democracy; what troubles Ceaser is the dilution of foundationalism, and how political actors can make democracy hospitable to nature or history (or religion?).

## From Foundations to Staging: Second-Story Concepts

I have raised questions about the meaning and use of foundational concepts, and I have canvassed what I see as the most serious weaknesses in Ceaser's attempt to link foundational concepts and American political development. In conclusion I want to question whether foundational concepts are either the most illuminating set of ideas for understanding APD or the ideas most needed for guiding political decision making today. I propose substituting "second-story," second-order concepts for foundations.

Before recommending a second-story approach to American political development, I cannot resist the observation that whether the subject is foundational concepts or others, the usual focus is on substantive content (nature, history, religion) rather than on styles of thought. This lapse is worth notice. Nothing is clearer in American history than the recurrent tension between those twins of political psychology: utopianism and paranoia. Ceaser is wrong to say that "no one dares to speak against progress." There are innumerable, politically influential conspiratorial accounts of history, perverse invocations of nature, apocalyptic religious thinking, and ferocious jeremiads. Conspiracism has proved to be a boundless resource for public discourse in America. It fuels political orientations (nativism, isolationism, anti-science); it is a persuasive force behind an identifiable array of policies. There are, in short, light and dark invocations of nature, history, and faith, and the tone and temper of these styles of thought may be more consequential for "general political orientation," persuasion, and mobilization than the concepts themselves.

That said, I want to pose a direct challenge to foundational concepts by proposing to replace foundations with "staging" in the study of American political development. Nature and history are Ceaser's chosen foundations. To use his own terms, why should we think they are the only foundational ideas? Why should we think they are foundational at all? In American political thought and practice, concepts such as liberty and equality may be foundational, for example, and nature and history may be epiphenomenal—ways of framing those deeper ideas. It is not necessary to decide which are foundational and which are "ground floor" to make my point, which is that second-story concepts provide the staging and a better vantage point on American political development than foundational ideas. Second-story concepts may invoke nature, history, or religion (or various combinations of these, or none); they may be associated with contested ideas of liberty and equality; in either case they are second story, not ground floor. But these second-story concepts provide a vantage point on the terms of argument and actors and dynamic of American political development. Some things are seen better from above. The only thing "higher" about foundational concepts is their higher level of abstraction.

I cannot attempt an exhaustive list of second-story concepts here. Any accounting would certainly include the idea of civil society, for example; a great deal of American political thought and institutional change turns on ideas about the status of associations (spontaneous and original? or artifacts of the state?) and the relation between civil society and government. I have only enough space to illustrate the challenge second-story concepts pose to foundationalism, using two candidate concepts: "majoritarianism" (key to legitimacy and decision making) and "constitutional reason of state" (key to national security and self-preservation). These second-story concepts provide an identifiable correspondence between political theory specifically (rather than philosophy broadly) and politics. They point—as nature and history do not—to concrete connections between ideas and defining political and institutional changes. These second-story ideas are the material of justification; "nature" can be invoked rhetorically, floating above institutional and policy questions; second-story concepts are indissolubly connected to both. We can see how they work politically. Finally, second-story ideas are demonstrably tied to distinctive aspects of American politics and institutions: separation of powers, judicial review, federalism, and the development of formal and informal societal-governmental connections.

Majoritarianism is a fairly straightforward example of a second-story concept. Majoritarianism has a mundane face, of course, as a decision rule employed in many settings—political and nonpolitical—when unanimity is impracticable. In American political life, however, majoritarianism is more than that. The will of the people is identified with the majority; it is the moral equivalent of popular sovereignty.[21] Presidents, especially, interpret election returns to tell the story of selection as not just garnering a literal majority of votes but as a mandate, or a declaration of popular will, so that using office to advance a program is obedience to the command of the people. As Tocqueville observed: "The parties have a great interest in determining the election in their favor, not so much to make their doctrines triumph with the aid of the president-elect as to show by his election that those doctrines have acquired a majority."[22] Parties contest for a majority wherever they can, Tocqueville went on, anticipating partisan invocations of silent and moral majorities. "When they lack it among those who have voted, they place it among those who have abstained from voting, and when it still happens to escape them there, they find it among those who did not have the right to vote."[23] The status of majoritarianism, when it is accepted and when it is rejected or constrained, how majorities relate to minorities—all are central to democratic theory in the United States and to institutional development. Majorities and minorities are "the basic units of political life around which so much reflection turns, . . . the primary realities of electoral politics and constitutional government."[24]

A key element in the design of institutions and rules is the periodic introduction of challenges and constraints on majoritarian decision making. I am thinking here less of constitutional civil liberties than of institutional qualifications on majorities, among them what Dennis Thompson has recently called the Madisonian and Hamiltonian "provisos." The Madisonian proviso limits majorities that would control membership in their own institutions in the future: self-perpetuation via party lock-ups and districting, for example, or letting representatives decide their own privileges. The Hamiltonian proviso constrains local and state majorities that would impair fair and just national representation.[25] The invention, interpretation, and institutionalization of majoritarianism and of qualifications are clearly central elements of the conceptual apparatus of American political development, and are directly implicated in political discourse and institutional design —as foundational concepts of nature and history are not.

Another example of a second-story concept is "constitutional reason of state." In the history of political thought, the idea of "reason of state" captures the deep, ineliminable tension between legal constraints on political power on the one hand and the grim political necessity for security and survival on the other. It is summed up in Bassiano's plea in *The Merchant of Venice*: "To do a great right, do a little wrong." In modern political thought, Machiavelli and Locke, most famously, provided the arguments and institutional models for addressing this tension: constitutional dictatorship and the prerogative power of the executive. We begin to see that "reason of state" is shorthand for the relation between national security and institutional development, and "constitutional reason of state" another key concept in American political development, not least because it is an undeniable example of American exceptionalism.

Rejecting more common institutional devices to deal with reason of state, American political theory and practice have insisted on *constitutional continuity* between dangerous times, including wartime, and presumably peaceful normal times. On this view, political actors can claim no special authority, and derogation from the law is impermissible; the discretionary is disallowed even as a "troubling exception."[26] The Constitution suffices for determining what is permissible during emergencies, as well as during periods of business-as-usual. "The Constitution of the U.S. is a law for rulers and people, equally in war and peace," and "no doctrine involving more pernicious consequences was ever invented by the wit of man than that any of its provisions can be suspended during any of the great exigencies of government."[27]

"Constitutional reason of state" has shaped the terms of debate about national security in the United States. It has also given rise to specific institutional arrangements. Executive action and administrative orders are one, and American presidential power is explained in part by this second-order idea. Enabling legislative action is another; Congress does not simply defer to the exercise of presidential authority during times of crisis, but materially enhances it.[28] Judicial review, too, is shaped by the norm of "constitutional continuity" and the need to translate emergency measures into doctrines of due process or equal protection. Constitutional reason of state also gives rise to the recurrent danger of corrosion of checks and balances: a combination of congressional irresolution, judicial abstention, and presidential defiance. Periods of American political thought and history are marked by pendular movements extending and retracting presidential authority, altering the separation of powers, reinterpreting (often shamefully) the meaning and scope of civil liberties.

This very brief illustration of second-story concepts challenges Ceaser's search for and claims for foundational concepts by indicating an interpretive perspective on American political development that is closer to the actual public philosophies, institutional changes, and policy conflicts at defining moments. I also draw attention to second-story concepts as a challenge to Ceaser's evaluative political purpose, which is to persuade us of the need for foundational concepts, natural rights above all. Ceaser argues that the weakness or absence of a single, foundational public philosophy rooted in natural right is the significant political failing of our time. He hopes that if foundational concepts are retrieved from the writings and speeches of past statesmen, present political actors will recognize them as resources. Interpretative and evaluative work that is tied, as Ceaser's is, to a sense of present political crisis is doubly vulnerable, because what I call "needy readers" can go wrong in two ways. They are in danger of reading into texts or speeches or policies questions the author never asked, much less answered—that is, of inventing conversations with the "reeducated dead." They are also liable to misunderstand the country's own needs. Nothing is more common than faulty analyses of America's own political predicament.

The urgent need in political life is not for foundational concepts articulated in persuasive public philosophies but rather for ways to advance common goals, such as fostering prosperity or protecting human rights. Our political distress stems not from a weak grasp on natural right but from disagreement or, as likely, general uncertainty about how to achieve agreed-on objectives.[29] Second-story concepts such as "majoritarianism" or "constitutional reason of state" suggest that appeals to nature or religion or historical narratives are not the best way to address the institutional deficits or justify the policies of our time. Ceaser is right: American political development, past and present, did not float on thin air and cannot rest on passing political moods. It needs support. But is the resource philosophy or more proximate political theory? Is the structural need foundations or staging?

# 4

WHAT IF GOD WAS ONE
OF US?

The Challenges of Studying
Foundational Political Concepts

*Rogers M. Smith*

JAMES CEASER'S THOUGHTFUL TOCQUEVILLE LECTURE challenges political scientists to engage in a new or at least insufficiently pursued type of inquiry: the study of "foundational concepts," ideas offered in public discourses as ultimate justifications for a variety of more specific political positions. He initially suggests we should do so because these concepts are a "potential variable" of some sort, and so they may account for some of the variance observable in political life. Puckishly, he asks if it is not our professional duty to seek to explain "every degree of variance." Given the finitude of human life, the clear answer to that question is, "No, we must choose priorities"; and especially in his conclusion, Ceaser gives us some reasons for making foundational concepts a priority.

He maintains that inquiries into foundational concepts are worthwhile, not so much because they can definitively answer social science questions about causality in human behavior and political development, but because they may help "supply a body of knowledge that can assist political actors to better perform their functions." Analyses of foundational concepts can do so by providing actors with a "framework" of the "field of ideas" available to them that can "guide their reflection." And Ceaser suggests

143

that, even though the study of foundational concepts may not settle issues of causality, it still may go some way toward helping political scientists understand better the political roles of foundational concepts. In particular, it may help them determine what types of concepts appear able "to meet certain political requirements," including accessibly informing the public without undue distortions, and guiding a healthy politics without undue dominance, in different times and places.

I find Ceaser's proposal highly commendable in its aims and partly commendable in its methods. My agreements far exceed my disagreements. Let me stress this at the outset, because Ceaser has already made the points I agree with more eloquently than I could. I will therefore focus here on some concerns about the way he pursues this valuable mode of inquiry and about the reasons he gives for undertaking it.

In brief, I think his choice to focus substantively on foundational concepts of nature and history, while largely setting religion aside, leads him to present the contrast between contemporary Republicans and Democrats so that it looks too much like a quarrel between two University of Virginia professors (one now Emeritus). Though he recognizes certain dangers in appeals to nature, Ceaser personally affirms the "validity of the analysis," advanced first by Leo Strauss, that anti-foundationalist "historicism" represents a debilitating "crisis for America." Ceaser believes that Strauss's position favoring foundations of natural right has now come to be "housed chiefly within the Republican Party," while anti-foundationalist views akin to those of his former Virginia colleague Richard Rorty have a "solid grip on large parts of the Left" and the Democratic Party today. It is hard not to see in this analysis an implication that to choose Democrats instead of Republicans today is to invite crisis. Bringing religious foundational concepts more fully into the analysis, however, might significantly alter Ceaser's depiction of America's past and present political contests in ways that would bring it more in line with what most political actors, leaders and voters alike, have perceived to be the issues at stake in those conflicts. It might also broaden the range of positions one can reasonably take on the main controversies in contemporary politics.

Methodologically, Ceaser does not call sufficient attention to some major problems confronting the inquiry he proposes, problems with which we all must struggle. The effort to "assist" and "guide" political actors by providing them with a catalogue of available foundational concepts that suggests those concepts' appropriate uses, likely consequences, and limits cannot in the end evade empirical claims about causality or normative judgments about consequences, as Ceaser recognizes. Analysts should therefore be as systematic as possible about the methods through which they determine the presence of foundational concepts in political discourse, and as explicit as possible about both the empirical and normative assumptions that shape their methods of investigation and evaluation.

Though I believe there is no substitute for some of Ceaser's preferred "old-fashioned" methods, especially the careful interpretation of texts, I think he should do more than he does here to define the relevant sources for study and to survey them systematically, so that we might have more confidence that the foundational ideas he focuses upon really are playing the prominent role he attributes to them. It is also striking that Ceaser chooses to focus on the two foundational concepts—"nature" and "history"—that he sees as "arrayed against each other" in today's partisan clashes, contests in which he endorses the "validity" of the views that form a "prominent face" of one party. Readers therefore must wonder whether Ceaser's decision to feature these two concepts, and his suggestions of their comparative political desirability, stem (in all good faith) from his prior academic and political views on the most important issues facing Americans today, as much as or more than from the "open-ended, empirical-analytical inquiry" that he endorses.

In fairness, no one can help approaching empirical and normative questions without some prior assumptions; it would not otherwise occur to us to undertake such inquiries. But for that very reason, in sound scholarship we need to explain our substantive judgments of what topics to study; we need to employ systematic methods to support any claims that particular patterns are dominant in the phenomena we examine; and we need to identify the normative standards we are invoking when we make evaluations. Otherwise we can fall prey to perhaps the worst offense of behavioralism: the presentation of highly politically charged categorizations and causal claims as the inarguable conclusions of value-free social science. On these points Ceaser's essay, though erudite, insightful, and illuminating, falls a bit short.

## The Value of Exploring Foundational Concepts

By way of clarifying just why I find Ceaser's enterprise commendable, let me acknowledge that my comments might be suspected of concealing a spirit of *ressentiment*. Ceaser begins by contrasting the type of inquiry he advocates with the efforts of those who study "traditions," and in a footnote he rightly identifies me as one of "those." He says a bit dismissively that this work examines "prefabricated essences" that analysts "import from the outside," instead of assigning analytic labels "virtually as they appear in political discourse" with only "the gentlest intervention of the researcher," as he promises to do. Ceaser concedes that we need something like the notion of a tradition for some purposes, but he thinks it is time to try a different approach.

Actually, he's right. Having wrestled with defining and analyzing "traditions" several times, I have also come to question whether we are sweeping too much into academic categories, some of which, particularly "liberalism," were almost never used during hundreds of the years to which we apply them.[1] I welcome his call for attention instead to the actual terms political actors use, and to any patterns or features in them that we can discern inductively. Despite my reservations about Ceaser's execu-

146

tion of his recommendations here, the refreshing approach he proposes may well help us to learn much more about how political writers and actors actually thought and argued, instead of endlessly poking at our own constructions of warring "isms."

Ceaser's suggestion that we can categorize some ideas visible in political discourse as "foundational concepts" because political actors regularly invoke them as unassailable first principles is also highly plausible. Insofar as we find patterns of political actors engaging in such conduct, we do indeed have a prima facie case for presuming that this practice is politically significant. To be sure, that claim raises important further questions: though actors may talk as if certain concepts are ultimate justifications for them, do they really think and act in ways consistent with their talk? Are foundational concepts foundational only to the thinking and acting of particular individuals, or do they also serve as unifying bonds for political coalitions or parties? Does a practice of invoking one sort of foundational concept rather than another actually have important consequences for political life? How can we tell?

But these questions indicate only that Ceaser is advocating promising directions of research, not that his suggestion is flawed. Though ultimately the utility of the category "foundational concepts," and claims for their political significance, must be sustained or invalidated by the products of such research, my guess is that these inquiries will prove fruitful. True, most people are probably not wholly clear on what their first principles are, and none of us think or act consistently with them all or even most of the time. Still, at any particular time in our lives, we generally do have core beliefs that we rely on as ultimate justifications for our courses of action. We may change these ideas over time, but at any given moment, we are likely to be both guided and limited by them in important ways as we seek to organize ourselves politically and intellectually, individually and collectively. Because these premises about human life seem right to me, I am less interested here in exploring whether Ceaser's proposed course of research is worth doing than in examining the problems of doing it as well as we can. In short, I'm on board with Ceaser; but I have some questions about how we should steer the ship.

## Ceaser's Choice of Foundational Concepts

Perhaps because we're both very insightful, more likely because we've had similar educations, Ceaser's characterizations of American intellectual and political history for the most part seem to me accurate, both in regard to broad trends and in regard to individual thinkers and actors. I also agree that the most obvious candidates for foundational concepts in American politics—probably politics in many other places as well—are nature, history, and religion. But I am puzzled why Ceaser chooses to focus here on nature and history only.

Some explanation seems called for, because in practice Ceaser cannot adhere entirely to his program. Doctrines of "Sacred History," "laws of nature and nature's God," Lincoln's evolution toward overtly religious civic conceptions, the "Social Gospel," the religious strains in the civil rights movement, and more, are too visible in American political development to ignore. Perhaps the very ubiquity of religious concepts explains Ceaser's decision to sideline them; but because his argument culminates in depicting what are presented to be fundamental contrasts between the two major parties today, it is peculiar to omit a foundational category that arguably has a longer history than any other and that has also been highly visible in recent political discourse. It is also true that, as Ceaser notes, in America religious concepts have frequently been complexly intertwined with concepts of nature and history, including modern scientific ones. This fact makes it hard to sort out what foundational concepts are primarily or distinctively "religious." The most obvious candidates are precepts whose adherents claim to find them in oral or written divine revelations, not in analyses of nature or history. And I concede that direct scriptural appeals, much less claims of personal communications with the Almighty, have probably not been so central to American political discourse as appeals to nature and history.

Still, they have not been absent in the past, even in Enlightenment tracts like Tom Paine's "Common Sense."[2] They are far from absent today, as is obvious in debates over abortion, stem cell research, same-sex marriage, and gay rights. Thus, there are costs to trying to keep religion at the margins of the discussion. When Ceaser suggests the "Jacksonian" Democratic Party embraced Idealist notions of universal history that were "wrapped up as well in a pantheistic form of Sacred History," he implies that their religiosity was merely window dressing for what were at core secular philosophic commitments, and theologically radical window dressing at that. I suspect that most Democrats saw their foundational concepts as, at bottom, forms of conventional Christianity, and heard George Bancroft's claim that the "Spirit of God breathes through . . . the people" as an encomium to common people of faith, not to German philosophy. Ceaser is probably right that Bancroft meant more the latter, but why should we set aside the understanding of their foundational concepts that most Democrats may well have embraced?

It is even more jarring to read Ceaser's effort to portray the antebellum controversies over slavery primarily in secular terms. The abolitionists, so often and not unjustly accused of religious fanaticism, are here seen as opposed simply for their "radical rationalist" policies. The religious justifications for slavery, which were more prominent than the scientific (but also religious) ones advanced by the American school of ethnology, are essentially ignored. The consequent great quarrels over religious principles and slavery that split many of America's Protestant denominations into hostile Northern and Southern wings lasting through much of the twentieth century disappear.[3]

It is also likely that many more Progressives, including Progressive political and intellectual leaders, saw themselves as carrying forward the Social Gospel than as embracing "the concept of History as the nation's primary foundational idea," as Ceaser would have it. As he notes, writing in the same period, Social Gospel evangelist Josiah Strong had far more readers than Lester Ward; so it is hard to know why Ward is the "most important figure in launching Progressivism," unless one takes its academic wing to be what really matters. That may be the case, and it is understandable that an academic should think so; but the priority of academic thinking over religious principles should be argued, not left as a matter of faith.

My greatest concern with Ceaser's choice not to consider religion as a foundational concept comes, however, in regard to his contemporary characterizations. He is after all using his inquiry to produce a guide to, and a guide for, political actors today. He is careful to note that in such an endeavor, there can be an "often unconscious" temptation to "bolster a favored current position," and he recognizes too that the connections between academic ideas, the phrases speechwriters favor, and what political leaders actually think and do are harder to discern than ever.

Even so, Ceaser does not hesitate to advance some strong claims. As I've noted, he contends that Leo Strauss and, following him, Walter Lippmann correctly contended in the 1950s that American "Progressive Liberalism" would crumble under the rise of relativistic, historicist philosophical perspectives, a development that would represent a "crisis for America." He believes the contemporary Democratic Party exhibits and contributes to that crisis, finding itself torn between New Left multiculturalists, tactically historicist communitarians, and the "idealistic anti-foundationalism" of Richard Rorty and other contemporary intellectuals. As a result, Democrats are in disarray, uncomfortable openly disavowing all foundations, uncomfortable affirming any.

In contrast, Ceaser presents today's Republican Party as fundamentally the party of nature and natural right, understood in something like the way Leo Strauss understood them. Ceaser recognizes that there are other variants of conservatism in the Republican ranks, particularly "traditionalism" and "libertarianism." But he believes that at least since the terrorist attacks of

September 11, 2001, President Bush and other Republican leaders have appealed to the foundational concept of natural right "with more frequency and emphasis," so that whatever the extent of the "internal theoretical battle" in the Republican ranks, the GOP's "prominent face" is as the party advancing the "foundational concept of nature," in opposition to the "idealistic antifoundationalism" of the "leading strains of thought" in the Democratic Party. Since in Ceaser's view Leo Strauss presented the "fundamental theoretical alternative" that human beings face as "between history and nature," Republicans are indeed the party of Strauss—and Ceaser—against Rorty and modern Democrats.

Let me acknowledge that I see a basis for everything Ceaser says; but in the end I do not find Ceaser's characterizations of modern Republicans, Democrats, or even Leo Strauss satisfactory. As I suggest below, many of our disagreements can and should be settled by more systematic analysis of recent political discourse than I have been able to undertake in the time available to prepare this response. But if we consider how foundational concepts of history, nature, and religion appear in a specified set of sources— the nomination acceptance speeches, inaugural addresses, and State of the Union addresses of the most successful representatives of both parties, their elected presidents over the past three decades—the patterns do not support Ceaser's claims.[4] There are differences in the parties, to be sure; but the leaders of both parties regularly affirm belief in the inalienable rights of the Declaration of Independence, as well as America's special role in promoting freedom and democracy in the world. And both Democratic and Republican presidents regularly refer to the nation's religious traditions and to history. The chief difference is that Democrats refer to religion somewhat less frequently, but more often via specific scriptural references. Republicans refer more often to a providentialist account of America's place in world history, without textual support. In these speeches, neither set of leaders explicitly refers to "nature" as a guide; and contrary to Ceaser's account, religious providentialism, not natural right, is both increasingly prominent in President George W. Bush's speeches over time, and more closely associated with justifications for specific policies, something that is absent in the Democratic addresses.

Begin with the Democrats. It is hard to detect any hint of "anti-foundationalism" in the major speeches of Jimmy Carter, Bill Clinton, or for that matter recent nominee John Kerry. In accepting his nomination in 1976, Carter praised America as the first nation clearly dedicated to "basic moral and philosophical principles" of human equality and to the "inalienable rights" of the Declaration of Independence, and in his Inaugural Address he affirmed America's dedication to those "absolute" rights while quoting the prophet Micah on the importance of doing justice, loving mercy, and walking "humbly with thy God."[5] In his 1978 State of the Union address, Carter insisted that "the very heart of our national identity is our firm commitment to human rights" and cited the Bible to assure Americans that they could "move mountains."[6] And in his 1979 State of the Union speech he also affirmed America's "special place of leadership in the worldwide struggles for human rights," without specifying the source of that "special place."[7]

Bill Clinton's 1992 nomination acceptance speech twice quoted "Scripture" on the importance of having an inspiring vision; and using religious terminology, Clinton promised a "New Covenant" with the American people to realize the "vision and values of the American people."[8] In his First Inaugural Address, he offered guidance from a reading of American history, as he and all other presidents have repeatedly done, saying: "From our revolution, the Civil War, to the Great Depression to the civil rights movement, our people have always mustered the determination to construct from these crises the pillars of our history." But Clinton also quoted Scripture while urging Americans to pursue their "timeless mission" of achieving "America's ideals"—realization of rights of life, liberty, and the pursuit of happiness, in America and "around the world."[9] His 1995 State of the Union address, especially, returned to this theme, holding that America's founders based their new country on a "single powerful idea," that "all men are created equal, endowed by their Creator with certain inalienable rights," that "every generation" of Americans since have sought to preserve that idea—the American Dream—and to "deepen and expand its meaning to new and different times."[10] His later speeches reassert these views, citing the prophet Isaiah in his 1997 State of the Union in support of renewed efforts to extend the American idea, "the most powerful idea in the history of nations."[11] Similarly, in his speech accepting the 2004 Democratic nomination, John Kerry invoked the "sons and daughters of liberty" who had given birth to "America's freedom" in Philadelphia as models for seeking a "new birth of freedom" today. He also professed his personal faith, but he disavowed any claim that "God is on our side," agreeing with Lincoln that we should pray to be on God's side.[12]

Bending over backward, one can perhaps detect a whiff of anti-foundationalist historicism in the emphasis of modern Democratic leaders on the responsibility of Americans to "construct" freedom in ways that would "deepen and expand" its meaning for "new and different times." In light of their other rhetoric, however, it seems more likely that the Democrats are simply trying to stress their rejection of past American violations of freedom and their determination to be the "Party of Progress" today. Although they do not speak of natural rights, their affirmations of American commitments to "absolute" human rights, to the "inalienable rights" as depicted in the Declaration of Independence, are innumerable.

It is true that, despite Clinton's call for "vision," their speeches are longer on particular reform recommendations than on any clear sense of the ultimate foundations of human rights and freedoms, whether in God, nature, or human choice. But so far as I can see, explicit "idealistic anti-foundationalism" still seems largely an academic phenomenon. And even Richard Rorty, when he writes in hopes of persuading his fellow citizens, distances himself from the "cultural left" and speaks of his democratic values as ones that Americans should embrace as their "civil religion," as constituting the "soul" of the nation.[13] It is probably true nonetheless that, with academics included, there are more anti-foundationalists in Democratic ranks than Republican ones. But based on this sample of the evidence of public discourse that Ceaser urges us to examine, it is far more likely that the Democrats, viewed as a whole, affirm their core commitments to human rights on the basis of the sort of "overlapping consensus" among different philosophical and religious positions that John Rawls has defended, than that Rorty-like sentiments of anti-foundationalism tacitly predominate.

Turn now to the Republicans. Modern GOP leaders from Ronald Reagan through George W. Bush have explicitly invoked a variety of foundational concepts, including history and, perhaps surprisingly, "stories." But they have repeatedly made clear that their conceptions of history and stories rest on religious providentialist concepts of America, which they have stressed far more than any other foundational theme. Insofar as they speak of nature, which they rarely do in major official speeches, it, too, is understood in light of this same religious foundational view.

No theme was dearer to Ronald Reagan than the notion that America was destined by "Divine Providence" to be the shining "city on a hill" that John Winthrop spoke of to the Pilgrims. Reagan invoked that image when he announced his candidacy for the presidency in 1979, in his 1984 nomination acceptance speech, and in his final State of the Union address, as well as on many other occasions.[14] In his inaugural addresses, he repeatedly made clear that he understood this to mean that America should be an "exemplar of freedom and a beacon of hope" to all the world, and that God "intended" and "called" the American people to play this role, so that God was the true "author" of America's "dream of freedom."[15] One of Reagan's most eloquent expressions of this view came at the 1986 Statue of Liberty commemoration, where the president celebrated the nation's history of welcoming immigrants by saying, "I have always believed there was some divine providence that placed this great land here between the two great oceans, to be found by a special kind of people from every corner of the world, who had a special love for freedom."[16]

This explicit providentialism does not appear in the comparable speeches of modern Democratic presidents, and in his 1984 State of the Union address, Reagan noted, in a defense of school prayer, that "we must be cautious in claiming that God's on our side, but I think it's all right to keep asking if we're on His side."[17] Reagan also often emphasized what he saw as the lessons of history and history's "calls" to Americans.[18] But this was clearly divinely guided history, and over time Reagan stressed more and more strongly that God had given the love of freedom and the right to freedom to all humanity and had "entrusted in a special way to this nation" a responsibility for the "defense" of freedom at home and around the world.[19] Reagan also increasingly emphasized over time that "the unborn child is a living human being entitled to life, liberty and the pursuit of happiness" granted by "our Creator."[20] In these latter two regards, particularly the last, he moved closer to suggesting that particular policies that he advocated were most consistent with divine intentions, though his religious rhetoric remained overwhelmingly an inspirational view of American identity in general, not a justification for specific positions.

President George H. W. Bush stated in his Inaugural Address, "my first act as president is a prayer" to use his new power to "help people, serve the Lord," and he then went on to say that a new chapter in history's "book of many pages" was beginning, one in which, as the "story unfolds," it seemed that "Freedom" was being "reborn."[21] He went on in subsequent State of the Union addresses to say, like Carter, that "freedom is at the very heart of the idea that is America" and to argue like both of his predecessors that America had a "unique responsibility" to promote freedom in the world, though he did not explicitly present this as a divine duty in the manner of Reagan.[22] But beyond his habit of ending speeches with "God Bless America," as Reagan and Clinton did often and Carter did rarely, the elder Bush did not speak extensively of religion in his major official speeches, nor did he stress providentialist themes.

His son, in contrast, has not only harked back to the religious foundationalism of Ronald Reagan; he has elaborated and extended those views. When George W. Bush accepted the Republican presidential nomination in 2000, he promised, like his father, to write "chapters in the American story."[23] This theme framed his ensuing Inaugural Address, when the new president told his fellow citizens that "we have a place, all of us, in a long story—a story we continue, but whose end we will not see. . . . It is the American story." Bush also stressed the "calling" of Americans to live up to the "ideals" visible in history, while indicating that ultimately this call did not come from history alone. The president concluded, "We are not this story's author, who fills time and eternity with His Purpose. Yet his purpose is achieved in our duty. . . . An angel still rides in the whirlwind and directs this storm."[24]

After the vicious September 11 attacks, Bush both heightened his reliance on this religious rhetoric and gave it increasing specificity. In his September 20, 2001 speech to the nation, the president identified Al-Qaeda and Osama bin Laden as the perpetrators of the attacks and Afghanistan's Taliban regime as their protectors, and he declared them the first targets in a new "war on terrorism." He argued that America was "called to defend freedom" in this way, and he concluded: "The course of this conflict is not known, yet its outcome is certain. Freedom and fear, justice and cruelty, have always been at war, and we know that God is not neutral between them."[25] In his 2002 State of the Union address, Bush stated that "History has called America" to "fight" and "lead" the campaign for liberty and justice, while he assured his fellow citizens that "God is near" amid these difficult events.[26] On September 11, 2002, he reaffirmed that Americans had heard "history's call," and he said: "We do know that God has placed us together in this moment . . . to serve each other and our country.

And the duty we have been given—defending America and our freedom—is also a privilege we share. . . . This ideal of America is the hope of all mankind. . . . That hope still lights our way." Using biblical language, the president concluded: "And the light shines in the darkness. And the darkness will not overcome it."[27]

In his 2003 State of the Union address, Bush asserted that "this call of history has come to the right country," and he added that though "we do not claim to know all the ways of Providence," yet we knew enough to "trust in them, placing our confidence in the loving God behind all of life and all of history."[28] In his most recent State of the Union speech, Bush argued, like Reagan, that "God has planted in every human heart the desire to live in freedom," and he assured Americans that they would fulfill their "mission" to "lead the cause of freedom" because of "that greater power who guides the unfolding of the years."[29] More recently, in his speech accepting his second presidential nomination, Bush returned to his theme of the "story of America," a "story of expanding liberty" in which "America is called to lead the cause of freedom" because freedom "is the Almighty God's gift to every man and woman in the world." He concluded that Americans "have a calling from beyond the stars to stand for freedom."[30]

This survey leaves little doubt, I think, that religious foundational concepts have long been central in George W. Bush's political discourse and show no signs of declining in favor of any other foundational concept. This is not surprising in a president who was "born again" after midlife struggles with alcohol, and whose staffers report that he reads the Bible each morning.[31] Perhaps this rhetorical pattern is not so important, if, as Ceaser contends, the president has also been appealing to "natural right" with "more frequency and emphasis as time has gone by." Yet Ceaser's only evidence for this claim is Bush's important 2003 speech to the National Endowment for Democracy, where Bush did indeed say that Americans "believe that liberty is the design of nature." But the president followed that phrase with one Ceaser omits: "We believe that liberty is the direction of history." Nature was not invoked against history, but in tandem with it. Earlier in the speech, moreover, Bush contended: "Liberty is both the plan of Heaven for humanity, and the best hope for progress here on Earth." He later concluded that "we can be certain that the author of freedom is not indifferent to the fate of freedom."[32] It is hard to see how this speech provides evidence that religious foundations are being submerged in favor of natural right. It is read more naturally as evidence that Bush continues to interpret both nature and history in providentialist terms.

Again, modern Democrats also invoke religious traditions regularly in their speeches—but with two differences. One is that, perhaps oddly, the Democrats tend to invoke Scripture directly more often than the Republicans. In the official speeches surveyed here, Reagan referred to a specific biblical passage only once, a passage that Clinton also later invoked; George W. Bush cited the Twenty-Third Psalm on the night of September 11, 2001, and he has sometimes echoed biblical language in his acceptance, inaugural, and State of the Union speeches, but he has not invoked specific scriptural passages.[33] This pattern may be related to a second, more significant difference: Reagan and the second Bush stress providentialist accounts of American history and destiny. And George W. Bush has often culminated his discussions of his policies aimed at combating terrorism with assurances that the "mission" he defines is a divine duty and that Americans can be confident they will prevail in these struggles because God sides with justice and freedom.

I do not wish to overstate: true, Bush has refrained from asserting that his specific measures are divinely authorized, and he has more than once stressed that we cannot know all of God's purposes and that our "calling is to align our hearts and action with God's plan, in so far as we can know it."[34] But I do not think it is possible to read through the quotations provided above without concluding that President Bush has frequently spoken in ways that strongly suggest his "war on terrorism" policies, including the war with Iraq, are in accord with God's will. These claims are controversial among those who take guidance from Scripture, a significant number of whom are pacifistic; so it is possible that the president prefers not to engage in scriptural justifications of his interpretations of divine Providence that might invite theological quarrels. Even so, his explicit foundational concepts remain religious, not appeals to natural right. I do not doubt that the various students of Strauss's writings in high Republican circles embrace and advocate nature as a foundational concept, but they appear to have embraced a Jerusalem/Athens alliance in which Jerusalem takes pride of place, out of political necessity as well as, sometimes, personal conviction. My perceptions here may be wrong; but they cannot be refuted on the basis of an analysis that sets religion aside without justification, and that does not engage in any explicit systematic analysis of the evidence concerning the appearances of foundational concepts in some specified realm of public discourse.

Ceaser might respond that I am placing too much weight on the public rhetoric of leading Republican and Democratic figures. Perhaps in less obvious ways, their real foundational concepts are the "anti-foundationalist" and "natural right" ideas that he depicts. But if so, we definitely need to know more about how Ceaser thinks foundational concepts should be discerned, because it seemed we were promised a reading of public "political discourse," not some kind of "insider" knowledge. Because his methods of analyzing such discourse remain unspecified (other than "old-fashioned"), and because his portraits of the two parties today in particular relies more on accounts of Strauss and Rorty than on examinations of the views of people directly involved in their political or intellectual leadership, it is hard not to suspect that Ceaser's choice to focus on concepts of "nature" and "history" but not religion arose because he is personally most engaged by the academic debate between the current versions of those more secular foundational concepts. That is a perfectly defensible interest on his part, but it may mar his analysis. Today's Democratic party seems to me to want to be much more the party of, at most, the multi-foundationalist John Rawls (if not the religious liberal Jimmy Carter) rather than the anti-foundationalist Richard Rorty; while the Republicans have rendered themselves unto the providence of God, not the nature of academia's Ceaser.

Let me add one other worry about Ceaser's choice of foundational concepts. He is surely right to argue that Leo Strauss believed that modern thought has undertaken a highly questionable turn from nature to history. Yet even if we take Strauss's diagnosis of the modern condition as a guide, it does not seem wise to ignore the presence of religious foundational notions in American political life. For Strauss not only diagnosed the modern condition—he analyzed the enduring dilemmas of the human condition, and in that regard he highlighted a different clash of fundamental alternatives. He regularly contended, "Whether the Bible or philosophy is right is, of course, the only question which ultimately matters." Nor did Strauss think that the differences between religion and natural right paled in comparison with their joint contrast to modern historicism. Although he believed the Bible and Greek philosophy had a certain "common ground," the "problem of divine law," he insisted that they "solve that problem in a diametrically opposed manner." Greek philosophy was "based on this premise: that there is such a thing as nature, or natures—a notion which has no equivalent in biblical thought." As a result, for Strauss philosophy and the Bible "are the alternatives, or the antagonists, in the drama of the human soul." It seems odd to take Strauss as a guide to modern American politics while omitting discussion of the role of one of these antagonists—all the more so because Strauss also averred that no one could ever credibly claim that "faith in America and the hope for America are based on explicit divine promises."[35] Yet the party that Ceaser identifies with Strauss now comes very close to doing so—far closer, it seems to me, than Democrats do to avowing the anti-foundationalist beliefs Ceaser detects.

## The Challenges of Discerning Foundational Concepts

But if Ceaser has indeed faltered somewhat in his quest to discern and analyze foundational concepts, I think this fact reveals real difficulties involved in his valuable endeavor that we all must face. The first difficulty comes in the effort to place terms visible in public discourse into appropriate categories. Perhaps if we immerse ourselves in such discourse, types of concepts and patterns of usage will emerge fairly plainly; but it is also possible, if not probable, that we will find many concepts used in many ways that lend themselves to many plausible categorizations. The gentle intervention of the analyst then *must* become more forceful: the analyst has to make choices about which concepts and which categorizations seem most pertinent to concerns that the analyst wishes to pursue.

I believe Ceaser has made such choices in constructing his lecture. For him, the clash between foundational concepts of nature and history is the deepest conflict of our times, perhaps of all time, and so he cannot resist looking for these concepts even if another is in fact more prominent. But I think we all must often make such choices in deciding what to study, and we must be alert to the possibility that we are doing so even when we believe that we are not. In these regards, our work may benefit from the discipline imposed by social science methods that require us to identify what we take to be the relevant universe of public political discourses and to justify our methods of surveying those discourses. The analysis of acceptance, inaugural, and State of the Union addresses I have done, for example, might well be extended throughout U.S. history to enable us to judge what sorts of foundational concepts have prevailed in different eras—though doing so might well require partial reliance on some type of "content-analysis" software.[36] I believe that scholars of the history of ideas should employ such procedures more than we customarily have done. I do not know if Ceaser would agree; again, if he has adopted any particular system in assessing the evidence in support of his claims here, he has not described it. Yet only such systematic, reproducible methods can provide readers with some assurance that the patterns an analyst claims to discern are empirical realities.

Still, I do not wish to overstate this problem. Often concepts and patterns that we did not expect to find do fairly leap out at us as we gain knowledge of our objects of study. I believe I've had that experience. Years ago, I began studying judicial decisions on citizenship, looking for "republicanism" and "liberalism," but during the 1990s I ended up writing mostly about racial and gender categories of second-class citizenship. I thought I did so not because these topics were then politically correct, but simply because, as I tried to survey all the federal judicial decisions governing a number of citizenship topics, I found that many of the largest early legal struggles over citizenship centered on those issues. I still believe that I simply arrived inductively at a categorization based on patterns evident in the primary phenomena, as Ceaser promises his approach can do.

Yet I have to admit that at other times, other scholars looking at those same cases have stressed different themes. Perhaps I read them more influenced by the concerns of my day than I knew. Even if so, I still believe strongly that we should try to do what Ceaser urges us to attempt. We should strive to identify the concepts that political actors actually use and try to build categories out of features immanent in those usages. And we will do those inquiries better, though never perfectly, if we recognize that we often are compelled to draw on categories and concerns that we bring to the enterprise in order to make sense of what we see. We ought then to do as much as we can to make readers aware of what our preliminary categories and concerns have been, so that they can judge how these preconceptions may have shaped the ensuing analyses. The point is not to provide autobiographies; it is, as math teachers rightly request, to show our work.

The problem of how far the categorizations of ideas we develop are shaped by our prior political concepts, concerns, and commitments leads to a further challenge facing the sort of inquiry Ceaser advocates. He hopes political scientists will produce "frameworks" mapping political concepts in ways that can tell political actors what conceptual options are available to them for effective political discourse. Those frameworks may also help both political actors and scholars to judge what political leaders and citizens are likely to get if they embrace some concepts rather than others. These are things well worth trying to do, but analysts cannot do them without relying both on their own notions of causality and their own normative judgments about what sorts of consequences are morally and politically desirable.

Political actors are likely to want to learn three types of things from a framework of available foundational concepts. They will first want to know what concepts will be persuasive to a sufficient number of constituents to create a successful political movement. Second, they will want to know the policy consequences over time of embracing certain concepts—who may benefit, who may be hurt, and in what ways? Third, being human, some will sometimes feel uncertain of their own commitments and conduct; so they will want to know what foundational concepts are not just politically potent, but morally and intellectually right. In sum, a typical political actor will ask of political scientists like Ceaser: If today I embrace natural right and not idealistic anti-foundationalism or scriptural revelation as my foundational concept in my public discourses, will I win? Will I govern in ways that benefit my constituents? Will I be doing what in the ultimate analysis can be seen as good?

Just as I suspect it is often impossible to sort out the blooming buzzing confusion of political discourse without some prior notions of what concepts and categories are important, I also think it is often impossible to answer these questions without fairly specific prior assumptions about causality and about the moral and intellectual soundness of different foundational concepts. If a scholar honestly believes that scriptural texts, properly interpreted, show that Americans are a providentially chosen people, it will be very hard for that analyst not to include such revelations as particularly potent foundational concepts. They are bound to be both available and efficacious; that's God's will. If a scholar instead believes that those scriptural claims are chauvinistic, superstitious nonsense, but that Americans as a people in history happen to be at a rare moment of historical opportunity or danger, the scholar is likely to suggest instead that historical conceptions can be advanced most persuasively.

If, on yet another hand, a scholar thinks that all foundational concepts are interchangeable window dressing for political endeavors driven by bedrock economic interests or passions for power, then it will be hard for that scholar to suggest that a framework of available foundational concepts provides political actors with any real guidance toward effective coalition building. Of course, such a scholar would probably not try to map the foundational concepts visible in public discourse in the first place. She or he would probably document the prevailing economic and political power structures instead. This fact only underlines, however, that the enterprise of studying foundational concepts already presupposes a confidence that they do have some sort of real, causal political role. This presupposition may be hard to test, as Ceaser suggests. Still, the scholar's particular causal assumptions should be acknowledged, elaborated, and justified as far as possible if the inquiry Ceaser urges is to be pursued in the most intellectually rigorous ways, and in the ways most likely to assist political actors. They will benefit from knowing just how and why an analyst thinks foundational concepts in general, and certain ones in particular, are likely to win constituents, shape policymaking, and generate governance with particular types of consequences.

Finally, not only in trying to answer whether certain foundational concepts are intrinsically right and good, but even in trying to discern the consequences that may follow from public embrace of a particular concept, analysts are again unlikely to be able to avoid relying on their own judgments about what concepts are normatively desirable as well as intellectually sensible. An analyst who believes that certain policies flow from the word of God is simply not likely to be able to see them as having, on balance, negative results. An analyst who finds concepts of natural right persuasive and who believes that they justify overthrow of regimes that violate human rights will probably see the complex consequences of wars like the one the United States has conducted against Iraq as, on balance, positive, even while acknowledging some accompanying failures, disappointments, and undesirable repercussions. A scholar who thinks that notions of America's providential mission are unjustified assertions and that notions of human rights need, at best, to be highly sensitive to varieties of social contexts may instead see such wars as indefensible forms of imperialism that will do the United States and humanity more harm than good in the end.

Ceaser's own closing admonitions to make sure that foundational concepts "meet certain political requirements," which include remaining within their "proper boundaries, allowing most political matters to be determined by political means," make these points clearly. His prescriptions presume that concepts do have causal consequences, that those not structured to remain within their limited compass will be harmful, and that we can decide normatively what their "proper" compass is and what constitute the harms that show they should be so confined. Clearly, in all these presumptions, notions of causality and of basic normative principles are quietly at work.

In so characterizing Ceaser's arguments, I mean not to refute them but to show that they do inescapably involve more than just openness to what we find empirically in the phenomena of political discourse before us. I still concur that we should try as hard and as honestly as we can to identify accurately the foundational concepts available to political actors, the consequences that have accompanied different uses of different foundational concepts, and whatever causal links we can discern between the concepts and the consequences. Though we cannot entirely avoid relying on our own preconceptions and convictions in these inquiries, we still can genuinely learn from what we see, and we will then have more to teach others. But I do think we ought to do one thing that Ceaser does not do. We are likely to produce more intellectually powerful and politically useful analyses if we are as clear as we can be with ourselves and our readers about the beliefs we have in regard to the causality and the intellectual and moral defensibility we ascribe to various foundational concepts.

To be consistent with my own argument and to clarify what it means, let me note the causal and normative premises that have shaped the critique of Ceaser's claims I have offered here. In recent years I have been arguing that political leaders need persuasive accounts of political identities and purposes to form coalitions broad and strong enough to support their visions of policy and community. This claim involves ascribing causal political force to what Ceaser terms "foundational concepts," which is probably why I have readily granted his similar attribution. I have also suggested that appeals to God and nature seem, both in logic and in practice, to be the most potent foundations for such accounts.[37] Such appeals appear to have been necessary in American experience to win support for the dangerous, uncertain endeavor of the American Revolution, for the enormously disruptive ending of slavery and later Jim Crow, and probably for sustaining faith in the American cause during the Cold War, among other tasks. As those examples suggest, I see these sorts of appeals as capable of doing enormous good.

I am nonetheless on record as being wary of all political discourses claiming authority from God and nature, since those have been used more routinely in America's past to justify racial, ethnic, gender, and religious hierarchies and exclusions that seem to me indefensible. Like many modern Democrats, I have urged instead that Americans see themselves as a people with a distinctive history and a special, advantaged position in today's world, rather than as a divinely chosen people, or as a people whose destiny is written in its racial or psychological traits.[38]

At the same time, I have always believed—I would say recognized—that history is far too complex and diverse to tell its own story or provide its own moral. We must ultimately appeal beyond history, to some larger account of a natural or divine order that we find morally meaningful, if we are to label some developments and tendencies in history as beneficial and desirable, others as destructive and deplorable.[39] In my most recent book, I have sided with what Ceaser terms "the increasing numbers of people on the Left" who are turning, however cautiously, to evolutionary biology for accounts of humanity's place in the natural order from which we may draw some normative lessons.[40] But I am vividly aware that this direction poses great political dangers and that it may well prove philosophically inadequate to upholding moral precepts. Even though I think we cannot credibly dispute that humanity is a product of evolving biology, and even though today we face momentous choices about how our actions will shape our future evolution, the atrocities committed in the name of evolutionary destiny in the past two centuries have been far too vast, and the complexities of moving from evolutionary history to contemporary human capabilities are far too great, for me to wish to see this foundational concept take center stage at present. That is why in politics I favor foundational concepts that are essentially interpretations of American historical experience—interpretations tempered by, but not grounded on, insights from major religious perspectives and scientific accounts of natural limitations.

I mention these points only so readers can consider how far they explain why I accept Ceaser's map of America's three basic foundational concepts, why I am more inclined than he is to deny that contemporary Democrats embrace radical anti-foundationalism, why I see the Republicans as stressing God as much as or more than natural right, and why I also see the consequences of the Democrats' more varied and historically oriented concepts as likely to be less dangerous than the providentialist and natural-right doctrines of the Republicans. I suspect that, though Ceaser probably agrees with my judgments about causality and about the need for ultimate appeals to some sorts of conceptions of natural or divine orders, he is much less wary than I am about the dangers of invoking nature as a direct political guide, and much more concerned than I am about the ways in which appeals to history may end up eroding confidence in any moral standards or limits whatsoever.

He may be right in his assumptions and judgments. He may also be right to focus on his two foundational concepts in public discourse, at the expense of religion. I have suggested that to some degree we can use systematically acquired and analyzed empirical data to settle the mapping disputes; and through reflection, study, and discussion we might over time even come to modify our causal and normative judgments, perhaps achieving greater convergence in the process. But I believe Ceaser should do more to acknowledge the presumptions that have shaped his analysis, rather than presenting his argument as almost purely the result of an inductive, open-ended empirical/analytical inquiry, as he does here. I think we are unlikely to make as much progress in any of these endeavors as we have the potential to do, if we do not include in our study of foundational political concepts an honest recognition and evaluation of the foundational concepts on which our own analyses rely. Only then can we fulfill our responsibility to inform readers in ways that can assist them in thinking critically, rather than, at most, inducing them to think as we do.

# 5

---

# FOUNDATIONAL CONCEPTS RECONSIDERED

*James W. Ceaser*

FOR THE INAUGURAL TOCQUEVILLE LECTURE, I presented a "political science of ideas" designed to shed light on the role played by different kinds of ideas in American political development and to assist thinkers and political leaders engaged in fashioning ideas for political life. Political scientists have written many works on American political thought, but there has been little effort to delineate the analytic categories that would enable all scholars, no matter what their viewpoint, to engage in common discussion. Science, even in the looser sense in which that term applies to the study of politics, must begin with shared concepts, so that each researcher does not, like Sisyphus, need to begin the task anew.

Since the Tocqueville Lecture consisted of a single talk, not a series, I was able to offer what amounted only to a syllabus of the topic. I selected one type of idea, "foundational concepts," for analysis, and even on this topic much had to be omitted or handled by assertion. (The text of the lecture published here is a much-expanded version of the original, but in fairness to the commentators, who prepared their initial responses at the time of the delivery of the lecture, no new conceptual arguments were added.) I am therefore grateful for the opportunity to have a final word.

I also wanted to express my appreciation to the three distinguished scholars who participated in this colloquy. Their essays go well beyond ordinary commentaries by presenting their own original perspectives. For my part, I will be more than satisfied with the result of this lecture and exchange if I can succeed in convincing some readers of the importance of the overall project. The fact that the three commentators made use of the categories in their own contributions, even while taking issue with many of the arguments, was, for me at least, a very gratifying sign.

In this essay, I will address some of the individual criticisms raised by the participants and then conclude with comments on two questions: What is the place of the foundational idea of religion? And what normative assessment can be made of the various foundational concepts that were discussed?

## Response to Jack Rakove

As I listened to the beginning of Jack Rakove's elegant commentary, I was almost afraid that he was going to claim, in a deprecating, aw-shucks manner, that he was just a simple academic historian, ill-suited to dealing with the analytic approach characteristic of the field of American political development. Happily, he stopped well short of any such display of false modesty and acknowledged that, if he is not a political scientist by training, he nevertheless is one where it counts: he is a member of a political science department, at Stanford University. He is also well known in political science for his works on the thought of some of the founders, including some notable discussions of—dare I say it?—their foundational thinking. Jack Rakove took the occasion to inch closer to our discipline when he noted that, in light of the disinterest for political history that currently reigns among academic historians, he could envisage the day when he might need to seek refuge in the warmer bosom of political science.

Jack Rakove's approach remains true to the best of classical historical studies in its reflection of a nominalist spirit that is skeptical of attempts to apply general categories (in this study, the concepts of "nature" and "History") across a series of specific cases (the ideas of the Founding era, of the Civil War era, and so on). The imprecision that results from trying to force particulars into broader categories costs more in our understanding than it yields. Given this reservation, Jack Rakove can take solace in the fact that he was not invited to discuss the more cutting-edge research going on in our field, where the passion for generalization extends much further. He might, for example, have been asked to comment on the celebrated theory of path dependency, which boldly argues that all things develop along established lines, except where they do not; or the hypothesis of electoral or regime cycles, where everything is said to repeat itself, except when something new or unique comes along.

While sympathetic to Jack Rakove's concern, I believe that social science has its uses, especially for those who do not study history full time and must content themselves with "dabbling" in secondary works. (Such people, alas, constitute a substantial portion of the population.) Since the occasion for our gathering was the Tocqueville Lecture, it is fitting to cite a theoretical reflection from *Democracy in America* that bears on this point: "General ideas do not attest to the strength of human intelligence, but rather to its insufficiency, because there are no beings in nature exactly alike: no identical facts, no rules indiscriminately applicable in the same manner to several objects at once. General ideas are admirable in that they permit the human mind to bring rapid judgments to a great number of objects at one time; but on the other hand, they never provide it with anything but incomplete notions, and they always make it lose in exactness what they give it in extent."[1]

Tocqueville's cost-benefit analysis applies to much of the work in the field of American political development. General categories are needed to help highlight important points in different contexts, so that we can locate a few of the forests before getting lost in the trees. This process allows the human mind in all its limitations to begin to build reservoirs of understanding. Still, as anyone engaged in social science research will acknowledge, the "fit" of a general idea to a particular case is never perfect; the broader the variable constructed, the less likely it is to capture perfectly the specific cases. Too many practitioners ignore this limitation and try to derive precise conclusions from synthetic variables.

How then can we use general categories in the study of political ideas, where the specific instances differ so greatly? Well-formulated general categories serve the purpose of allowing entrance into the treatment of a subject at an interesting and meaningful point, after which they invariably break down somewhat and require qualification and clarification. Every important classification scheme I know of, from Aristotle's and Montesquieu's designations of regime types to Tocqueville's distinction of historical ages (aristocracy and democracy), possesses both this attribute and this liability. In this respect, I felt no special concern that, beginning with a simple scheme of three foundational concepts (nature, History, and religion), it became necessary at times to combine categories.

The main reason for adopting general categories, however, is not to facilitate historical investigation, but to build political science. Political science, as I understand it, is a practical discipline whose aim is to develop knowledge that can help political actors—"those who direct society," to use Tocqueville's phrase—in their ongoing and future activities. Without general categories, this kind of political science is impossible. In more formal terms, one can distinguish between two forms of political science: political science 1, which aims at knowledge that tries to explain historical variance (how, and in what measure, A causes B), and political science 2, which is concerned with knowledge that provides guidance for those who act. Political science 2 begins by elaborating general categories or factors in a way that has depth and intelligibility to political actors; it then proceeds, to the extent possible, to develop probabilistic "equations" expressing contemporaneous analytic causality (if A is chosen, B would be more likely to follow).

A direct connection exists between these two forms of political science. Historical inquiry is the best place to identify larger variables and flesh out their meaning. By investigating specific instances in which foundational ideas have appeared, one begins to get a sense of what a foundational idea is, far better than by just throwing around general terms like "metaphysical notions," or "essentialisms." Each foundational concept is permitted to speak and to present its case. The articulation of these ideas in specific contexts, in which they often respond to one another, provides a richness of argument akin to that offered by the interlocutors in a philosophical dialogue. Historical investigation also provides a laboratory in which to study the relationships among key elements.

Historians, who by definition are interested chiefly in historical causality, often ignore the fact that political scientists have a different objective, and they become too dismissive of the political scientists' more general approach. But if we had followed the historians' method for studying ideas in American history, I doubt very much that the discussion would ever have opened up to a treatment of the contemporary role of foundational ideas—the sort of treatment, for example, found in the commentaries of Nancy Rosenblum and Rogers Smith. We would instead have confined ourselves to further inquiries on the probative value for American Revolutionary thought of the radical Whig critique of the post-Walpole British constitution, or to the effect of Herbert Spencer on the ideas of the late nineteenth-century Republican Party. These are no doubt important issues, but they are historians' questions, not questions that are central to political science. Besides, it is past time for political scientists to acknowledge that historians—if they would only stick to their task—do a much better job of writing history; historians, after all, possess no constitutional aversion to visiting a library or spending time in an archive.

For the reason of comparative disadvantage alone, therefore, it is regrettable scholars of American political development do so little to cultivate political science 2. To my mind, it is the more important form of knowledge in our discipline. Studies into historical causality should be pursued more often with this end in mind, rather than with the sole objective of explaining additional variance. Long before political science became an academic enterprise, with its professional awards, its specialized journals, and its elaborate conferences—in other words, long before the "profession" created a little world unto itself—it was conceived as a discipline whose function was to address the prospective actor or legislator. We should not wander too far from our foundations.

Jack Rakove raises another criticism when he asks whether the foundational ideas I identified are the deepest causes of action. He suggests as an alternative the role of fundamental "values"—in particular, liberty and equality. (In speaking of equality, he was polite enough not to invoke the authority of Tocqueville, who famously treated "the love of equality" as a dominant feature of our times). This criticism provides a welcome opportunity to reiterate a point that may unfortunately have been obscured by the weight or pretentiousness of the term "foundational," which can easily suggest more than I meant. For this reason, I toyed with using other words, like "fundamental ideas" (not much different), or "background ideas" (too weak), or even the German *Grundbegriff* (impressive, admittedly, but too professorial), before settling finally on "foundational," which at least had the advantages of having been used in political life itself and of being employed in political theory today.

Whatever word is used, however, it is the meaning that counts. The term "foundational" is intended to locate the place of an idea within a structure of thought, not to claim anything a priori about its historical importance. Foundational ideas are identified according to how they fit in a chain of reasoning in public discourse, where they serve as primary causes or justifications for political orientations. There were two reasons I did not base the classification system of ideas on their causal importance. One is that thinkers and political actors, in presenting their ideas, are concerned with making sound or effective choices. It is enough that each level of idea has at least some causal importance to make it worthwhile for such people to attempt to avoid mistakes and select well. The scheme is intended not to explain causality, but to help deepen arguments and improve the quality of thinking about political ideas. The second reason is that no one now yet knows the respective degree of influence of various kinds of ideas. If the three commentaries prove anything, it is that the question of causality remains in dispute—among three leading experts no less. Assessing causal importance is a matter for investigation, not something to be decided in advance by an analytic scheme.

Nevertheless, so as not to claim too little for foundational ideas, one must emphasize that thinkers and political actors often assert that these ideas have great importance. Practical people usually do not persist in doing things in vain. The recurring use of nature and History as ideas in American politics is also an indication of their significance. As for their relative importance compared to the "values" Jack Rakove has identified—and which appear and would be analyzed under the category of the "ends of government and society"—it is admittedly difficult to separate the two, because they almost always appear in combination. The argument from natural rights, for example, has been connected to the values of equality and of liberty. Yet foundational ideas are not the same thing as values. A "value," whatever exactly it may be, can be justified on the basis of a foundational idea, whereas the reverse is not the case. When conflicts emerge about what is meant by a value such as liberty or equality, some political actors proceed to raise the theoretical level of the discussion, seeking clarification or justification in foundational ideas. Whether "liberty" meant the right to hold slaves, or the right to be free of being held in slavery, was sometimes debated in terms of different accounts of nature.

## Response to Nancy Rosenblum

Nancy Rosenblum is a political theorist who, unlike Jack Rakove, claims no affiliation with a second academic discipline. From her spirited essay, filled with imagination and big theoretical concepts, no one, certainly, could ever accuse her of wishing to join a history department. She expresses none of Jack Rakove's reservations about general ideas. On the contrary, Nancy Rosenblum begins by taking me to task for not assigning more causative power to them, contending that I did not show that foundational concepts "are the exclusive or even most important concepts at work, much less that they actually shape these periods." My project is thereby "diminished," and I will be unable to make the mark on APD that I might have hoped to.

Touched as I am by Nancy Rosenblum's solicitude for my reputation, her reach on my behalf exceedeth my grasp. It would no doubt have made for a more powerful lecture—it certainly would have made for a simpler one—to have described foundational ideas as constituting an omnipotent *Geist* moving through American history and bending everything else to its sway. Unfortunately, there is this little obstacle known as reality, which can put a crimp in the boldest of theories. The discussion of foundational ideas was intended as a *supplement* to, not a replacement for, the study of ideas on other levels. A network of ideas operating on different levels influences American political life; only at certain moments have foundational ideas been the most conspicuous element of political discussion. The focus of debate in some periods has been on theories of governance (the constitutional arrangements of strict versus loose constructionism, the distribution of power among national institutions, and national versus state power); at other periods it has been on the scope of government power ("big government" versus limited government) or on America's role in the world. Whether, when, and to what extent these more usual kinds of political ideas are derived from or seek justification from foundational concepts is a question I began to investigate.

Let me take this opportunity to emphasize again that I did not appear, with an *F* on my blazer, to serve as a cheerleader for foundational concepts. Unlike some political theorists who have grown cold or bored studying their texts, I have no stake in trying to boost the importance of theoretical ideas in political life beyond what they actually exercise. If anything, I made clear my disapproval of that species of intellectual that lies in wait for the slightest mention of these ideas, so that it can come out of hiding and shout to the world, "Yes, we too have a variable!"

These quibbles are merely preparatory, however, to Nancy Rosenblum's central charge, which is that I am in reality a closet normativist. I cooked the historical books. In the world of construction and product development, a frequent approach, known as reverse-order engineering, consists of beginning from a desired result and then working back to what will bring the product into being. In Nancy Rosenblum's view, this was my technique. I reverse engineered a "narrative" of American political development in order to campaign for the Republican Party and to vindicate the political philosophy of Leo Strauss.

It may be that I broke all precedent in the field of American political development by mentioning the name of Leo Strauss. I did so, however, not to invoke him as an authority or to discuss his political philosophy, but primarily to draw on his assessment of the status of foundational ideas in American intellectual life in the 1950s and to explain a major development in contemporary conservative thought. His observation was that Progressive intellectuals were no longer convinced, as they once had been, that the idea of Progress was an objective truth; at the same time, they had long since abandoned belief in the truth of the concept of natural right. Strauss might well have been describing, for example, the trajectory of the Progressive Charles Beard, who by the 1930s argued, in his presidential address to the American Historical Association, entitled "Written History as an Act of Faith," that the notion of a "science of history embracing the fullness of history" was an "illusion"; each era—each historian within each era—had to choose a frame of reference, which ultimately was a "subjective decision."[2] Strauss's assessment of the intellectual situation at that time is neither exceptional nor, I think, even particularly controversial. Others concluded the same thing.

Let me now therefore make a heterodoxical claim: the mere fact that Leo Strauss happened to say something does not make it untrue.

I had no reason, in any case, to discuss the intellectual situation of the 1950s, and would not have done so, if it were not for the fact that it informed the political situation of the 1960s and shed light on the fracturing of the Democratic Party, which was home to most Progressive intellectuals. Along with the South's defection from the Democratic Party in the 1960s, it was the split between the New Left and the Old Left that accounts for the great electoral transformation of the current era in which the Democratic Party lost its status as the majority party. The New Left openly brought into the political arena the doubts expressed about progress that had emerged in the 1950s. Nancy Rosenblum's left-handed compliment—that my only point of originality in APD periodization was to select the 1960s as a decisive moment, which I allegedly concocted to support my reverse-engineered narrative—is unfounded both as to fact and motive. To treat the 1960s as a moment that opened the door to fundamental change is hardly original to me; it is consistent with the position of Nancy Rosenblum's colleague Samuel Beer, who located the collapse of the New Deal public philosophy in the 1960s, as well as with the view of some of the best scholars in the field of electoral politics.[3] One need not embrace a fetish for periodization—David Mayhew, among others, has called this project into doubt—in order to acknowledge that the "rolling realignment" that has remade electoral politics may well have begun at this point.[4] In the 1960s the Democratic Party was the majority party; in 2004 the Republican Party is in the majority. I would call this a "real" event in American political development, one that meets the current canonical threshold, set down by Orren and Skowronek, of something that contributes to a "durable shift in governing authority."[5]

As for my intentions, who can see into a person's heart? I treated the 1960s no differently from the 1830s or the 1870s— both periods, incidentally, where a shift in foundational ideas does not perfectly track with the standard periodization schemes of electoral realignment. In all of these cases I began from important developments in American politics and then inquired into the foundational ideas that had some bearing on their emergence or justifications. I never knowingly sought to adapt facts to norms; I drew my analysis not from my prejudices but from the reality before us. Nancy Rosenblum also found me a bit hard on the 1960s, taking exception to my mention of Norman O. Brown as a major figure of New Left thought. I do not know if her reaction would have been much different if I had named Paul Goodman, Tom Hayden, or Charles Reich.[6] It is not my fault, surely, that this movement was so filled with vague thoughts and bathetic sentiments, so that it is often counted, even by thinkers on the Left today, as an intellectual embarrassment. In any event, some of the intellectual currents I discussed on the Right might easily qualify for no less harsh criticisms.

The charge of reverse-engineered history is wide of the mark for another reason. My closet normativism is said to derive from my embrace of the same intellectual crisis of which Leo Strauss spoke in 1953. But we are more than a half-century from that time, which by my reckoning is nearly a quarter of all American history since the Founding. Why should I wish to dwell in the past? The most notable fact about the status of foundational ideas in political life in America today is how different it is from their status in the 1950s. One of our major parties has turned to foundational ideas, openly embracing an account of nature in some combination, as Rogers Smith points out, with religion. That party's president, George W. Bush, is frequently either accused or praised for being—let us be impartial and just say "identified as"—the most foundationalist president since Abraham Lincoln. I never spoke of a contemporary "crisis." If there is such talk today, it comes most often from intellectuals who, when they are not decrying the grip of Christianity over the Republican Party, are deploring the influence of "Straussians," usually with an equal misunderstanding of both. If one strips these analyses of their polemical or paranoid dimension and considers them in their descriptive aspect, the alleged "crisis" of American politics today is not what Leo Strauss defined it to be, but just the opposite: it is a surfeit, not a dearth, of "foundationalism."

If the chief purpose of my lecture had been evaluation, I would not have proceeded in such a roundabout way, elaborately wrapping a normative judgment inside a historical inquiry and sealing it in a strategic silence about religion. Insofar as the lecture was related to evaluation, its aim was to provide a data set of real examples of how foundational ideas have been used, so that others might have at their disposal more information when setting about the task of theorizing. The need for this information is obvious. There is much talk in political theory today about foundations, but little examination of the actual cases in which foundational ideas have been used. We have theorizing that is divorced from experience. Survey the literature and you will see that many of the greatest works have practically no reference to actual facts or data. Take a look, for example, at the index of John Rawls's classic *Political Liberalism,* and you will see "Adams" listed once, but the reference is to a contemporary academic, Robert Adams, not John; Thomas Jefferson appears twice, once in a footnote. All this would be of no consequence if the discussions of foundational ideas referred merely to formal arguments of political theory, with no reference to the political world. But their intent is to be apposite to American politics. We in political science would think it odd in the extreme if someone, other than a rational-choice theorist, sought to study political parties or Congress without bothering to inquire into how these institutions have actually functioned. Is it not equally strange to encounter learned discussions of foundational ideas that do not consult the record of how they were used? The fault here, however, does not lie chiefly with the philosophers and theorists, who are only following their own nature; instead, the responsibility belongs to political scientists, who need to take the lead in developing a political science of ideas.

For the same reason, Nancy Rosenblum misconstrues my purpose when she says that I wrongly characterized the state of political theory today. Characterizing contemporary political theory was the furthest thing from my mind. I discussed foundational ideas insofar as they entered prominently into the realm of experience, as part of American political development. I did not treat—I never intended to treat—the many interesting speculations about the same general kinds of ideas that are taking place in political theory, but that have yet to make a huge impact in American politics. Among the ideas omitted were not just those from the school of "democratic theory" with which Nancy Rosenblum identifies, but also those from the schools of ecologism and sociobiology, which may well enter the political realm next. If I slighted anyone in academic political theory, it was certainly not by intention. Some of my best friends are democratic theorists.[7] It was just that, in making the circuits in Washington, D.C., I haven't run into very many political leaders claiming to be Millian perfectionists or Kantian autonomists.

If, however, I erred in my analysis of the ideas that have influenced American politics, then I have come up short by my own criterion. Nancy Rosenblum suggests that I did not rightly portray the contemporary political Left and the Democratic Party. Describing the status of foundational ideas in the current period, as I admitted, is a difficult task, especially for the Left. Others have expressed a similar perplexity. An anecdote may help to clarify—or perhaps further to obscure—this problem. A journalist friend of mine recently told me that when a major new Democratic think tank opened in Washington, he asked its director which philosophical schools would be most prominent in setting the intellectual direction of the institute. The director hesitated and said he would get in touch later with a response. He never did (and my friend never expected that he would). By contrast, Republican think tanks are abuzz with squabbles among proponents of different theoretical schools, often openly identified. The point of this story is not to claim that the contemporary Left is less intellectual than the contemporary Right. One need only look at how much support, both political and financial, went from the Harvard faculty to John Kerry as opposed to George Bush in the 2004 election to know which side in America owns the hearts and minds of the intelligentsia. What the story indicates is something, I think, that most acknowledge, however differently they might evaluate it. The Republican Party today, to use modern jargon, is more "comfortable" with deploying foundational ideas, while Democrats hesitate or decline to do so.

So how to describe the Left on this dimension today? For insight I turned to analyses by Richard Rorty. I was frankly surprised that Nancy Rosenblum finds him to be every bit as radioactive as, well, Leo Strauss. I thought it would be an honor for the Left to be associated with a thinker who has the reputation of being America's greatest contemporary philosopher. Nancy Rosenblum cites as authorities a few other thinkers, including Dennis Thompson, Samuel Freeman, and John Dunn, eminent scholars all; but I know Richard Rorty, and Dennis Thompson is no Richard Rorty. It may also be that I was influenced by Richard Rorty's prominence, since he is so frequently cited in places like the *New York Times*. Indeed, I happened to run into him in 1998 at the coffee cart outside my office at the University of Virginia when he was still flush with the afterglow of his celebrated Second Voyage from Charlottesville to Washington, where he dined with the president of the United States, whom he described to me as "charming." The substance of this first-ever encounter between a postmodern president and a postmodern philosopher has been ably preserved in Benjamin Barber's book *The Truth of Power: Intellectual Affairs in the Clinton White House,* a work in which the author carefully chronicles the influence of many intellectuals, his own included, on the Democratic Party. Although few of these thinkers went as far in a theoretical direction as Richard Rorty in explaining to the president that "liberal practices [are] worthy even in the absence of liberal foundational purposes," the tenor of all of the discussions recorded generally corroborates an absence of foundational concerns.[8]

On the basis of Nancy Rosenblum's testimony, I am prepared to enter a guilty plea, though only in the second degree, to exaggerating Richard Rorty's influence. But if Richard Rorty, for whatever reason, is an unwelcome figure, perhaps because of his skepticism about truth on theoretical issues, let us set his views aside and go straight to the heart of the political matter, which revolves around the claim that a foundational concept is authoritative for the political community and helps define what constitutes a people. A foundational idea in this sense is not a theorist's argument in an academic journal about his or her personal fidelity to Mill or Kant, but rather—in Lincoln's words—a statement of "philosophical public opinion," aimed at having a definitive public impact. If speaking of *anti*-foundationalism is an error, then let me substitute the longer phrase: "political non-foundationalism." Under this formulation, I think it is correct to describe the current political controversy, at least as seen by many on the Left, as one between political non-foundationalism and foundationalism. The position of political non-foundationalism joins together not just Richard Rorty and John Rawls (post-1985), but also, evidently, Nancy Rosenblum, who writes, with great verve, that "we are a political culture of subcultures, there are a lot of spooks running around in the dark of the foundational basement, and my 'nature' may be positively ghoulish to you." The Left today is ambivalent on this question, wishing neither to reject foundational ideas outright, nor to embrace them. It is a case of wishing not to have your foundational cake but to eat it too.

To avoid favoring the non- or anti-foundationalist position, it is important on each occasion to reiterate that characterizing this issue as a conflict between political non-foundationalism and foundationalism already adopts the language of the non-foundationalists. "Foundationalists" should understand that this categorization scheme is a trap used for rhetorical purposes, in order to taint all foundations with the guilt of some, as in Richard Rorty's clever attempt to somehow equate "Marxists" and "Straussians."[9] As one examines the different ideas that non-foundationalist thinkers stuff into the category of "foundationalism" or "essentialism"—comprising no less than every theoretical view expounded before the birth of John Dewey—it becomes ever more clear that this category is so broad as to be almost meaningless. Anything from the most obscure speculations of astrology to the subtlest philosophic and scientific explorations can be labeled, at the author's discretion, "metaphysics." The science or philosophy of one era often turns out to be the metaphysics of the next. It may be only a matter of time, if it has not happened already, until someone begins denouncing the metaphysics of anti-foundationalism.

Nancy Rosenblum's final criticism of my lecture has to do with the discussion of the relationship of theory to political activity. Because her point requires some digging to formulate accurately, I cite the entire passage:

> He fails to speak to the question of the expressivism or the shaping power of foundational concepts for politics at all. I conjecture that the reason the constitutive relation between ideas and political experience does not make an appearance in Ceaser's essay is that holism and hermeneutic interpretation fail to capture the deliberate election of foundational ideas. Ceaser wants to claim autonomy for these ideas, and to accent the agency of political leaders who find themselves in situations in which they "need to actively engage foundational concepts." Foundational concepts in his account are chosen by political actors for strategic purposes. Ceaser turns out not to be particularly interested in the sociology of knowledge but

simply in the fact that concepts of nature and history are used by political actors.

Before turning to the substance of this critique, I wish to say in fairness to me—and to whom would I wish to be fairer?—that it was not I who put myself into the camp of "sociology of knowledge," but Nancy Rosenblum who placed me there. After she initially conferred this honor on me, I am pleased that she later saw fit to withdraw it, as it only serves to deflect attention from the concerns of political science. In line with sociology of knowledge, I am aware that human thought does not take place in a vacuum. We are all part of a civilization, speak a particular language, and are shaped by vast currents of thought or "structures," known sometimes by such vague names as enlightenment rationalism, Romanticism, scientism, and postmodernism. Like everyone else, political actors live and act within a context influenced by these structures, and like almost everyone else, most of them, most of the time, tend unreflectively to follow prevailing currents.

Granting all this, Nancy Rosenblum is correct to charge me with focusing considerable attention on the choices of political actors in selecting foundational ideas. But I am at a loss to understand why this admission should be considered a basis for criticism. First, is it an error? Political actors find themselves in a historical and philosophical context, but they often possess a margin of choice. A context is not a prison, but a set of circumstances. Oftentimes political actors live in transitional eras when the great ideational "structures" themselves are in conflict with one another, as in the decades of the 1820s and 1830s when Romanticism was vying with rationalism. At other times, their choices can seem oddly out of step with putative "trends" of thought. Lincoln's return to natural right in the 1850s was not evident from an account of sociology of knowledge. This is even more the case with the reappearance today of the foundational concepts of religion and natural right. For decades the sociology of knowledge had staked its credibility on the thesis of the inevitable secularization of modern life, only to have to reassess this view in the past decade. Many European analysts have been as dumbfounded as they have been disconsolate by the unexpected return of strong foundations in American politics in a postmodern age. I would be more impressed with the claims of sociology of knowledge if it had a better track record. All such theories aside, the more important point is what we discover by observing political actors. They often select among competing foundational ideas.

But if it is not an error to claim agency for political actors, then is it a crime? What is the harm in calling attention to, or even "accentuating," so long as one does not distort, the potential for human choice—for both its nobility and ignobility—in political life? If speaking in this way excludes me from the theorists' club of "holists and hermeneuticists," I at least have the solace of knowing that I can keep my membership in the American Political Science Association.

Nancy Rosenblum's objection to my effort to recognize political action relates to a closet normative concern she seems to have about statesmen acting for "strategic" reasons. But strategy is intimately connected to the "world" of the political actor. Good or right in the political world is brought about by actions in particular cases. The civilization in which we live is shaped not just by ideas, but also by events and political acts. These include the choices made by American political leaders at critical moments, as in the 1770s, the 1850s, the 1940s, and the 1980s. The force and power of certain ideas, which are admittedly causes of political action, are also the effects of political action. Where would the idea of natural rights be in our world today without John Adams, Thomas Jefferson, Abraham Lincoln, or Ronald Reagan? Nancy Rosenblum is of the party that believes that hermeneuticists and narrativicians are the sole legislators of the world. I am of the party that believes that legislators are also the legislators of the world. I embrace this party not because I wish things to be this way, but because the phenomena of the political world show me that this is so. I do not know if observation in this sense carries much weight with many thinkers today. Narrativicians do not accept the facticity of the phenomena of the political world. They live in a field of dreams, believing that if you narrate it, it will be.

How does the inclusion of the theme of political action relate to the question of foundational ideas? An enigmatic phrase by Aristotle says something to the effect that while certain things in political life are naturally just or right, they "are nevertheless always changeable, as are all things human."[10] This phrase might be interpreted to mean that philosophical doctrines of right or formulae are insufficient by themselves to be the bases for action in the political world. Because of the imprecision of our intellectual concepts, and because each new circumstance is unique—compelling us, when we confront one, to see things in a different way—the exact bundle or package needed to express right in any particular era can be grasped and expressed only with the aid of the political art. The modern political world is obviously different from the classical one—as Aristotle says, all human things are changeable—and it is therefore entirely plausible to argue that in our world, where an overlay of philosophy and religion has already developed, it is essential to rely on general doctrines of right. There is nevertheless still something to be learned from Aristotle. The way in which any doctrine is articulated, including the degree of emphasis given to it and the exact mix with other foundational ideas, will depend on the situation and circumstances. The political art is needed to make such determinations.[11]

Let us move from abstraction to a real case. Nancy Rosenblum thinks that, under my portrayal, Abraham Lincoln's stature is diminished by his "strategic" actions on foundational thinking. She writes that I explain "the shifts in Lincoln's appeals to foundational ideas by the specific political context and tasks at hand; by his strategic political needs." It was my intention, however, to suggest that Lincoln's stature is enhanced by his strategic steps—not, perhaps, as a political theorist, but as a statesman. His shift from the Whig Party to the Republican Party is an instructive lesson of how strategy operates in the articulation of foundational ideas. There is nothing to deplore in Lincoln's attachment to the Whig Party in the 1840s, as the Northern wing of that party never denied the doctrine of natural rights, even if it did not always trumpet it. Its position arguably offered, for the time, a reasonable formulation of right for the needs of the nation. When, however, circumstances changed, and the doctrine of natural rights came under attack, Lincoln shifted to make a public declaration of natural rights, unmodified by Whig embellishments from the Historical School, the central doctrine of the Republican Party. A similar point can be made of Lincoln's articulation of Sacred History in the 1860s, which also furthered the cause of natural right under a new set of circumstances. To return to the plane of abstraction, no theoretical doctrine of right by itself can ever quite get right fully right. Part of what is right is what does right, and what does right will always need to adapt in its formulation. This is what I meant when I concluded the lecture by saying that the task of reformulating and refining a nation's foundation is never-ending.

## Response to Rogers Smith

The final essay is by Rogers Smith, the one pure political scientist of the group. Because he has been involved in the field of American political development (even before it had the name), and because he has produced some of its finest works, Rogers Smith had the least difficulty in appreciating the aim of my project. Instead of trying to ignite idle theoretical disputes, Rogers Smith went directly to work pointing out both the problems and possibilities of this enterprise. His comments are on occasion the most critical of all, but they are also the most constructive. His essay shows the progress that can be made in a discussion that adopts this framework as a starting point of analysis.

Rogers Smith also does what I never thought to do. Instead of trying to prove the causal importance of foundational ideas by accumulating historical evidence, he turns to the device of a psychological description of how people think (at least some of the time). His little experiment indicates the importance that foundational concepts often play in our thought processes. By appealing to ordinary experience, Rogers Smith provides a better answer than any of the responses I offered to the theoretical objections that these ideas are merely "epiphenomenal." Obviously, his exercise does not settle the issue of the exact degree of causality of these ideas, nor did he intend it to do so. But it provides further ground to confirm what observation and common sense already indicate: that foundational ideas are of sufficient importance to merit attention and analysis.

There are, of course, differences in style or temperament between Rogers Smith and myself. He argues with great conviction that, in addition to supplying reasons and analysis, an author does best to set his/her preconceptions or concerns out on the table for all to see. He justifies this truth-in-scholarship provision by contending that, because preconceptions always play a role in what one's formal thinking seeks to prove, an open avowal of them will not only make things clearer, but also reveal—and thus correct for—an author's inadvertent errors or prejudices. Stating one's preconceptions is therefore an act not of "autobiography" or therapeutic self-revelation, but of intellectual probity and humility that will diminish error. All who have read Rogers Smith's books know of his admirable frankness, which once prompted me to refer to him, with no ill-will intended, as the Alceste of our profession. At least until recently, I held a different view on this matter. To my way of thinking, there was nothing other than the text and the argument. Arguments must stand on their own, with only their strengths to vouch for them or their deficiencies to impeach them. One's values or concerns should carry no additional weight. But I have now begun to see the wisdom of Roger Smith's position. If you state your values and concerns in advance, perhaps you will be able to avoid having others impute the worst motives to you, such as that you are working to promote conservative or Republican causes.

It is always unbecoming to appear overly defensive. So as not to place myself for too long in this position, I will mention one point of sensitivity and then move on. In the lecture, I identified three main foundational ideas—nature, History, and religion—but discussed only the first two. All of the commentators called attention to this fact, offering on occasion some rather creative speculations for the omission. But the real reason is as banal as it is, I think, understandable: a lack of space within the confines of a single lecture. If the event had been a series of five lectures, the sequence I would have followed is fairly evident: (1) the state of the study of political ideas in the field of American political development; (2) the concept of nature; (3) the concept of History; (4) the concept of religion; and (5) evaluative implications. The only reasonable solution to the misunderstanding is for Theda Skocpol to book me for the Tocqueville Lecture for the next four years.

With my excuse thus stipulated, I not only accept but endorse Rogers Smith's contention that the current text is an incomplete treatment of the theme of foundational ideas. The full picture, even in outline form, of how foundational ideas have functioned has not been presented. To support his point about the importance of religion, Rogers Smith proves himself to be a far better Straussian than I, noting that if it were permissible to draw on Leo Strauss's thought to conceptualize the theme of foundations, one would not stop at treating the categories of nature and History, but would proceed to what Strauss referred to as the "theologico-political" problem.[12] Rogers Smith undertakes to conduct his own investigation, and he is surely correct to say that the Republican Party today, along with being a natural-right party, is also in some sense a God-centered party. (How much this is so, and in what ways, might be matters on which we would have slight differences.) Evaluation is important for Rogers Smith, and although I could not tell for certain what effect this reliance on religion had on his own estimation of the Republican Party, he seems to think that its presence would diminish the party in mine. The religious element, he says, is not in keeping with what "various students of

Strauss's writings in high Republican circles" want. These students, he suggests, prayed for Athens, but found that they had to take Jerusalem in the bargain.

Rogers Smith also argues that the Democratic Party today is more open to foundational ideas than I made out, and he cites much evidence of Democrats' use of these concepts in political speeches. While I concede that the Left is eager to speak of its commitment to certain values, many of its thinkers are reluctant to anchor them in any foundational concepts. Rogers Smith states that Democrats "affirm their core commitments to human rights on the basis of a sort of 'overlapping consensus' among different philosophical and religious positions." I do not know whether this observation so much contradicts as it confirms my point, since it suggests an eclecticism that draws down the capital of foundational concepts without seeking to replenish it. But whatever the exact position of most Democratic thinkers may be, political strategists in the party have recently begun to discuss what they now call their "values" problems, by which they really mean their foundations problem. If not from theoretical conviction, then from a practical concern about electoral politics, they have called attention to the gap between their intelligentsia's ambivalence about foundational concepts and what large segments of the American public now think. The public is not yet nearly as indifferent to foundations as many thinkers hoped it would be. Rogers Smith's essay addresses this same theme, but on a more theoretical and principled level than any of these strategists. It should be required reading in Democratic think tanks.

## Conclusion

I come, at the end, to a dilemma. Two topics at the edge of my lecture proved of great interest to the commentators: an assessment of religion as a foundation and an evaluation of the different foundational ideas. It would be easiest to say that I will address these subjects on another occasion, offering the excuse that both are as large as anything treated in the lecture itself. I hesitate, however, to close off matters so abruptly, not only because both subjects are legitimate outgrowths of matters raised in the lecture, but also because some suppositions were raised about my intentions for which silence might mistakenly be taken as acquiescence. Nancy Rosenblum, for example, offered that I may have "dropped" religion from the discussion because I believe it to be "dangerous, profitless, or untrue and so cannot meet the political requirements of foundational concepts." Suggestions of this sort also seemed to be designed to elicit from me a summary declaration of a normative position. Curiosity about norms seems almost to go automatically with the subject of foundational ideas, making the study of this subject anything but a "normal" science.

Unable to fully resolve this dilemma, I will use the brief space remaining to at least make clear certain views that I do not hold. To treat religion as a foundation would require breaking it down into four different "modes," since religion in American political discourse does not appear in a single form. The first two modes occupy roughly the same "space" as foundational ideas of nature that speak of permanent laws. The first mode offers revelation, in the form of clear laws and injunctions, as the primary political foundation of the community, without reference to another standard. Some say, for example, that America is first or essentially a Christian, perhaps even Anglo-Protestant nation, whose core is formed by sacred declarations. The second mode offers revelation as evidence for a standard that can be confirmed on the basis of human reason and philosophy. This mode contains an important subdivision, usually overlooked, between the claim that God set the world in motion in such a way that everything that can be learned about it comes from scientific observation, and the claim that religious teachings and revelation provide additional insights, which can be supported by reason, that would not likely have occurred to the human mind in the absence of revelation.

The third and fourth modes relate to religion's role in the temporal realm and occupy the same "space" as discourse on history.

The third holds that revelation operates in and through God's action in history, and that aspects of God's providential plan can serve as a direct guide to the political community. As in some late nineteenth-century versions of the Social Gospel, this use of religion parallels Philosophy of History. The final mode also holds that there is a Divine Providence assuring that the historical realm does not end in chaos or meaninglessness. Providence, however, has the character that it precludes any purely human understanding of the course of history, whose ultimate movement must remain a mystery to us. Providence cannot serve as a specific guide or foundation. This view, best articulated by Lincoln in his Second Inaugural, intrudes more into the realm of reason (or what some have supposed to be within the realm of reason) than is generally supposed, because it denies the possibility of a science of time— "a science of history embracing the fullness of history," to use Beard's formulation—that can know the future.

Examples of each of these modes can be found in American history, with some playing a much more prominent role than the others. As in the analysis of the other foundations, a political science of ideas would encourage an investigation of the different instances of the uses of religion as a foundation; and it would do so without prejudgment. I am aware today of a favorite pastime of certain intellectuals, which is to consider the introduction of religion into political life as proof of backwardness and ignorance. If religious foundational thinking in America can be charged with occasional excesses, its sins seem to have been no greater—they have almost certainly been less—than those committed in the names of science and philosophy. Some of the most egregious crimes ascribed to religion apply, in spades, to rational thought. Was biblical racialism of the 1850s worse than the racialism that derived from the science of natural history? Was Christian Providentialism of the late nineteenth century more imperialistic than some strands of scientific Darwinism? It would also be unwise to ignore the fact that biblical religion has been consonant with this nation's tradition and has served, in combination with other foundations, as a support of liberty. Tocqueville considered a joining of what he called the "spirit of religion" with the "spirit of freedom" as a key to the success of democracy in America.[13]

Since I have not systematically treated religion here, I see no basis on which anyone should want to ascribe to me a position, above all one of hostility. Nothing in anything I have ever written warrants such a conclusion. Just the contrary. Perhaps the reason for this charge has something to do with the authority accorded to a strange syllogism that has been circulating in parts of the intellectual community, and that once again has something to do with Leo Strauss. It proceeds as follows: (1) Leo Strauss is hostile to religion; (2) Person X is a Straussian; (3) therefore Person X is hostile to religion. Each term in this equation is more simple-minded than the next. What Leo Strauss thought about many larger questions, in particular religion, is not settled and is open to discussion. People influenced by Leo Strauss's writings are not part of a single group, but include a large and prominent contingent of "faith-based" thinkers. Finally, instances, admittedly rare, have been reported of individuals from this school having conceived a thought of their own.[14]

This brings me to the final issue of an evaluation of foundations. In taking an initial step in a political science of ideas, it seemed to me to be premature to try to arrive at a summary conclusion or to produce a simple ranking. This was not a paper of political philosophy, and absent a full argument on this score, any pronouncements I might have made should be of no interest. The aim at this stage is to examine the historical record of foundational thinking. But so as not to profess a Puritanical zeal for a value-free approach that I do not subscribe to, and which would be inappropriate to this subject matter, it was obvious that certain inferences, rather close to the surface, followed from an examination of the historical record. I pointed to abuses that derived from certain foundations, tracing the problem in many cases to a tendency to employ foundational concepts to excess, especially where the concepts have drawn on truths (or what have been thought to be truths) from realms external to politics. The explanation, if there is one, for this overreaching seems to be a human desire for a unified account of truth and a yearning for greater precision and certainty than can ever be had in the realm of political life. For foundational ideas to play a constructive part in a modern society, their place, while significant, must be limited. Foundational reasoning cannot replace political reasoning. The existence of these and other abuses that have been caused by foundational concepts did not, however, lead me to endorse the convenient hope, as yet unsubstantiated, that eliminating all foundations can be the solution to these difficulties. A more reasonable, and certainly a more prudent, approach is to continue to seek foundational remedies to the problems most incident to foundational thinking.

# NOTES

## 1. FOUNDATIONAL CONCEPTS AND AMERICAN POLITICAL DEVELOPMENT

1. Tocqueville met with Jared Sparks on September 19 and Josiah Quincy on September 20, 1831. The influence of the Josiah Quincy interview is discussed by James Schleifer in *The Making of Tocqueville's Democracy in America*, 2nd ed. (Indianapolis: Liberty Fund Press, 2000), 67, 68, 78. Sparks's memo to Tocqueville can be found in Herbert Baxter Adams, *Jared Sparks and Alexis de Tocqueville* (Baltimore: Johns Hopkins University Press, 1898). I am indebted to my colleague Olivier Zunz for background information on Tocqueville's relationship to Harvard University.

2. John Adams, *The Works of John Adams* (Boston: Charles C. Little and James Brown, 1850), II:371 (emphasis added).

3. The phrase "laws of nature" appears in the Declaration of Independence. *Federalist* 43 refers to "the transcendent law of nature and of nature's God." See Alexander Hamilton, James Madison, and John Jay, *Federalist* 43, in Clinton Rossiter, ed., *The Federalist Papers* (New York: New American Library, 1961).

4. Edward Gibbon, *Decline and Fall of the Roman Empire* (New York: Modern Library, 1995), I:60.

5. I develop this distinction further in James Ceaser, "The Idol of History," *Social Philosophy and Policy* 20:1 (2003), 38–58.

6. Abraham Lincoln, *Selected Speeches and Writings* (New York: Library of America, 1992), 257, 216. From "Speech at New Haven" (1860) and "Letter to Henry L. Pierce, and Others" (1859).

7. Woodrow Wilson, *The New Freedom*, www.hax0r.org/~dragon/nf/progress.html (accessed November 15, 2004).

8. Thomas Jefferson, Letter to John Cartwright, June 5, 1824, in *The Portable Thomas Jefferson*, ed. Merrill Peterson (New York: Penguin, 1975), 578. Jefferson's claim is a remembrance of an event of a half-

century earlier and is not offered here as a statement that, necessarily, accurately depicts the situation in 1776.

9. Woodrow Wilson, *The Papers of Woodrow Wilson,* ed. Arthur S. Link (Princeton: Princeton University Press, 1911), 23:33–34, speech of May 12, 1911.

10. Woodrow Wilson, *Constitutional Government in the United States* (New York: Columbia University Press, 1961; orig. pub. 1908), 56, 57.

11. Lester Ward, *Applied Sociology* (Boston: Ginn, 1906), 41. See Virgil's *Aeneid,* VI:727; and Comte's *Cours de philosophie positive,* vol. 1 (Paris: Bachelier, 1830), 40–41.

12. This is the title of a book by Richard Weaver, *Ideas Have Consequences* (Chicago: University of Chicago Press, 1948).

13. See Louis Hartz, *The Liberal Tradition in America* (New York: Harcourt, Brace, 1955); Samuel Huntington, *American Politics: The Promise of Disharmony* (Cambridge, Mass.: Harvard University Press, 1981); idem, *Who Are We?* (New York: Simon and Schuster, 2004); and Rogers Smith, *Civic Ideals: Conflicting Visions of Citizenship in U.S. History* (New Haven: Yale University Press, 1997).

14. The exception is Rogers Smith. See his essay "Beyond Tocqueville, Myrdal, and Hartz: The Multiple Traditions in America," *American Political Science Review* 87 (1993). See also Smith, *Civic Ideals,* 507, n. 5.

15. Theodore Lowi, *The End of Liberalism* (New York: Norton, 1969), 3; Samuel Beer, "In Search of a New Public Philosophy," in Anthony King, ed., *The New American Political System* (Washington, D.C.: American Enterprise Institute, 1978), 5. The term "public philosophy" was coined by Walter Lippmann in a book entitled *Essays in the Public Philosophy* (Boston: Little, Brown, 1955), but Lippmann used it in a normative sense. Lowi first adopted it as a term for use in social science in his article "The Public Philosophy: Interest Group Liberalism," *American Political Science Review* 61 (1967).

16. Michael Sandel, *Democracy's Discontent: America in Search of a Public Philosophy* (Cambridge, Mass.: Harvard University Press, 1996), 4.

17. Lowi, "The Public Philosophy," 5. For Beer, a public philosophy is needed to lift the nation above a situation in which "warring groups, emptied by any vision of the social whole . . . quarrel over the spoils." Beer, "In Search of a New Public Philosophy," 44.

18. See James W. Ceaser, "The Theory of Governance of the Reagan Administration," in Lester Salamon and Michael S. Lund, eds., *The Reagan Presidency and the Governing of America* (Washington, D.C.: Urban Institute, 1984); idem, *What Is the Public Philosophy?* (Oxford: Oxford University Press, 2000).

19. The phrase "errand in the wilderness" comes from a sermon by Samuel Danforth in 1660. It is also the title of a book by Perry Miller, *Errand into the Wilderness* (Cambridge, Mass.: Harvard University Press, 1966).

20. From Cotton Mather, *Magnalia Christi Americana; or, The Ecclesiastical History of New-England, from Its First Planting in the Year 1620 unto the Year of Our Lord 1698* (London: Thomas Parkhurst, 1702), "General Introduction," sect. 3. Online at xroads.virginia.edu/~DRBR/cotton2.html (accessed on August 24, 2005).

21. Abraham Keteltas, "God Arising and Pleading His People's Cause," sermon delivered in Newburyport, Mass., 1777. In Ellis Sandoz, ed., *Political Sermons of the American Founding Era: 1730–1805* (Indianapolis: Liberty Press, 1990), 593–595.

22. J. G. A. Pocock, *The Ancient Constitution and the Feudal Law* (New York: Norton, 1957), 36, 37. Pocock explains the character of Customary History in ch. 1.

23. See H. Trevour Colburn, *The Lamp of Experience: Whig History and the Intellectual Origins of the American Revolution* (Chapel Hill: University of North Carolina Press, 1974); David Mayer, *The Constitutional Thought of Thomas Jefferson* (Charlottesville: University Press of Virginia, 1994); Reginald Horsman, *Race and Manifest Destiny: The Origins of Racial Anglo-Saxonism* (Cambridge, Mass.: Harvard University Press, 1981).

24. This phrase from Tacitus was widely cited by authors at the time, including Montesquieu and Gibbon.

25. Since I have mentioned Jefferson in regard to other foundations, it needs to be pointed out that Jefferson at various times supported a number of different foundational concepts.

26. Thomas Jefferson, Letter to Pendleton, August 13, 1776, as found at www.yale.edu/lawweb/avalon/jefflett/let8.htm (accessed on August 24, 2005). Spelling has been updated. See also Horsman, *Race and Manifest Destiny,* 18; and Smith, *Civic Ideals,* 73 and 523, n. 10.

27. The American pamphlet authored by "Demophilus" (probably George Bryan) is entitled "The Genuine Principles of the Ancient Sax-

ons or English Constitution" and is reprinted in Charles Hyneman and Donald Lutz, eds., *American Political Writing during the Founding Era, 1760–1800* (Indianapolis: Liberty Press, 1983), 340–367.

28. David Gress, *From Plato to NATO: The Idea of the West and Its Opponents* (New York: Free Press, 1998).

29. From *Federalist* 14.

30. Karl Löwith, *Meaning in History: Theological Implications of the Philosophy of History* (Chicago: University of Chicago Press), 1. For a discussion of the origin of the term, see Reinhart Kosselek, *Futures Past: On the Semantics of Historical Time* (Cambridge, Mass.: MIT Press, 1985), 30–32.

31. Both names were used to describe this group. One of the most interesting treatments of the Economists can be found in Tocqueville's *Old Regime and the Revolution,* bk. 3, ch. 3.

32. Jean Antoine Nicolas Caritat, marquis de Condorcet, *Sketch for a Historical Picture of the Progress of the Human Mind* (New York: Noonday, 1955). This work was originally published in 1795. Turgot's carlicr cssay, written in 1750, is entitled "On the Successive Advances of the Human Mind." It can be found in Jacques Turgot, *Turgot on Progress, Sociology and Economics,* trans. and ed. Ronald Meek (Cambridge: Cambridge University Press, 1973).

33. *Federalist* 6 and 28.

34. For an account of the historiography of this period, see Lester Cohen, *The Revolutionary Histories* (Ithaca, N.Y.: Cornell University Press, 1980).

35. This last sentence is a paraphrase from Richard Hildreth, *History of the United States* (New York: Harper, 1880), I:vii.

36. Adams, *Works,* 374 (debate of September 8, 1774).

37. Ibid., 370 (debate of September 8, 1774).

38. The distinction between "destructive" and "constructive" is from Edwin Corwin, *The "Higher Law" Background of American Constitutional Law* (Ithaca, N.Y.: Cornell University Press, 1955), 82.

39. Michael Zuckert has written that, for Thomas Jefferson, rights in the full sense "arise when human beings come to recognize a need for reciprocity in rights, when they recognize that to claim a right for oneself requires accepting the same right in others." Zuckert, *The Natural Rights Republic* (South Bend, Ind.: University of Notre Dame Press, 1999), 74.

40. Thomas Engeman and Michael Zuckert, eds., *Protestantism and the*

*American Founding* (South Bend, Ind.: University of Notre Dame Press, 2004), esp. the essays by Peter Lawler and Wilson Carey McWilliams. Also see James T. Kloppenberg, *The Virtues of Liberalism* (Oxford: Oxford University Press, 1998), 45–48.

41. Kloppenberg, *The Virtues of Liberalism,* 46.

42. In some formulations, the science of nature or politicalized psychology was a part of political science; but the full breadth of the discipline, or what could be referred to as ordinary political science, rested on an examination of experience. For an explanation of this usage and a fuller treatment of the meaning of "political science," see John Adams, *Discourses on Davila* (New York: Da Capo Press, 1973). The original version appeared in 1790.

43. The theoretical concepts of the contract and of sovereignty do not appear in discussions of the Gothic constitution; accordingly, there was no original alienation of power from individuals or local groups to the collectivity. The relationship between center and periphery was one of ongoing accommodation between primary local communities and a central state.

44. Cited in Robert Nisbet, *History of the Idea of Progress* (New York: Basic Books, 1980), 207.

45. Alexander Hamilton, "The Examination No. 9, January 18, 1802," in *Papers of Alexander Hamilton,* ed. Harold C. Syrett (New York: Columbia University Press, 1961–1987), 25:501.

46. Zoltan Haraszti, *John Adams and the Prophets of Progress* (New York: Grosset and Dunlap, 1964), 246, 247.

47. Harvey Mansfield, *Machiavelli's Virtue* (Chicago: University of Chicago Press, 1996), 136; see also 109–122.

48. For a history of the term "progress," see Nisbet, *History of the Idea of Progress.* The decisive work that broke with the Progressive understanding of progress is Marvin Meyers, *The Jacksonian Persuasion* (New York: Vintage, 1960).

49. See John Dinan, "'The Earth Belongs Always to the Living Generation': The Development of State Constitutional Amendment and Revision Procedures," *Review of Politics* 62 (2000), 645–674.

50. Daniel T. Rodgers, *Contested Truths: Keywords in American Politics since Independence* (Cambridge, Mass.: Harvard University Press), 71.

51. Thomas Paine, *Common Sense,* in Jack Greene, ed., *Colonies to Nation, 1763–1789* (New York: Norton, 1975), 271.

52. In 1787 Condorcet followed with the publication of a book, in the form of a set of "letters" from a fictitious citizen of New Haven to a fictitious citizen of Virginia, in which he argued for the superiority of a single legislative chamber. Jean Antoine Nicolas Caritat, marquis de Condorcet, *Lettres d'un bourgeois de New Haven à un citoyen de Virginie,* 1788; cepa.newschool.edu/het/profiles/condorcet.htm (accessed August 25, 2005).

53. François Quesnay, *Le Droit Naturel,* 1765; www.ecn.bris.ac.uk/het/quesnay/drtnat.htm (accessed August 25, 2005). In ch. 5, Quesnay draws a direct analogy between human natural law and the order of the heavens, as discovered by Newton. In his study *The Physiocratic Conception of Natural Law* (Chicago: University of Chicago Press, 1943), John Mourant writes of the Physiocrats: "Their whole argument is essentially an effort to convert a descriptive natural law based on the physical order into a prescriptive law that will apply to the actions of men" (21).

54. The term *laissez faire* seems to have predated the Physiocrats and was used by a few French thinkers earlier in the eighteenth century.

55. George Logan, *Letters Addressed to the Yeomanry of the United States* (Philadelphia: Oswald, 1791), 11. The letters were syndicated, being published first in Philadelphia in the *Independent Gazette* and later the *National Gazette.*

56. Ibid., 12.

57. See *Federalist* 31.

58. See ibid. and *Federalist* 11.

59. These terms were first applied by R. W. Lewis in *The American Adam* (Chicago: University of Chicago Press, 1955), 2.

60. The term "historical sense" was introduced by Friedrich Carl von Savigny, *Vom Beruf unserer Zeit für Gesetzgebung und Rechtswissenschaft* (Hildesheim: Georg Olms, 1967; orig. pub. 1814), 5. Savigny is usually credited with being the founder of the Historical School.

61. The wording is Hegel's. See Georg Hegel, *The Philosophy of History,* trans. J. Sibree (New York: Dover, 1956), 63.

62. One of the first to suggest a full science of organic development was Goethe in his work *Theory of Colors* (1810), in which he proposed a conception of nature different from that found in Newton's mechanistic account. See Johann Wolfgang von Goethe, *Theory of Colours,* intro. Deane B. Judd (Cambridge, Mass.: MIT Press, 2000), esp. 283–304. This proposal, which Hegel also sought to develop, never gave

birth to a genuine or respected science. See Ernst Mayr, *The Growth of Biological Thought* (Cambridge, Mass.: Harvard Press, 1982), 387–391. Not until Darwin did an evolutionary view of nature begin to carry more empirical weight.

63. Rufus Choate, *The Works of Rufus Choate,* ed. Samuel Gilman Brown (Boston: Little Brown, 1862), I:339, from the oration "On Illustrating New England History" (1833). For the background on New England Whig thought, see Jean Matthews, *Rufus Choate: The Law and Civic Virtue* (Philadelphia: Temple University Press, 1980); and Daniel Walker Howe, *The Political Culture of the American Whigs* (Chicago: University of Chicago Press, 1979).

64. Alexis de Tocqueville, *Democracy in America,* trans. Harvey C. Mansfield and Delba Winthrop (Chicago: University of Chicago Press), 403–404.

65. Choate, "The Age of the Pilgrims, Our Heroic Period" (1843), *The Works of Rufus Choate,* I:380.

66. George Marsh, *The Goths in New-England* (Middlebury, Vt.: J. Cobb, 1843). Marsh writes: "The Goths, the common ancestors of the inhabitants of North Western Europe, are the noblest branch of the Caucasian race. We are their children. It was the spirit of the Goth that guided the *Mayflower* across the trackless ocean; the blood of the Goth that flowed at Bunker's Hill" (14). This is likewise the theme of the celebrated work by John Lothrop Motley, *The Rise of the Dutch Republic* (London: J. M. Dent, 1913).

67. Choate, *The Works of Rufus Choate,* I:339. Choate also speaks of the "useful truths" of history (I:340).

68. Ibid., I:340. Choate is speaking here of historical romance—or what we would call historical fiction—but he is obviously suggesting that history itself might be shaded in the same direction.

69. Ibid., I:429.

70. See Choate, "The American Bar as an Element of Conservatism in the State," *The Works of Rufus Choate,* I:414–438; Lincoln, "Address to the Young Men's Lyceum of Springfield, Illinois," January 27, 1838, in *Selected Speeches and Writings,* 17.

71. Russel Nye, *George Bancroft, Brahmin Rebel* (New York: Knopf, 1944), 100.

72. George Bancroft, "Address at Hartford, February 18, 1840" (Hartford, 1840).

73. Bancroft, "Speech to the New-York Historical Society, 1858 (New

York, 1858)." If this sounds like Hegelianism, the simplest explanation is that it almost certainly was. Bancroft, like a number of other prominent historians at the time, did his advanced work in Germany. He attended a course of Hegel's in Berlin, which he described as "unintelligible half the time"—a fact that proves beyond any doubt that he understood Hegel better than any of his contemporaries.

74. Bancroft, *History of the United States from the Discovery of the American Continent* (Boston: Charles C. Little and James Brown), IX:499, 500–501.

75. Ibid., II:145.

76. George Bancroft, *Literary and Historical Miscellanies* (New York: Harper, 1855), 425.

77. Edward L. Widmer, *Young America: The Flowering of Democracy in New York City* (Oxford: Oxford University Press, 1999), 43, 3.

78. Abraham Lincoln and Stephen A. Douglas, *The Lincoln-Douglas Debates of 1858,* ed. Robert W. Johannsen (New York: Oxford University Press, 1965), 91, 92. See also Harry V. Jaffa, *Crisis of the House Divided* (Chicago: University of Chicago Press, 1982), 63–104.

79. John C. Calhoun, "Speech on the Oregon Bill" (1848), in *Union and Liberty: The Political Philosophy of John C. Calhoun,* ed. Ross M. Lence (Indianapolis: Liberty Fund, 1992), 565.

80. James Hammond, *Selections from the Letters and Speeches of Hon. James H. Hammond,* ed. Clyde Wilson (Spartanburg, S.C.: Reprint Company, 1978), 193, xvii (quote is from 1845).

81. John C. Calhoun, "A Disquisition on Government," in *Union and Liberty,* 44.

82. There is a side debate, which I will not go into here, of whether the different races were in fact part of the same species—i.e., different "varieties" of the same species or different species altogether. I have discussed this question at much greater length in *Reconstructing America* (New Haven: Yale University Press, 1997). See also Bruce Dain, *A Hideous Monster of the Mind: American Race Theory in the Early Republic* (Cambridge, Mass.: Harvard University Press, 2002).

83. Harry Cleveland, *Alexander H. Stephens* (Philadelphia: National Publishing, 1866), 721.

84. Republican Platform of 1856, www.presidency.ucsb.edu/platforms .php (accessed August 15, 2005).

85. Choate, "Letter to the Maine Whig Central Committee" (1856), in *The Works of Rufus Choate,* I:214.

86. Lincoln, Speech at Springfield, Ill., May 29, 1856, in *The Essential Abraham Lincoln*, ed. J. G. Hunt (Avenel, N.J.: Portland House, 1993), 99 (from notes by Henry Whitney in 1896 that followed Lincoln's arguments). Lincoln responded in his letter to Henry Pierce, April 6, 1859, "It is now no child's play to save the principles of Jefferson from total overthrow in this nation. . . . The principles of Jefferson are the definitions and axioms of free society. And yet they are denied and evaded, with no small show of success. One dashingly calls them 'glittering generalities'; another bluntly calls them 'self-evident lies.'" *Selected Speeches and Writings*, 216.

87. Choate, "Speech at Lowell" (1856), in *The Works of Rufus Choate*, II:412, 411.

88. This conclusion confirms the earlier suggestion that the two schools or variants of History were by the mid-nineteenth century moving closer together. Philosophy of History, in its Hegelian or Idealist phase, had accepted the development of history throughout particular (national) spirits and had spoken more of organic developments. The Historical School, by its organic way of looking at the past and tradition, had begun to acknowledge a slow process of immutable growth or progress stretching into the future.

89. Lincoln, "Lecture on Discoveries and Inventions" (1859), in *Selected Speeches and Writings*, 200, 201, 202.

90. Abraham Lincoln, "Speech at Springfield," October 4, 1854, in *Collected Works of Abraham Lincoln*, ed. Roy P. Basler (New Brunswick, N.J.: Rutgers University Press, 1953), II:245.

91. Lincoln, "Speech on the Dred Scott Decision," June 26, 1857, www.freemaninstitute.com/lincoln.htm (accessed August 30, 2005). This speech indicates the close attention Lincoln paid to the ethnological arguments about nature.

92. Lincoln, "Speech at Peoria" (1854), *Selected Speeches and Writings*, 98.

93. Lincoln had suggested earlier, in his eulogy for the great Whig Henry Clay, that a shift from the Whig Party might have had Clay's blessing: "But I would also, if I could, array his name, opinions, and influence against the opposite extreme—against a few, but an increasing number of men, who, for the sake of perpetuating slavery, are beginning to assail and to ridicule the white man's charter of freedom—the declaration that 'all men are created free and equal.'" Lincoln, "Eulogy on Henry Clay" (1852), in *Selected Speeches and Writings*, 88.

94. Charles Francis Adams, "The Sifted Grain and the Grain Sifters," *American Historical Review* 199 (January 1901).

95. George M. Fredrickson, *The Inner Civil War: Northern Intellectuals and the Crisis of the Union* (Champagne: University of Illinois Press, 1993), 192. Fredrickson then goes on: "[It] can hardly be denied that it [Social Darwinism] contributed to the later Northern decision to permit the fall of the Southern radical governments and the return to the 'natural condition' of white supremacy" (193).

96. Andrew Delbanco, *The Death of Satan: How Americans Have Lost the Sense of Evil* (New York: Farrar, Straus, Giroux, 1995), 151–153.

97. William Graham Sumner, "Socialism," in Sumner, *On Liberty, Society, and Politics*, ed. Robert C. Bannister (Indianapolis: Liberty Fund, 1992), 172, xxiii.

98. Ibid., 172.

99. Andrew Carnegie, "Wealth," *North American Review* (1889), excerpted at academics.uww.edu/lscore/cc120/industry/rspind7o.htm (accessed August 30, 2005). See also Carnegie, *"The Gospel of Wealth" and Other Timely Essays,* ed. Edward C. Kirkland (Cambridge, Mass.: Harvard University Press, 1962.

100. Progressive Party platform of 1912, www.presidency.ucsb.edu/platforms.php (accessed August 30, 2005).

101. Quoted in Theodore Lowi, "The Old Public Philosophy," in Lowi, *The End of Liberalism,* 3–21.

102. Theodore Roosevelt, *The Winning of the West: From the Alleghanies to the Mississippi* (1889), www.gutenberg.org/dirs/1/1/9/4/11941/11941.txt (accessed August 30, 2005).

103. Kloppenberg, *The Virtues of Liberalism,* 48.

104. Josiah Strong, cited in Ernest Lee Tuveson, *Redeemer Nation: The Idea of America's Millennial Role* (Chicago: University of Chicago Press, 1968), 166–167.

105. Josiah Strong, *Our Country* (New York: Baker and Taylor, 1885), 170–171.

106. John Dewey, *The Political Writings,* ed. Debra Morris and Ian Shapiro (Indianapolis: Hackett, 1993), 81.

107. Lester Ward, *Dynamic Sociology* (New York: Appleton, 1897), I:xxvi.

108. John Dewey, *Liberalism and Social Action* (New York: Putnam, 1935), 45, 50.

109. See Ernst Breisach, *American Progressive History* (Chicago: University of Chicago Press, 1993).

110. Vernon Parrington, "Introduction," in J. Allen Smith, *Growth and Decadence of Constitutional Government* (New York: Holt, 1930), xi.

111. Herbert Croly, *Progressive Democracy* (New Brunswick, N.J.: Transaction, 1998; orig. pub. 1914), 77.

112. John Dewey, *Freedom and Culture* (New York: Prometheus, 1989), 120; idem, *Reconstruction in Philosophy* (Boston: Beacon, 1957; orig. pub. 1920), 44.

113. Carl Becker, *The Declaration of Independence* (New York: Knopf, 1951; orig. pub. 1922), 277.

114. Charles Beard, *The Republic* (New York: Viking, 1943), 39.

115. *The Political Writings of John Dewey*, 45.

116. From *Federalist* 49.

117. Franklin D. Roosevelt, State of the Union Address, January 6, 1941, www.janda.org/politxts/State%20of%20Union%20Addresses/1934-1945%20Roosevelt/FDR41.html (accessed August 30, 2005).

118. Franklin. D. Roosevelt, State of the Union Address, January 11, 1944, www.fdrlibrary.marist.edu/011144.html (accessed August 30, 2005).

119. See G. Edward White, *The Constitution and the New Deal* (Cambridge, Mass.: Harvard University Press, 2000), 198–236.

120. Lionel Trilling, *The Liberal Imagination* (New York: Viking, 1950), ix.

121. Twelve Southerners, *I'll Take My Stand* (New York: Harper, 1930), ix.

122. Russell Kirk, "Prescription Authority and Ordered Freedom," in Frank S. Meyer, ed., *What Is Conservatism?* (New York: Holt, Rinehart and Winston, 1964), 7.

123. Russell Kirk, "Burke and the United States Constitution," *Intercollegiate Review* (Winter 1985–1986), 6.

124. Friedrich von Hayek, *Our Moral Heritage* (Washington, D.C.: Heritage Foundation, 1963), 10.

125. Friedrich von Hayek, "Why I Am Not a Conservative," in Hayek, *The Constitution of Liberty* (Chicago: University of Chicago Press, 1960), 399, 398.

126. James Bryce, *Modern Democracies* (New York: Macmillan, 1892), II:555.

127. Beer, "In Search of a New Public Philosophy."

128. Port Huron Statement, coursesa.matrix.msu.edu/~hst306/docu ments/huron.html (accessed August 15, 2005).

129. Norman O. Brown, *Life against Death* (Middletown, Conn.: Wesleyan University Press, 1959), 236.

130. Hannah Arendt, *On Revolution* (Harmondsworth: Penguin, 1965), 51.

131. Michael Walzer, "Michael Sandel's America," in Anita Allen and Milton Regan Jr., eds., *Debating Democracy's Discontent* (Oxford: Oxford University Press), 175.

132. Richard Rorty, *Achieving Our Country* (Cambridge, Mass.: Harvard University Press, 1998), 11.

133. Walter Lippmann, *Essays in the Public Philosophy* (Boston: Little, Brown, 1955), 96, 97, 99. Lippmann went on to argue that the decline of Western society could not be reversed if the "prevailing philosophers" oppose the "restoration of the public philosophy" and "if they impugn rather than support the validity of an order which is superior to the values" that each man is now told he has a license to invent (178). Lippmann adopted much of his argument from Leo Strauss's *Natural Right and History* (Chicago: University of Chicago Press, 1953), although one may doubt whether Strauss would have approved of advocating a doctrine of this kind, especially under the label of "the public philosophy."

134. Cited in Spencer Warren, "Reagan and Churchill Closer Than You Might Think," Claremont Institute website, October 6, 2004, www .claremont.org/writings/041005warren.html (accessed July 11, 2005).

135. Ward Connerly, "One Nation Indivisible," www.hooverdigest.org/ 011/connerly.html (accessed August 30, 2005).

136. See Iris Marion Young, *Justice and the Politics of Difference* (Princeton, N.J.: Princeton University Press, 1990), 99, 111.

137. George W. Bush, "Remarks by the President at the 20th Anniversary of the National Endowment for Democracy," November 6, 2003, www.whitehouse.gov/news/releases/2003/11/20031106-3.html (accessed July 11, 2005).

138. For an expression of this view by European philosophers, see Giovanna Borradori, interviewer, *Philosophy in a Time of Terror: Dialogues with Jürgen Habermas and Jacques Derrida* (Chicago: University of Chicago Press, 2003).

139. Mark Lilla, "The Closing of the Straussian Mind," *New York Review of Books,* November 4, 2004, 58.

140. Leo Strauss, *On Tyranny,* rev. ed. (New York: Free Press, 1991), 210.

141. For an early survey of this historical literature, which is partly appreciative and partly critical, see Gordon Wood, "The Fundamentalists and the Constitution," *New York Review of Books* 35, no. 2 (February 18, 1988).

142. Alexandre Kojève, "Tyranny and Wisdom," in Strauss, *On Tyranny,* 174.

143. Richard Rorty, *Contingency, Irony, and Solidarity* (Cambridge: Cambridge University Press, 1989), 86; idem, *Essays on Heidegger and Others* (Cambridge: Cambridge University Press, 1991), 135.

144. Rorty, *Essays on Heidegger and Others,* 132–133.

145. Tocqueville, *Democracy in America,* 407.

## 2. CAN WE KNOW
## A FOUNDATIONAL IDEA WHEN WE SEE ONE?

1. My epitaph, I sometimes half-joke, should read: "He tried to make the old history respectable (again)."

2. Thomas Paine, *Common Sense* (Philadelphia, 1776), in *Thomas Paine: Collected Writings,* ed. Eric Foner (New York: Library of America, 1995), 36. On the other hand, the 2003 and 2004 annual meetings of the Organization of American Historians, the principal scholarly association devoted to the study of American history since 1789, included rousing sessions where political historians, themselves heartened by the success of APD, expressed hope that a corner has been turned within the discipline. One of these sessions, at the 2004 meeting in Boston, was occasioned by the publication of Meg Jacobs, William J. Novak, and Julian Zelizer, eds., *The Democratic Experiment: New Directions in American Political History* (Princeton: Princeton University Press, 2003), which is a useful volume showing what the field looks like today.

3. Does this mean, therefore, that foundational concepts act as "trumps," in the sense in which Ronald Dworkin speaks of appeals to rights, or only that they possess certain self-insulating properties that render them relatively immune to attack?

4. Jack N. Rakove, *The Beginnings of National Politics: An Interpretive History of the Continental Congress* (New York: Knopf, 1979), 52–

62; John Phillip Reid, *The Constitutional History of the American Revolution*, vol. 1, *The Authority of Rights* (Madison: University of Wisconsin Press, 1986), 65–66.

5. Or perhaps I speak too quickly, since "republicanism," that now-depleted concept that was so much in vogue in the 1970s and 1980s, is cited as one example. For its emergence, rise, and decline (at least among historians), see Daniel T. Rodgers, "Republicanism: The Career of a Concept," *Journal of American History* 79 (1992), 11–38.

6. Montesquieu, *The Spirit of the Laws*, bk. 11, ch. 5, in Philip Kurland and Ralph Lerner, eds., *The Founders' Constitution* (Chicago: University of Chicago Press, 1987), I:624. Kurland and Lerner quote the eighteenth-century translation by Thomas Nugent.

7. John Phillip Reid, *The Concept of Liberty in the Age of the American Revolution* (Chicago: University of Chicago Press, 1988. See also Bernard Bailyn, *The Ideological Origins of the American Revolution*, enlarged ed. (Cambridge, Mass.: Harvard University Press, 1992), 55–93; and, for a broader (but economical) treatment, Michael Kammen, *Spheres of Liberty: Changing Perceptions of Liberty in American Culture* (Madison: University of Wisconsin Press, 1986).

8. Mary Ann Glendon, *Rights Talk: The Impoverishment of Political Discourse* (New York: Macmillan, 1991).

9. On this point, see Peter S. Onuf, *Jefferson's Empire: The Language of American Nationhood* (Charlottesville: University of Virginia Press, 2000), ch. 1. The quoted phrase comes from Jefferson's famous (and in some circles notorious) discussion of his proposed (but never introduced) bill for emancipation in Query XIV of his *Notes on the State of Virginia*. The relevant passage is reprinted in Kurland and Lerner, eds., *The Founders' Constitution*, I:534.

10. Pauline Maier, *American Scripture: Making the Declaration of Independence* (New York: Knopf, 1997), 197–208.

11. Jefferson, *Notes on the State of Virginia*, Query XIV, quoted in Kurland and Lerner, eds., *The Founders' Constitution*, I:534.

12. I can never refer to Filmer without recalling a lunchtime conversation in Harvard's Leverett House, circa 1974, with the late Judith Shklar pronouncing a final judgment on the subject: "But Filmer was crazy."

13. To historians of the American Revolution, this distinction seems painfully familiar, replicating as it does long-standing disputes between Progressive and neo-Progressive scholars on the one hand, and neo-Whig or ideological historians on the other.

14. Douglass Adair, "'That Politics May Be Reduced to a Science': David Hume, James Madison, and the Tenth Federalist," in *Fame and the Founding Fathers: Essays of Douglass Adair,* ed. Trevor Colbourn (Chapel Hill: University of North Carolina Press, 1974). This essay gave rise to a veritable cottage industry of scholarship.

15. J. G. A. Pocock, *The Machiavellian Moment: Florentine Political Thought and the Atlantic Republican Tradition* (Princeton: Princeton University Press, 1975).

16. Forrest McDonald, *Novus Ordo Seclorum: Intellectual Origins of the Constitution* (Lawrence: University Press of Kansas, 1985), 186–203.

17. William H. Riker, *The Strategy of Rhetoric: Campaigning for the American Constitution* (New Haven: Yale University Press, 1996); idem, "Why Negative Campaigning Is Rational: The Rhetoric of the Ratification Campaign, 1787–1788," *Studies in American Political Development* 5 (1991), 224–283.

18. Terence Ball and J. G. A. Pocock, eds., *Conceptual Change and the Constitution* (Lawrence: University Press of Kansas, 1988), especially the essay by James Farr, "Conceptual Change and Constitutional Innovation," 13–34.

19. Jack N. Rakove, "Thinking Like a Constitution," *Journal of the Early Republic* 24 (2004), 1–26, punning on James Scott, *Seeing Like a State: How Certain Schemes to Improve the Human Condition Have Failed* (New Haven: Yale University Press, 1998).

20. Bruce Ackerman, *We the People,* vol. 1: *Foundations* (Cambridge, Mass.: Harvard University Press, 1991), vol. 2: *Transformations* (Cambridge, Mass.: Harvard University Press, 1998).

21. What follows is a distillation of a teaching exercise I impose on students, requiring them to identify the diverse kinds of arguments that Bailyn makes about political ideas and the explanatory mechanisms on which each of these arguments relies. You could try it yourself sometime! References to particular sections of *Ideological Origins* are effectively found in the chapter headings cited in the succeeding paragraphs. One could conduct similar exercises with Gordon Wood, *The Creation of the American Republic, 1776–1787* (Chapel Hill: University of North Carolina Press, 1969), and (I am brash enough to claim) my own *Original Meanings: Politics and Ideas in the Making of the Constitution* (New York: Knopf, 1996).

22. How and why this came to be is the subject of the companion set of lectures published as Bernard Bailyn, *The Origins of American Poli-*

*tics* (New York: Knopf, 1968). In its own way, this slim but provocative volume could also be designated a contribution to APD, because it asks how differences in the effective post–Glorious Revolution settlements in Britain and America rendered the structure of governance in the latter, and with it the structure of politics, more brittle and rough-edged than in the former. Bailyn concludes the third lecture by intimating that the origins of what might be called anti-statist political attitudes in America could be traced to the same configuration of factors that gave late colonial politics its distinctive tone.

23. See Gordon S. Wood, "Conspiracy and the Paranoid Style: Causality and Deceit in the Eighteenth Century," *William and Mary Quarterly,* 3rd ser., 39 (1982), 401–441, tacitly renouncing views expressed some years earlier in "Rhetoric and Reality in the American Revolution," ibid., 23 (1966), 3–32.

24. Bailyn, *Ideological Origins,* 319.

### 3. Replacing Foundations with Staging

1. Alexis de Tocqueville, *The Old Régime and the French Revolution,* trans. Stuart Gilbert (New York: Doubleday, 1955), 139.

2. Karl Mannheim, *Ideology and Utopia,* trans. Louis Wirth and Edward Shils (London: Routledge and Kegan Paul, 1940; orig. German ed. 1929), 1.

3. I appreciate Ceaser's reasons for abjuring the phrase "public philosophy." Nevertheless, I use it at times in this essay because by his own account "foundational concepts" are not abstractions but must be put to political use over the long term. In the context of this discussion, "public philosophy" captures this more precisely than the even more elusive phrase "public political discourse."

4. Mannheim, *Ideology and Utopia,* 36.

5. Ceaser concedes that certain foundations in nature, particularly those drawn from anthropology, physics, and biology, are unsuited to the world of politics.

6. Rogers Smith argues against this facile conflation in *Civic Ideals* (New Haven: Yale University Press, 1997).

7. Leo Strauss, *Natural Right and History* (Chicago: University of Chicago Press, 1953), 2–6. It is not clear whether Ceaser agrees with Strauss's position that nature, history, and religion are mutually ex-

clusive, antagonistic foundations, so that mixing and overlapping are dysfunctional.

8. Ibid., 7.

9. Notice the puzzling relation Ceaser raises between truth and efficacy at the end of his essay. When he writes, "A foundation needs to be true, which is a matter for philosophers or scientists to consider, but it also needs to meet certain political requirements," is "but also" two-directional? Is truth something political actors propagating public philosophy must conjure with, or at least benefit from, because truth is necessary for efficacy? Ceaser does not develop this provocative suggestion. But the overall tenor of his essay suggests that political requirements may be undercut by the hubris of Richard Rorty's claim in *Achieving Our Country:* "I think there is no point in asking whether Lincoln or Whitman or Dewey got America right. Stories about what a nation has been and should try to be are not attempts at accurate representation, but rather attempts to forge a moral identity." Richard Rorty, *Achieving Our Country: Leftist Thought in Twentieth-Century America* (Cambridge, Mass.: Harvard University Press, 1998), 13.

10. Bruce Ackerman, *We the People,* vol. 1: *Foundations* (Cambridge, Mass.: Harvard University Press, 1991).

11. Conor Cruise O'Brien, *God Land: Reflections on Religion and Nationalism* (Cambridge, Mass.: Harvard University Press, 1988).

12. Carl Schmitt, *Political Theology,* trans. George Schwab (Cambridge, Mass.: MIT Press, 1985), 15.

13. "Remarks by the President at Victory 2004 Rally," Brown County Veterans Memorial Complex, Ashwaubenon, Wisconsin, Saturday, October 30, 2004. From www.whitehouse.gov/news/releases/2004/10/20041030-5.html (accessed November 1, 2004).

14. Nancy L. Rosenblum, "Religious Parties, Religious Political Identity, and the Cold Shoulder of Liberal Democratic Thought," *Ethical Theory and Moral Practice: An International Forum* 6:1 (March 2003).

15. Bernard Manin, *The Principles of Representative Government* (Cambridge: Cambridge University Press, 1997; orig. French ed., 1995), 226; Joshua Cohen, "Procedure and Substance in Deliberative Democracy," in Seyla Benhabib, ed., *Democracy and Difference: Contesting the Boundaries of the Political* (Princeton: Princeton University Press, 1996), 412.

16. Maurice Duverger, *Political Parties: Their Organization and Activity in the Modern State,* trans. Barbara North and Robert North, 2nd English ed., rev. (New York: Wiley, 1963; orig. French ed. 1951).

17. See Michael Rosen, *On Voluntary Servitude: False Consciousness and the Theory of Ideology* (Cambridge, Mass.: Harvard University Press, 1996), 156.

18. Keith E. Whittington and Daniel P. Carpenter, "Executive Power in American Institutional Development," *American Political Science Review* 1:3 (September 2003), 495–513.

19. John Rawls, *The Law of Peoples, with "The Idea of Public Reason Revisited"* (Cambridge, Mass.: Harvard University Press, 1999), 573.

20. For a thorough discussion of different conceptions of public reason, see Samuel Freeman, "Deliberative Democracy: A Sympathetic Comment," *Philosophy and Public Affairs* 29:4 (2000), 371–418.

21. It may not matter whether elections are seen as mechanisms for identifying a presumptively preexisting popular will or whether the popular will just is the outcome preferred by a majority—that is, whether voting (at least under certain conditions) is evidence of popular will because it defines it.

22. Alexis de Tocqueville, *Democracy in America,* trans. and ed. Harvey C. Mansfield and Delba Winthrop (Chicago: University of Chicago Press, 2000), 127 (I, 1.8).

23. Ibid., 230 (I, 2; ch. 6).

24. Judith N. Shklar, "The American Idea of Aristocracy," in Shklar, *Redeeming American Political Thought,* ed. Stanley Hoffmann and Dennis F. Thompson (Chicago: University of Chicago Press, 1998), 147.

25. Dennis Thompson, *Just Elections* (Chicago: University of Chicago Press, 2002), 124, 126ff.

26. Kathleen Sullivan, "War, Peace, and Civil Liberties: American Identity," Tanner Lecture, Harvard University, November 2001. See Nancy L. Rosenblum, "Constitutional Reason of State: The Fear Factor," in Austin Sarat, ed., *Dissent in Dangerous Times* (Ann Arbor: University of Michigan Press, 2005).

27. *Ex Parte Milligan,* 71 U.S. 2 (1866).

28. Congress has passed myriad statutes authorizing executive action to meet new dangers (statutes such as the Tonkin Gulf resolution), adding to the powers of the executive branch (the post-9/11 U.S. Patriot

Act), creating new agencies like the Department of Homeland Security, and expanding law-enforcement authority.

29. Or, according to the grim view expressed by one misanthropic theorist, from the fact that for many citizens today "there just are no patently rational political strategies of the faintest ambition, . . . no lines of conduct the rational appeal of which is sufficiently robust and salient to carry to most potential agents." Unless such lines of conduct exist, this profound observation proceeds, it may not greatly matter how democratic or not, how effective or not, how "foundational" or not, government is. John Dunn, *The Cunning of Unreason: Making Sense of Politics* (London: HarperCollins, 2000), 286.

## 4. What If God Was One of Us?

1. Rogers M. Smith, "Beyond Tocqueville, Myrdal, and Hartz: The Multiple Traditions in America," *American Political Science Review* 87 (1993), 563n4; idem, *Civic Ideals: Conflicting Visions of Citizenship in U.S. History* (New Haven: Yale University Press, 1997), 507n5; idem, "Liberalism and Racism: The Problem of Analyzing Traditions," in David F. Ericson and Louisa B. Green, eds., *The Liberal Tradition in American Politics: Reassessing the Legacy of American Liberalism* (New York: Routledge, 1999), 11–18.

2. Thomas Paine, *Common Sense,* in Merrill Jensen, ed., *Tracts of the American Revolution, 1783–1776* (Indianapolis: Bobbs-Merrill, 1967), 409–413.

3. Sydney E. Ahlstrom, *A Religious History of the American People* (New Haven: Yale University Press, 1972), 635–389; David Brion Davis, *Challenging the Boundaries of Slavery* (Cambridge, Mass.: Harvard University Press, 2003).

4. There is, fortunately, an easily accessible archive of presidential speeches at www.geocities.com/americanpresidencynet/archive.htm.

5. Last accessed on December 19, 2004, at www.geocities.com/rick matlick/nomacarter76.htm and also at www.geocities.com/american presidencynet/39thinaugural.htm.

6. Last accessed on December 19, 2004, at www.geocities.com/ presi dentialspeeches/1978.htm.

7. Last accessed on December 19, 2004, at www.geocities.com/ presidentialspeeches/1979.htm.

8. Last accessed on December 19, 2004, at www.4president.org/speeches/billclinton1992acceptance.htm.

9. Last accessed on December 19, 2004, at www.geocities.com/americanpresidencynet/43ndinaugural1.htm.

10. Last accessed on December 19, 2004, at www.geocities.com/presidentialspeeches/1995.htm.

11. Last accessed on December 19, 2004, at www.geocities.com/presidentialspeeches/1997.htm.

12. Last accessed on December 20, 2004, at www.johnkerry.com/pressroom/speeches/spc_2004_0729.html.

13. Richard Rorty, *Achieving Our Country: Leftist Thought in Twentieth-Century America* (Cambridge, Mass.: Harvard University Press, 1998), 10, 15, 18.

14. Last accessed on December 18, 2004, at www.geocities.com/presidentialspeeches/announcereagan79.htm (Reagan's announcement speech); www.geocities.com/rickmatlick/nomareagan84htm (Reagan's nomination acceptance speech); www.geocities.com/presidentialspeeches/1988.htm (Reagan's last State of the Union address).

15. Last accessed on December 19, 2004, at www.geocities.com/americanpresidencynet/40thinaugural1.htm (Reagan's First Inaugural); www.geocities.com/americanpresidencynet/40thinagural2.htm (Reagan's Second Inaugural).

16. Last accessed on December 20, 2004, at www.reagan.utexas.edu/resource/speeches/1986/70386d.htm.

17. Last accessed on December 19, 2004, at www.geocities.com/presidentialspeeches/1984.htm.

18. For example, Reagan's 1985 State of the Union Address, last accessed on December 19, 2004, at www.geocities.com/presidentialspeeches/1985.htm; 1986 State of the Union Address, last accessed on December 19, 2004, at www.geocities.com/presidentialspeeches/1986.htm.

19. For example, Ronald Reagan, 1985 State of the Union Address; 1987 State of the Union Address, last accessed on December 19, 2004, at www.geocities.com/presidentialspeeches/1987.htm; 1988 State of the Union Address.

20. Reagan, 1986 State of the Union Address; 1988 State of the Union Address.

21. Last accessed on December 19, 2004, at www.geocities.com/americanpresidencynet/41stinaugural.htm.

22. Last accessed on December 19, 2004, at www.geocities.com/ presidentialspeeches/1990.htm and www.geocities.com/presidential speeches/1991.htm.

23. Last accessed on December 19, 2004, at www.geocities.com/ rickmatlick/nomawbush00.htm.

24. Last accessed on December 19, 2004, at www.whitehouse.gov/news/ inaugural-address.html.

25. Last accessed on December 19, 2004, at www.whitehouse.gov/news/ releases/2001/09/20010920-8.html.

26. Last accessed on December 19, 2004, at www.geocities.com/ presidentialspeeches/2002.htm.

27. Last accessed on December 19, 2004, at www.bushcountry.org/bush_ speeches/president-bush-speech-091202.htm.

28. Last accessed on December 19, 2004, at www.geocities.com/ presidentialspeeches/2003.htm.

29. Last accessed on December 19, 2004, at www.geocities.com/ presidentialspeeches/2004.htm.

30. Last accessed on December 19, 2004, at www.georgebush.com/ News/Read.aspx?ID=3422.

31. Judy Keen, "White House Staffers Gather for Bible Study," *USA Today,* October 13, 2002, last accessed on December 19, 2004, at www.usatoday.com/news/washington/2002-10-12-bible-usat_x.htm.

32. Last accessed on December 19, 2004, at www.whitehouse.gov/news/ releases/2003/11/20031106-2.html.

33. Last accessed on December 19, 2004 at www.geocities.com/ presidentialspeeches/1985.htm (Reagan) and www.yourcongress .com/ViewArticle.asp?article_id=1758.

34. George W. Bush, "2003 National Day of Prayer Remarks," last accessed on December 19, 2004, at www.christianitytoday.com/global/ printer.html?/ct/2004/135/41.0.html.

35. Leo Strauss, *The Rebirth of Classical Rationalism: An Introduction to the Thought of Leo Strauss—Essays and Lectures by Leo Strauss,* ed. Thomas L. Pangle (Chicago: University of Chicago Press, 1989), 206, 248, 253, 260.

36. For an overview of such software, see Will Lowe, "Software for Content Analysis: A Review," Harvard Identity Project, 2002. Last accessed on December 20, 2004, at www.wcfia.harvard.edu/misc/initiative/identity/.

37. Rogers M. Smith, *Stories of Peoplehood: The Politics and Morals*

*of Political Membership* (Cambridge: Cambridge University Press, 2003), 66.

38. Ibid., 186–212.
39. Smith, *Civic Ideals,* 501–502.
40. Smith, *Stories of Peoplehood,* 164–174.

## 5. FOUNDATIONAL CONCEPTS RECONSIDERED

1. Alexis de Tocqueville, *Democracy in America,* trans. and ed. Harvey C. Mansfield and Delba Winthrop (Chicago: University of Chicago Press, 2000), 411.

2. Charles Beard, "Written History as an Act of Faith," American Historical Association Presidential Address, 1933, online at www .historians.org/info/AHA_History/cabeard.htm (accessed February 1, 2005).

3. Byron Shafer, "The Notion of an Electoral Order," and Walter Dean Burnham, "Critical Realignment Dead or Alive?" both in Byron Shafer, ed., *The End of Realignment? Interpreting American Electoral Eras* (Madison: University of Wisconsin Press, 1991), especially 51 and 106–107. For Beer's analysis, see Samuel Beer, "In Search of a New Public Philosophy," in Anthony King, ed., *The New American Political System* (Washington, D.C.: American Enterprise Institute, 1978), 5.

4. David Mayhew, *Electoral Realignments: A Critique of an American Genre* (New Haven: Yale University Press, 2002). In light of Mayhew's book, Nancy Rosenblum's attachment to periodization might be questioned by some in the field of American political development today.

5. Karen Orren and Stephen Skowronek, *The Search for American Political Development* (Cambridge: Cambridge University Press, 2004), 123.

6. Norman O. Brown is named as being one of the three most important intellectuals in the movement both by Beer ("In Search of a New Public Philosophy," 17) and by Morris Dickstein (*Gates of Eden* [New York: Basic Books, 1977], 69–70).

7. I take the opportunity in this context to recommend works by three of my colleagues at the University of Virginia which have made notable contributions to the field of democratic theory: Stephen White, *Sustaining Affirmation: The Strengths of Weak Ontologies in Politi-*

*cal Theory* (Princeton: Princeton University Press, 2000); Colin Bird, *The Myth of Liberal Individualism* (Cambridge: Cambridge University Press, 1999); and George Klosko, *Democratic Procedures and Liberal Consensus* (Oxford: Oxford University Press, 2000).

8. Benjamin Barber, The *Truth of Power: Intellectual Affairs in the Clinton White House* (New York: Norton, 2001), 230.

9. Richard Rorty, "Marxists, Straussians and Pragmatists," *Raritan* (Fall 1998), 128–136. Rorty in this article reviews a book by a fictional Straussian named "James Caesar." The same character is discussed further in Anne Norton's fable *Leo Strauss and the Politics of American Empire* (New Haven: Yale University Press, 2004).

10. Aristotle, *Ethics,* Book V (1134b, 29). The translation of this passage was provided by Professor Jenny S. Clay of the Department of Classics at the University of Virginia.

11. For a treatment of these themes, see the excellent article by Charles Kesler, "The Founders and the Classics," in J. Jackson Barlow, Leonard Levy, and Ken Masugi, eds., *The American Founding: Essays on the Formation of the Constitution* (New York: Greenwood, 1988), 58–90.

12. Leo Strauss, *Spinoza's Critique of Religion* (Chicago: University of Chicago Press, 1997). The expression comes from Spinoza's *Theologico-Political Treatise.*

13. For one of the few treatments of the role of religion in American political development, see James Morone, *Hellfire Nation: The Politics of Sin in American History* (New Haven: Yale University Press, 2003).

14. For one of the best accounts of Leo Strauss's views on religion, as well as a collection of some of his important writings on the subject, see Leo Strauss, *Jewish Philosophy and the Crisis of Modernity,* ed. Kenneth Hart Green (Albany: SUNY Press, 1997). There are a number of scholars greatly influenced by the writings of Leo Strauss who include religion as a major focus of their work. Among them are Daniel Mahoney, Peter Lawler, and Robert Kraynak in America and Philippe Bénéton and Pierre Manent in France.

# ABOUT THE AUTHORS

JAMES W. CEASER is Harry F. Byrd Professor of Politics at the University of Virginia.

JACK N. RAKOVE is the W. R. Coe Professor of History and American Studies and Professor of Political Science at Stanford University.

NANCY L. ROSENBLUM is the Senator Joseph Clark Professor of Ethics in Politics and Government at Harvard University.

ROGERS M. SMITH is the Christopher H. Browne Distinguished Professor of Political Science at the University of Pennsylvania.

# INDEX

Abolitionism, 44–45
Ackerman, Bruce, 107–108, 121
Adams, Charles Francis, 53–54
Adams, John: on foundational concepts, 5–6, 23; criticizes Physiocrats, 28, 30–31
Affirmative action, 77, 78, 100
Anti-Federalists, 21, 111, 123
Anti-foundationalism, 74–76, 81, 85–87, 104, 120–121, 124, 132–134, 150, 153, 185
Arendt, Hannah, 74
Aristotle, 174, 189
Austin, J. L., 132
Authenticity, 72–73

Bailyn, Bernard: *Ideological Origins of the American Revolution*, 108–112
Bancroft, George, 40–43, 51, 54, 149
Barber, Benjamin, 184–185
Beard, Charles, 61–62, 63, 179–180
Becker, Carl, 63
Beer, Samuel, 13–14, 72–73, 180
Belknap, Jeremy, 22
Bible, 16–17
Blackstone, William, 18
*Brief History of the Warr with the Indians in New-England, A* (I. Mather), 16

Brown, Norman O., 73, 120, 181
Bryce, James, 71
Buchanan, James, 48
Buffon, Georges Louis Leclerc, comte de, 45
Burke, Edmund, 68
Bush, George H. W., 155–156
Bush, George W., 78–79, 125; and religious rhetoric, 151–152, 154, 156–158; and foundational ideas, 181–182

Calhoun, John C., 36, 44–45
Carnegie, Andrew, 56, 57
Carpenter, Daniel, 132
Carter, Jimmy, 152
Causality, 82–83, 104, 121–122; and foundational ideas, 164, 166, 177, 190–191
"Chicago School," 69
Choate, Rufus, 37–39, 47–48
Civil rights, 52, 65, 78, 148
Civil War, 52–53, 55, 173
Clay, Henry, 52
Clinton, Bill, 152–153, 158, 184–185
Coke, Edward, 18
Cold War, 77, 130, 166
Collective rights, 29
Communitarianism, 15, 74
Comte, Auguste, 11, 20

Condorcet, Jean Antoine Nicolas Caritat, marquis de, 20, 21, 27, 30–31; *Sketch for a Historical Picture of the Progress of the Human Mind,* 28; and Philosophy of History, 35, 40, 61

Connerly, Ward, 78

Considine, Terry, 3

Constitution, U.S.: and Philosophy of History, 21, 29; and Darwinism, 58–59; Progressives' opposition to, 61–62; Liberalism's view of, 66; and foundational concepts, 106–107; and reason of state, 136, 138–140

Continental Congress (1774), debates in, 5–6, 23, 98, 130

Croly, Herbert, 62, 72

Customary History, as foundational concept, 16, 18–20, 26–27, 74

Darwin, Charles, 58

Darwinism, 53–59

Declaration of Independence, 74; and concept of nature, 6; and rights of British constitution, 17–18, 48, 68–69, 101, 152, 153

*Democracy in America* (Tocqueville), 3–4, 173, 196

*Democracy's Discontent: America in Search of a Public Philosophy* (Sandel), 15

Democratic Party: and Philosophy of History, 33, 34, 40–44, 48–49; and concept of nature, 53; New Left, 72–73, 76, 120, 180, 183; and concept of history, 75,

168; and foundational concepts, 151–152, 183–184, 193

"Demophilus," on Saxon principles, 19

Dewey, John, 61, 62–63, 73, 75, 186

Douglas, Stephen, 43, 47, 48–49

*Droit Naturel, Le* (Quesnay), 31

Dunn, John, 184

Duverger, Maurice, 127

*Ecclesiastical History of New-England, The* (C. Mather), 16

Economics, and spontaneous order, 31–32, 69–70

Enlightenment: and Philosophy of History, 28; and foundational concepts, 72, 87–88

Equality, as a foundational concept, 100–102, 110–111, 136, 174

Ethnology, 44, 45–46, 49–50, 54

*Federalist, The,* 17, 19–20, 21, 32–33

Federalist Party, 27–28, 29–33, 111, 123

Fillmore, Millard, 48

Filmer, Sir Robert: *Patriarcha,* 102, 103

Foundational concepts: definition of, 4–6, 96–102; Customary History, 16, 18–20, 26–27, 74; Philosophy of History, 16, 20–21, 27–31, 80; Sacred History, 16–18, 40, 50–51, 149, 190; Real Whig History, 18–19, 26–27, 94–95, 99–100; in modern society, 71–89, 117–121; "second-story," 117, 135–140. *See also* Equality; Liberty; Religion

Foundationalism, 63, 81, 132–135

Founders, and natural rights, 10, 12, 16, 62; and Providential plan, 17, 51; and Philosophy of History, 21–22; and religion, 24–25; and laws of nature, 32–33, 35, 45; opposition to, by Progressives, 61–64; and political science, 64–65

Founding, 15, 20–22, 26, 38–39, 46–47

Frederickson, George, 54

Freeman, Samuel, 184

French Revolution, 27, 34, 43–44, 45

Germany, and discipline of history, 34–35

God, 154, 158–159

Gothic, historic tradition of, 18, 19, 26, 38

Great Britain: constitution of, 17–18, 48, 68–69, 101, 152, 153; as source of foundational ideas, 102–103

Hamilton, Alexander, 31

Hammond, James, 44–45

Hartz, Louis, 12

Harvard University, and Tocqueville, 3–4

Hayek, Friedrich von, 69, 70

Hegel, Georg Wilhelm Friedrich, 7, 35

Historical School, 33, 34–36, 48, 80; southern, 44–45, 67–68

History: as a foundational concept, 5, 7, 18–19, 26–27, 33–44, 80–81, 94–95, 99–100; 177; Sacred History, 16–18, 124; Whig, 18; and the Founders, 21–22; and Democratic Party, 75, 168; intellectual, 104. *See also* Philosophy of History; Sacred History

*History of New England, The* (Winthrop), 16

Hobbes, Thomas, 15, 102–103

Hofstader, Richard, 94, 108

Holmes, Oliver Wendell, 57

Human nature, and natural rights, 24, 27, 50

Hume, David, 106

Idealism, study of, 11–12

Ideas, in political realm, 13, 14–15, 83–84, 95–96, 105

Jay, John, 23

Jefferson, Thomas: on nature, 8; on idealists, 11; *Summary View of the Rights of British America,* 19; associated with Philosophy of History, 27–28; and racial argument, 46; on equality, 101

Jeffersonian Republicans, 27, 29–32

Johnson, Lyndon, 72

Judgments, normative, 14, 15, 130, 145–146, 163, 165–168, 194

Justification (first cause), 5, 6, 7, 52, 97, 100, 131–135; religious causes of, 149

Kerry, John, 152, 153, 184

Kirk, Russell, 68

Kloppenberg, James, 25
Kuhn, Thomas, and theory of ideas, 14

Laissez-faire, 31, 57–58
Legislature, unicameral, 30–31
*Letters Addressed to the Yeomanry of the United States* (Logan), 31–32
Liberalism, 12, 15, 60, 65–67, 120, 146
Libertarianism, and philosophy of history, 67, 69–70
Liberty: as a foundational concept, 100, 109–110, 177–178; as "second story" concept, 136
Lilla, Mark, 79
Lincoln, Abraham: and natural rights, 8, 43, 187; on historical consciousness, 39–40, 195; and foundational thinking, 47–52, 185, 189–190
Linneaus, Carolus, 45
Lippmann, Walter, 71–72, 77, 150
*Lochner v. New York*, 56–57
Locke, John, and concept of nature, 35–36, 102–103, 138
Logan, George, 31–32
Lowi, Theodore, 13, 14, 56
Löwith, Karl, 20

Machiavelli, Niccolò, 106, 138
Madison, James, 106
Majoritarianism, 136–138
Manifest Destiny, 42–43
Mannheim, Karl, 115, 116, 126
Marsh, George Perkins, 38
Marshall, John, 22
Marx, Karl, 7, 20

Marxism, 11
Materialists, 11, 105
Mather, Cotton: *The Ecclesiastical History of New-England*, 16
Mather, Increase: *A Brief History of the Warr with the Indians in New-England*, 16
Mayhew, David, 180
McDonald, Forrest, 106
Missouri Compromise, 36
Monarchy, and history, 18
Montesquieu, Charles Louis de Secondat, 21, 100, 174
Multiculturalism, 73, 78, 150

Narratives, as foundational concepts, 15, 75, 86, 124, 127, 179–180, 188–189
Natural history, 45–46
Natural rights: and Lincoln, 8, 43, 187; as foundational concept, 12, 24, 27, 29, 44, 120; and race, 45–46; and Republican Party, 47–48, 76–79, 81, 120–121, 150–151
Nature: as a foundational concept, 5, 6, 22–26, 29–32, 99–100, 177; as metaphysical, 23, 25; and Democratic Party, 40–44; in the late 19th century, 52–53; and Darwinism, 58–59
Neo-conservatism, 79
New Deal, 66
New England, Whigs in, 38–40
Normans, 18, 19

O'Brien, Conor Cruise, 124
Orren, Karen, 181
O'Sullivan, John, 42–43

Paine, Thomas, 30, 149
Paradigms, 14
Paranoia, 135
Parrington, Vernon, 62
Periodization, 94, 117, 121–124, 180–181. *See also* Founding
Philosophers, and foundational concepts, 7, 9, 115–116
Philosophy of History: as foundational concept, 16, 20–21, 27–31, 32, 55–59, 80; and Democratic Party, 33, 34, 35, 40–44, 48–49; and Progressivism, 60–62; and Liberalism, 66; and Libertarianism, 67, 68–80
Physiocrats, 20, 31
Pilgrims, 38, 154
Pocock, J. G. A., 18
Poets, 7, 11
Political parties: and foundational concepts, 31, 33–44, 77, 126–128, 182; and Tocqueville, 137
Political science, 173–174, 176; and Founders, 64
Political scientists, 9–11, 83, 162–163
Political theory, 39, 43, 117, 128–129, 131–132, 136–138, 182
Politicians, and ideology, 115–116
Polk, James K., 40
Port Huron Statement, 73
Progress, law of, and Philosophy of History, 20–21, 27–29, 32, 35, 42–43, 55–59
Progressives, 56, 149–150
Progressivism, 20; and concept of nature, 23; and concept of progress, 28–29, 60; and Philosophy

of History, 60–62; collapse of, 71–75, 179
Providentialism, 17, 151–152, 154–155, 158–159, 165, 195
Psychology, 32, 45–46, 49–50
Public philosophy: and study of ideology, 13–16, 22, 56, 66–67, 99; and politics, 121–124
Puritans: and Sacred History, 16–17; and founding thesis, 38–39

Quesnay, François: *Le Droit Naturel*, 31
Quincy, Josiah, 3

Race: and natural rights, 45–46; and natural selection, 57–58; and equality, 101
Rakove, Jack N.: on foundational ideas, 93–112; response from Ceaser, 172–178
Ramsay, David, 22
Ransom, John Crowe, 67
Rationalism, 25; Lockean, 35–36
Rawls, John, 15, 133–134, 154, 160, 182, 185
Reagan, Ronald, 77, 154–155, 157
Real Whig history, and Saxon antecedents, 18–19, 26–27
Reason, and law of nature, 6
Reconstruction, 54
Reid, John Phillip, 98, 100
Religion: and Founders, 24–25; as foundational concept, 97, 99, 120, 124–126, 194–196; and Progressives, 149–150. *See also* Republican Party, and religious foundations
Republicanism, 15

Republican Party, 44–45, 47; and natural rights, 47–48, 76–79, 81, 120–121, 150–151; and concept of nature, 52–53; and idea of progress, 57; and religious foundations, 154–155, 167–168, 192–193

Revelation, 25, 87, 148, 164, 194–195

Revolutionary War, 19, 107–112

Rights, individual, 29, 42, 101. *See also* Natural rights

Riker, William, 106

Rodgers, Daniel, 29

Roosevelt, Theodore, 57, 60, 65–66

Rorty, Richard: anti-foundationalism of, 75, 85, 104, 144, 150–151, 159–160, 184–186; and human rights, 153–154

Rosenblum, Nancy L.: on American Political Development, 113–140; response from Ceaser, 178–190

Sacred History: as foundational concept, 16–18, 40, 50–51, 124, 149, 190; and Darwinism, 57–58

Sandel, Michael, 15, 65

Saxons, 18–19, 38

Science: as a foundational concept, 22–23, 88; and influence on concept of nature, 24, 45, 49–50

Scott, James, 107

Scripture, and political justification, 102, 148, 151, 152, 158–159

*Sketch for a Historical Picture of the Progress of the Human Mind* (Condorcet), 28

Skocpol, Theda, 4

Skowronek, Stephen, 181

Slavery, 43, 45–46, 50, 149

Smith, Adam, 21, 31

Smith, Rogers M.: on religion as foundational concept, 143–168; Ceaser responds to, 190–193

Social Gospel, 57–58, 149–150, 195

Social science, 60, 61, 64, 161

Sociologists, 7

Sociology, 55, 61

Sociology of knowledge, 129, 186–188

Southern Agrarians, 67–68

Spanish-American War, 57

Sparks, Jared, 3

Spencer, Herbert, 55–57

Spencerianism, 55–59

Stephens, Alexander, 46

Strauss, Leo, 71–72, 77, 79–80, 144, 150–151; *Natural Right and History,* 120; and Republican Party, 159–161; political philosophy of, 179–180, 192; and religious views, 196

Strong, Josiah, 58, 150

*Summary View of the Rights of British America* (Jefferson), 19

Sumner, William Graham, 55–56, 57

Supreme Court, 56–57

Tacitus, Cornelius: *Germania,* 19

Tate, Allen, 67